Assimilation in American Life

"Would you tell me, please, which way
I ought to go from here?" [asked Alice]

"That depends a good deal on where
you want to get to," said the Cat.

Alice in Wonderland
chapter vi

Assimilation
in American Life

The Role of Race, Religion, and National Origins

MILTON M. GORDON
UNIVERSITY OF MASSACHUSETTS

New York OXFORD UNIVERSITY PRESS

In this work appear selections from the following: *Catholic–Protestant–Jew* by Will Herberg, Copyright © 1955 by Will Herberg. Reprinted by permission of Doubleday and Company, Inc. *Jews in Suburbia* by Albert I. Gordon, Copyright © 1959 by Albert I. Gordon. Reprinted by permission of the Beacon Press.

Printed in the United States of America
printing, last digit: 29 28 27 26 25

Acknowledgments

I am grateful to the Russell Sage Foundation for financial assistance which made it possible for me to carry out this study. My appreciation also goes to Dr. Donald Young, President of the Foundation, who provided wise counsel at several stages in the work's development.

In the study's final phases, a grant from the University of Massachusetts Research Council enabled me to obtain secretarial assistance which greatly facilitated its completion. I wish to acknowledge this grant with thanks and also the encouragement of Dr. J. Henry Korson, Head, Department of Sociology and Anthropology at the University of Massachusetts.

Professors Gordon W. Allport, David Riesman, and Oscar Handlin of Harvard University and E. Digby Baltzell of the University of Pennsylvania were helpful when called upon for advice. They have my thanks. Any scholar who draws upon materials from the field of American immigration history owes a special debt to the work of Professor Handlin, and that debt is hereby admiringly acknowledged.

I am grateful to the *American Association of University Professors Bulletin* for permission to use certain portions of my article, "Social Class and American Intellectuals," which appeared in the Winter, 1954-55 issue (Volume 40, Number 4), and to the following publishers and authors for permission to quote from their copyrighted works: The American Sociological Association, D. Van Nostrand Co., the National Education Association, Doubleday and Company, Beacon Press, Isaac B. Berkson, Joshua A. Fishman, August B. Hollingshead, and Horace M. Kallen.

Amherst, Massachusetts   M.M.G.
November 1963

To the memory of
my father and mother

Contents

Assimilation in American Life

1

Introduction

This book is concerned, ultimately, with problems of prejudice and discrimination arising out of differences in race, religion, and national background among the various groups which make up the American people. It is different, however, from most books written on this theme in that little of it will be focused directly on overt discriminatory acts or even on scientific studies of the personality factors which "cause" or predispose some American citizens to deny some of their fellow citizens equal opportunities in American life and to harbor hostile or negative feelings toward them because of a difference in skin color, religion, or country of origin. Rather, we shall concern ourselves with what, to my mind, is the equally important, logically prior, and substantially neglected problem of *the nature of group life itself* within a large, industrialized, urban nation composed of a heterogeneous population. Our laboratory of investigation will be American society, but our conclusions, insofar as they are valid, will have more than token applicability to other nations and areas of the world which have undergone, are now undergoing, or in the next century will undergo, similar processes of urbanization and industrialization, and which have a population base of diverse racial, religious, and cultural backgrounds. In point of fact, this means most of the rest of mankind.

In one sense it is not difficult to understand why the nature of group life—the social structure of our racial, religious, and national groups and their various interrelationships—has received minimal attention on the American scene. Americans are known to be a "practical," hard-headed, empirically minded people. We tend to perceive and be concerned with the immediate, the clearly tangible event. When a Negro is beaten up by a gang of village toughs in Mississippi or is frightened away from the polling booth in Georgia, when a Jew is turned away from a "restricted" hotel in upstate New York, or an American of Japanese descent is denied the right to buy a house in a "white" neighborhood in California, these occurrences have the flavor of immediacy and, supposing we are "liberals," activate the sense of outrage and concern which leads to investigation, discussion, and perhaps, sooner or later, to attempts at remedial action. All this is well, though the deeper roots of the problem may not thus be upturned. Furthermore, the nature of group structure in the United States is, for the most part, "legally invisible." If, for the moment, one excludes the special situation of the American Indian, and bars from consideration the remaining Jim Crow laws of the South and the laws forbidding interracial marriage in a number of states, mostly Southern and Western (ultimately, all of these laws are doomed as a result of the United States Supreme Court's entirely reasonable interpretation of the "equal protection of the laws" clause of the Fourteenth Amendment to the Constitution), then it is correct to say that the American political and legal system recognizes no distinction among its citizens on grounds of race, religion, or national origin. From the legal point of view, there are simply 190 million discrete American individuals, most of them citizens,[1] involved in kinship and marriage relationships and

[1] In 1957, 2,833,732 resident aliens reported under the Alien Address Program. Source: Table No. 114, *Statistical Abstract of the United States, 1958,* U.S. Government Printing Office, Washington, D.C.

falling into age categories which have some legal relevance, but whose communal life as Negroes, Jews, Catholics, or Protestants, insofar as it exists, is, broadly speaking, a matter of formal indifference to the body politic and is not recognized or delineated by law.[2] This means that the social outlines of racial, religious, and national groupings in the United States are more or less invisible; they must be inferred from either casual or scientific observation of the social relationships, communal organizations, and community institutions which make up American community life. Their existence, then, though in a sociological sense distinctly real, is formally unrecognized and thus tends to be obscured from accurate appraisal. What emerges in the public mind is a collection of vague perceptions and half-truths about the nature of the communal life of groups other than one's own. Many of these imperfect perceptions and the lack of understanding of the nature of American group life in general constitute fertile soil, it may be presumed, for the growth of prejudiced attitudes. Indeed, the white Protestant American is rarely conscious of the fact that he inhabits a group at all. *He* inhabits America. The *others* live in groups. One is reminded of the wryly perceptive comment that the fish never discovers water. We shall have more to say about this point later.

It is a little harder to understand why social scientists themselves have given so little research and theoretical attention to the nature and implications of American communal group life. There are signs of an increasing recognition of the phenomenon in the theoretical literature, and, more and more, research studies dealing with racial and religious groups and problems of prejudice and discrimination are published which have some bearing on the broader problems of

[2] There are some "fringe" exceptions to this principle: for example, the chaplaincy in the armed forces, the granting of civil standing to marriages performed by the clergy, and the use of racial classification in the federal decennial census. There is also a glaring historical exception to the principle in recent American history. I refer, of course, to the evacuation and "relocation" (internment) of American citizens of Japanese descent from the West Coast during World War II.

social structure with which we are here concerned. Also, a significant portion of the recent ever-widening stream of studies dealing with social classes on the American scene have much of value to say about ethnic group life in the United States. We shall have occasion to refer to the most relevant of these discussions and studies in later pages. However, the general neglect of investigation of the nature of ethnic communal life in the United States is a condition which any student of "racial and cultural relations" must face and which may probably be attributed to several factors.

In the first place, social scientists have probably been affected by the lack of clear and obvious visibility of many of the lines which divide ethnic communal life in the United States. The division between the white and the Negro social communities has been uniformly recognized, and research has been carried out on this basis; in recent years, too, some studies of Jewish communal life have appeared, although a full-scale study of Jewish social structure at all class levels in a metropolitan setting is yet to be done. Catholic communal life has been little researched[3] and, indeed, until the publication of Will Herberg's perceptive study, *Protestant—Catholic—Jew*,[4] had been little articulated in the public consciousness. Much of the social science discussion concerning religious and national groups is still concentrated on their cultural behavior—that is, the question of to what extent the immigrants and their children have taken on the values and behavior patterns of the dominant American culture. This is an important question and one to which we shall address ourselves, but the question of social structure is one

[3] The studies of Joseph H. Fichter, S.J., have begun to contribute to our knowledge of the internal structure and dynamics of Catholic community life in this country. See his *Southern Parish*, Vol. I, *Dynamics of a City Church*, Chicago, University of Chicago Press, 1951; *Social Relations in the Urban Parish*, Chicago, University of Chicago Press, 1954; and *Parochial School; A Sociological Study*, Notre Dame, Indiana, University of Notre Dame Press, 1958.

[4] Will Herberg, *Protestant—Catholic—Jew*, New York, Doubleday and Company, Inc., 1955.

of equal importance, and the most fruitful approach is one which considers them together.

Another significant factor in the relative lack of preoccupation by social scientists with communal structure in the United States is the cumulative force of research trends in other directions. The post-World War II publication of "Studies in Prejudice,"[5] a large-scale investigation of the personality correlates of prejudice, commissioned by the American Jewish Committee, attracted considerable attention to this facet of intergroup relations and reinforced the traditional concern of social psychologists with personality and attitude dynamics. Sociologists have devoted considerable attention in the post-war years to studies of "small groups" in various settings[6] and the dynamics of behavior in various organizational situations such as a factory or a hospital.[7] Such research and theoretical trends have tended to keep in the background of attention the existence of larger social structures such as that of the ethnic group itself. In a sense, then, this book may be considered an essay into the sociology of "large groups," a social phenomenon which I

[5] See particularly, T. W. Adorno, Else Frenkel-Brunswik, D. J. Levinson, and R. N. Sanford, *The Authoritarian Personality*, New York, Harper and Brothers, 1950; Nathan W. Ackerman and Marie Jahoda, *Anti-Semitism and Emotional Disorder*, New York, Harper and Brothers, 1950; Bruno Bettelheim and Morris Janowitz, *Dynamics of Prejudice*, New York, Harper and Brothers, 1950; Leo Lowenthal and Norbert Guterman, *Prophets of Deceit*, New York, Harper and Brothers, 1949.

[6] See Robert F. Bales, "Small-Group Theory and Research" in Robert K. Merton, Leonard Broom, and Leonard S. Cottrell, Jr. (eds.), *Sociology Today, Problems and Prospects*, New York, Basic Books, Inc., 1959; and A. P. Hare, E. F. Borgatta, and R. F. Bales (eds.), *Small Groups: Studies in Social Interaction*, New York, Alfred A. Knopf, Inc., 1955.

[7] See Alvin W. Gouldner, "Organizational Analysis," in Merton *et al.*, *Sociology Today, Problems and Prospects*, op. cit.; Robert K. Merton, Ailsa P. Gray, Barbara Hockey and Hanan C. Selvin (eds.), *Reader in Bureaucracy*, Glencoe, Ill., The Free Press, 1952; Peter M. Blau, *Bureaucracy in Modern Society*, New York, Random House, 1956; Alfred H. Stanton and Morris S. Schwartz, *The Mental Hospital*, New York, Basic Books, Inc., 1954.

believe deserves considerably more scientific attention than it has yet received. Of course, "large groups" are made up of "small groups" and "personalities" in various kinds of interaction, but it is precisely this kind of interaction and the form of the resulting larger wholes that need attention. Only perhaps in the burgeoning interest in social class divisions in America has "large group" analysis been adequately represented. As I shall endeavor to show, it is in the combination of ethnic group and social class dynamics that the area of "large group" analysis most fruitful for our purposes will emerge.

The consequence of this relative lack of attention to the structure and structural interrelationships of ethnic groups by both the lay public and professional scientists is that, by and large, there is no informed and sophisticated discussion of social structural goals in intergroup relations taking place in American intellectual life today. "Liberals," well-meaning people, and professional intergroup relations workers (not necessarily mutually exclusive categories) know that they are against racial, religious, and nationality prejudice and discrimination and want to see these phenomena eliminated from American life. They are "for" equality of opportunity in all areas for all men regardless of "race, creed, or national origin." Faced with the concrete reality of an overt discriminatory act in employment or housing, they are concertedly against it. But the question of whether Negroes, or Jews, or Catholics, or Mexican-Americans, should maintain or lose their group identity in this America of the future is one which, for the most part, receives no thoughtful attention or is dealt with largely in clichés. Do we want "total assimilation," "the melting pot," or "cultural pluralism"? And, more pointedly, what implications does each of these phrases have, concretely, for friendship patterns, organizational affiliations, civic participation, self-identification, value conflict and value integration, political life, prejudice and discrimination, and American unity? No well-considered answer is forthcoming. Not only is there little informed discussion of projected guidelines for the future, in this dimension, but a perceptive analysis of where we stand now with regard to social structure is similarly lacking. I exaggerate only slightly when I state that, *in terms of the crucial considerations of social structure,* intergroup relations work in the United States proceeds like a race horse galloping along with blinders. He doesn't know where he's been, he doesn't know where he is, and he doesn't know where he's going. But he's making progress!

I have carried out, as a part of this study, a series of interviews with officials of intergroup relations and intragroup communal life organizations in the United States. Most of these organizations are concerned with interracial, intercultural, or interreligious relations in America and strive to eliminate discrimination and prejudice wherever they exist. A few of the agencies are of the intragroup nature, concerned largely with the development of communal activities within the ethnic group; some of the agencies have both functions. I interviewed twenty-seven officials, representing twenty-five different agencies. All of these officials were in highly responsible positions in the work of their respective organizations.[8] These agencies constitute most of the well-known private national organizations working in the field of intergroup relations in the United States today, together with several state-wide and city-wide agencies, both governmental and private.[9] Table 1 gives a breakdown of the ethnic focus (auspices, sponsorship, or area of principal concern[10]) of the agencies interviewed.

[8] Twenty-five were formal interviews carried out with the aid of a specially prepared schedule of questions (modified in a few cases to fit special conditions); two of the interviews were informal discussions with the Research Directors of the respective agencies.

[9] A list of the agencies interviewed is obtainable on request to me by any interested scholar.

[10] In most cases sponsorship and area of principal concern coincide. There are a few exceptions. For instance, the two "Indian" agencies are concerned with Indian problems but are sponsored by whites. Two of the "Protestant" agencies deal largely with problems of racial discrimination.

TABLE 1. ETHNIC FOCUS OF AGENCIES INTERVIEWED

Jewish	4
Catholic	4
*Intergroup	4
Negro	3
Protestant	3
Governmental	3
Indian	2
Japanese-American	1
Italian-American	1
Total	25

* No one ethnic group sponsorship or concern

In these interviews my principal objective was to find out how much thought and consideration had been given by these agencies to problems of social structure, theories and models of "assimilation," "integration," and "group life," of whatever nature, and long-range goals of social structure in the United States.[11] I discovered that the vast majority of these agencies (nearly three-fourths) had given little or no attention to these problems. That is, they have no clearly articulated set of principles and observations which a) describes adequately the nature of group and communal life in America, b) sets up the desired or preferred (in terms of the group's own philosophy) structural goals with respect to communal life in this country, in any kind of sociologically sophisticated fashion, and c) considers in depth and richness of articulation the implications of such a preferred theory of social structural goals for the various facets of their own program.

I do not wish to be misunderstood. I am not, in the slightest degree, criticizing the work of these agencies in their day-to-day activities, or even in the way they go about achieving their stated goals. As a specialist in the field of intergroup relations, I was familiar in a

[11] I also examined the publications of these agencies which describe their work and specify their goals.

general way with the programs and activities of most of these organizations before I began this study, and I had developed a healthy respect for their accomplishments. My series of interviews with leading officials of these agencies has heightened rather than diminished my confidence in the intellectual and practical cogency of the work which these agency executives are carrying out in the fight against racial and religious discrimination in America. As I think back on the long conversations which I had with these men and women in their headquarters in New York, Washington, Philadelphia, Boston, and elsewhere, as I review their frank and incisive discussions of agency programs and problems, I am fairly persuaded that there is no other body of workers in any professional field of social concern on the whole more dedicated or more able. But these agency officials face a continuous wave of daily, practical problems and decisions, directly focused on overt cases of prejudice and discrimination or immediate communal concern. In this context, long-range issues of social structure are likely to be slighted and, in the long run, effectively ignored. As one agency executive put it, "The Commission has been terrifically busy with immediate day-to-day problems. We do not have time at Commission meetings to sit down and discuss these [social structural] issues."

Let us turn our attention, for a moment, to those few "group relations" organizations which did report some substantial consideration of problems of social structure. Most of these were agencies concerned with either Indian or Jewish affairs. The Indian agencies are virtually forced into a consideration of social structural issues since Indian reservation life is obviously communal, with a distinct geographical base and a history of treaty relationships as groups with the American federal government, and since the question of whether the Indians should maintain their communal societies and culture or disappear into the mainstream of American life is the precise focus of governmental policy debate, private concern, and Indian self-examination. It is well known that the various Indian groups, by and large, wish to preserve their own societies and cultures and that governmental policy throughout much of America's history has been, directly or indirectly, inimical to this wish. The private "Indian" agencies are enthusiastic supporters of the principle of "letting the Indians decide for themselves" and are therefore, in fact, committed currently to the principle of Indian communal life. This commitment, however, does not arise out of any general viewpoint or theory about "group life" in the United States, but is highly specific to the Indian group with its historically unique factors of subjection to colonial conquest and persecution, treaty relationships with the American government, and the remoteness of ancestral Indian culture from the general European or Western nature of the rest of American culture. In fact, unlike most other intergroup relations agencies in the United States, the Indian agencies, so far as I can see, do not concern themselves even in a modest peripheral way with general problems of discrimination and prejudice in American life. They are the most highly concentrated in their deliberations and efforts of all the group relations organizations.

Those agencies which are focused primarily on the life of Jews in the United States and the relations of Jews to other Americans tend to have some awareness of "group life" problems and to have devoted some thought to them. This is hardly surprising since the position of the Jews within the imperial entities and nations of an overwhelmingly culturally Christian Europe and, later, America, has been an issue with a history as long as the Christian era. The rise of the modern democratic state in the late eighteenth and nineteenth centuries and the coming of the industrial and urban revolutions placed the issue in an entirely new setting. Finally, in the twentieth century, the demonic development of Naziism with its program of mass genocide and the later phoenix-like birth of the state of Israel contributed new elements which would naturally have stimulated American Jewish religious and communal leaders to continued reflection on the relations of Jews in the United States to their fellow Americans. Most of these agencies (the American Council for Judaism is a conspicuous exception) support in varying forms and degrees the "cultural pluralist" conception of American life—a point of view which offers legitimization of the preservation of sub-national communal life and some cultural differences for the nation's various ethnic groups, and justifies the result as providing a more democratic, more interesting, and more dynamically fruitful culture for all Americans than one in which uniformity was the norm. We shall have more to say about this conception later.

Of the Jewish agencies, probably the American Jewish Committee and the American Council for Judaism have in recent years devoted the most extensive and most considered thought to problems of social structural adjustment on the American scene. The American Jewish Committee sponsored, in 1956, a Conference on Group Life in America, at which a number of leading scholars and social scientists considered the problem.[12] The American Council for Judaism, with its highly articulated anti-Zionist and anti-Jewish communal life ideology and program, and its minority position within contemporary American Jewish life, has naturally found itself concerned with problems of social structure and cultural adjustment, and its publications reflect this interest.[13]

It should not be inferred from the above remarks that it is only the Indian and most of the Jewish agencies that support the cultural pluralist conception of America. On the basis of my interview materials and an examination of the published literature which

[12] Some of these papers were published in the symposium "Ethnic Groups in American Life," *Daedalus: The Journal of the American Academy of Arts and Sciences*, Spring, 1961.
[13] See American Council for Judaism, "An Approach to an American Judaism," (pamphlet), 1953; Elmer Berger, *Judaism or Jewish Nationalism*, New York, Bookman Associates, 1957; and George A. Lundberg, "Pluralism, Integration and Assimilation," New York, American Council for Judaism, (pamphlet) 1957.

these agencies distribute outlining their programs and goals, I would conclude that nineteen out of the twenty-five organizations, or 76 per cent, support the cultural pluralist idea in some degree. That is, they support the *right* of ethnic groups to maintain some degree of cultural difference and some degree of ethnic communality, and regard this cultural variation as essentially beneficial for American culture as a whole.

Of the remaining six agencies—that is, those which expressed little interest in or enthusiasm for cultural pluralism—the major Negro agencies bulked large. This does not mean that they are necessarily opposed to the idea for other groups, nor that they have taken an official position on the matter or would oppose Negroes otherwise inclined, but my inference from the interview materials and published statements is that they do not envisage the retention of a Negro subcommunity with its own institutions as a desirable long-range goal for Negroes in the United States—that is, one to be consciously sought. One official of one of the Negro agencies, when asked about the position of his organization on the question of Negro communality, put it this way: "We would like to see complete freedom of choice exist. We stand very firmly on the distinction between public situations and private relationships. As far as friends and associates are concerned, this is a matter of private likes and dislikes. We don't regard this as susceptible to the operations of law. *We believe, however, that eventually, under equal-status contact, these private mixed associations will take place, and we regard this as desirable when taking place naturally.* [And later] *The logic of our position is obviously anti-insularity—anti-communal;* [however] we assume that there will be a definable Negro group in the foreseeable future" (italics mine).

This indifference to Negro communality is not difficult to understand when we consider that the vast majority of Negroes are Protestants and thus have no distinctive religious values to preserve which differ from those of the dominant American culture, and that their ties to their various ancestral cultures are extremely tenuous or nonexistent. Even here, some exceptions must be noted. The Black Muslim movement, whose appeal to the disadvantaged Negro masses has drawn some response in recent years, stresses an extreme form of Negro communal separation, its own version of a non-Christian religious faith, and identity with the peoples of Asia and Africa.[14] A new organization was formed in 1956 by a group of Negro intellectuals at the other end of the socio-economic and cultural spectrum. It is called the American Society of African Culture, and its purpose is to stimulate interest on the part of Americans, and especially Negro Americans, in African culture, past and present, and to disseminate knowledge of African culture and African cultural contributions to American life. At a conference on Africa and African culture sponsored by the society, its president, Dr. Horace Mann Bond, noted American Negro educator, was reported by *The New York Times* as stating that (in the newspaper's words) "the American Negro's traditional aversion to Africa and things African as a humiliating part of his heritage was quickly changing to intense interest and sympathy." The *Times* account added that "A spokesman for the society predicted that the conference would mark a significant step in the American Negro's progress away from the 'native son' attitude and toward a belief in cultural pluralism combined with pride in his singular identity."[15] The rise of the independent African states and the entrance onto the stage of world history of powerful and consequential native African political leaders are events which have undoubtedly had a bracing and salutary effect on the American Negro's collective self-image,[16] but how much influence these developments will have in

[14] See C. Eric Lincoln, *The Black Muslims in America*, Boston, Beacon Press, 1961, and E. U. Essien-Udom, *Black Nationalism: The Search for an Identity*, Chicago, University of Chicago Press, 1962.
[15] *The New York Times*, June 27, 1959.
[16] See Harold R. Isaacs, *The New World of Negro Americans*, New York, John Day, 1963, for some evidence and a persuasive discussion of this point.

creating a desire for perpetual Negro communality and unique cultural identity on the part of the large majority of American Negroes remains to be seen.

While the viewpoint of "cultural pluralism," in some form or other, is dominant among intergroup relations agencies at the present time, it should not be thought that these agencies have given careful consideration to the meaning of this conception and its implications, particularly for the various facets of social structure and institutional life in the United States. As I have pointed out above, for the most part quite the contrary is the case. There is a distinct tendency to confine consideration of cultural pluralism to the issue of cultural differences in behavior and to slight or ignore pertinent issues of social structure and their relationship to communal group life. Even in the area of cultural behavior as such, questions relating to possible conflict in the value-assumptions of various ethnic groups tend to be overlooked or to be kept below the surface of articulation, and the question of possible limits in value variation for a functionally effective national culture is sometimes raised but not conspicuously dealt with in depth. Among the various questions and types of questions which I put to the agency officials whom I interviewed, in the attempt to elicit their thoughts on group life in America, was one direct query: "What would you say is meant by cultural pluralism?" Following are some characteristic replies (Each numbered reply is a separate one and is given in full) :[17]

1. "The ability of many religious, racial, and nationality patterns to coexist in helpfulness instead of harm. Written in the very nature of human life is vanity. We don't ask that people be less Jewish, less Protestant, or less Catholic. We want them to understand and appreciate those of other groups."

2. "A recognition of the value of different groups and some approval of their holding on to differences. It implies a kind of equality without conformity."

[17] In one case the answer was volunteered in another context.

3. "I would guess it meant several cultures touching upon each other but not mixed. It would enrich the person from the other culture. It could conceivably strengthen the concept of brotherhood, if people realized that even with these differences, there is an essential spirit running through all groups. If there is too much separateness, it is harder to feel the spirit of brotherhood."

4. "The concept of subgroups in the total American culture, retaining their identity and aspects of their parent culture and thus contributing not only to their own welfare and development but also to that of America as a whole. We plan a pamphlet on cultural pluralism for next year. We intend to deal with this problem in more depth."

5. "The right and value of diverse cultures working on those things they have in common, preserving those facets of their culture they wished to, as long as those cultural facets did not impinge on others. The right of diverse cultures to exist side-by-side and to preserve whatever they wish as long as they do not interfere with the rights of others. A positive approach to diversities."

6. "The acceptance of cultural differences both religiously and in terms of ethnic and cultural groups. These differences are important to the members of the group. One of the rights in America is the right to be different. As long as the practices and ideas don't conflict with each other or the national culture, people ought to have the right to preserve these differences. We do not strive to make everybody the same, nor are we trying to eliminate all tension resulting from differences but to reduce it to a tolerable level. There are limits—where anyone is getting hurt as a result of differences. I believe that national culture patterns are abrasive of group differences and wear them down. There is a strong tendency on the part of religious groups to produce ethnic neighborhoods."

7. "A complete and honest respect for cultural variation. No barrier in citizenship. I assume that some cultural diversity is desirable, but how much a stable social system could tolerate, I don't know."

8. "The possibility for people of different cultural identities to retain these identities within the framework of this nationality."

We note in these replies, in addition to their brevity, the emphasis on cultural behavior and the almost complete lack of attention to social structure. In some there is a recognition of the possibility of value-conflict; in others there is none. By and large, they suggest an absence of the opportunity for considered discussion, thought, and debate on long-range goals of social structure and group life.

If the organizations devoted to intergroup relations and ethnic group communal concerns in American life have devoted so little considered reflection to problems of social structure and long-range social structural goals in the United States, it may safely be presumed that the American public as a whole has devoted even less. That is why this book is being written. What I hope to do in the following pages is to make a contribution toward filling the gap that now exists in the discussion and articulation of problems of intergroup relations in the United States. This demands, above all, close and careful consideration of what it means for social relationships, organizational life, and social institutions, as well as for value-conflict and integration, to have a society composed of groups of varying racial, religious, and national backgrounds functioning within the context of modern industrialism and urbanization and operating under a democratic political system formally unconcerned with whatever degree of ethnic communality might arise within its borders. In this consideration I shall develop what may be called a "theory" of group life. I shall try to show its relationship to other theories of group life in America and to test it against the research findings of social scientists who have devoted skilled and patient labors to the study of group divisions and group relations on the American scene. Finally, I shall attempt to extract the implications of this theory for those efforts designed to attain the eminently desirable goal of eliminating the strands of prejudice and discrimination based on race, creed, or national origin from the warp and woof of American life.

2

The Subsociety and
the Subculture

What does a man answer when he is asked, or asks himself, a question as old as the time when some Pleistocene hunter, strayed far from his reassuring campfire and making his way fearfully through the dark tree-dense forest, came upon a stricken man, bested by his quarry, and realized that he had never seen him before—the first stranger? That question is "Who are you?"

If the stranger is a member of an Old, or more assuredly New, Stone Age band he will reply I am a Zuni, or an Arapesh, or a Kariera—these are my people—*the* people—so-an-so is my mother and thus-and-so is my mother's brother and this is our land, which is the world. In other words, he places himself in a group which is a political unit, which is culturally uniform, and which occupies a definite geographical place (at the center of the universe), and within this group he occupies more specific relationships of kinship.

The subsequent history of mankind, apart from those isolated pockets of pre-literate society, steadily and irretrievably dwindling in number, which have been by-passed by what we immodestly choose to call civilization, is from one point of view a record of a

series of events which have challenged with ever-increasing force
and complexity this simple model of self-identification.

The coming of settled agriculture and animal domestication
brought with it the possibilty of accumulating food surpluses,
which, in turn, allowed some members of the society to withdraw
from the previously society-wide demand of hunting and gathering
or fishing for the daily supply of edibles, and to devote themselves
to the specialized pursuits which a better-fed and growing population required: the extraction and smelting of ore to create more ef-
ficient metal tools, the propitiation and cultivation of the gods, the
governing of the larger and more complex community. These occupations tended to become differentially evaluated and rewarded and
to create various life-styles, and the occupational specialization
might be passed down to the sons and the sons of sons, and thus
social class divisions arose. Ultimately these agricultural surpluses
made it possible for some men to live apart from the agricultural
community itself, to reside together in walled towns and cities
where busy markets allowed them to trade their services and hand-
made goods for the agricultural staples brought in by farmers from
the outlying area, driving their donkeys and camels along with a
stick and muttering suspiciously of the flesh-pots and wicked dis-
tractions to be found in this community of men who did not labor
and sweat in the sun to grow their daily food—who did not "work."
As the farmers entered the city, they would see the Ruler's soldiers,
haughty in their special garb, with swords clanking at their sides.

And from inside the palace there came occasionally in the clear
night to these peasants, sleeping fitfully on beds of straw in the ill-
smelling stable beside their beasts of burden and the wheat as yet
unsold, the sound of the voices of the courtiers, high-spirited but
thick with wine, and the tantalizing musical laughter of beautiful
women—women dressed in fine linen and rubbed with fragrant oint-
ments—women such as they knew they would never see in their
own village and by their own hearthsides.

THE SUBSOCIETY AND THE SUBCULTURE

Now what was a man to answer when asked who he was? I am an Assyrian, yes, but I am also a scribe in the palace and sit at the right hand of the King. My companions at table are priests and nobles and my daughter shall marry one of their sons. I live in the city and know nothing of the way in which barley is sown and reaped. Those who labor in the fields or clean out my stable are of my people, and yet we are not the same, and it is good that each of us knows his special place, for is this not the way it was decreed by the great god Ashur? And so he identifies himself as a member of a people, but also of a particular social class within that group and in a particular ecological segment of the society—that is, the urban segment.

As if this were not complex enough, simultaneously came the wars and conquests and migrations, and here is now a *people* subjugated by another *people* and transferred to the conquerors' land space, some as slaves, some not. I am a Jew but I dwell in Babylon. God speed the day of my return to the land of my fathers. Or the conquerors come and establish their rule in the land. I am a Hellene but the governor of my city and the collector of my taxes are Romans. And complexity compounded! Whereas in the days of my ancestors all of us worshipped the gods of Olympus, now there are some of us who have transferred their allegiance to the Roman gods, others who adhere to the commands of Mithras, and I have heard tell of a new cult in our city which follows the teachings of one Jesus of Nazareth, a Jew who was crucified during the reign of Tiberius and whose disciples call themselves Christians.

In distant India, under Hinduism, a religion which had developed, scholars speculate, out of the civilization of invaders from the northwest, there was taking form a rigidly hierarchical and hereditary system of castes and subcastes which carefully marked out a person's status, his life-space, his occupation, and his sense of identity. I am a Brahman, a keeper and interpreter of the sacred lore. All who are not Brahmans are my inferiors and must defer to me.

The winning of Europe by Christianity after the fall of Rome eventually imposed a substantial measure of religious uniformity over the peoples of Western Europe. Eastern Europe went its own way under the banner of Byzantium and Eastern Orthodoxy. The political units, however, such as the Holy Roman Empire and the Frankish Kingdom, were loosely organized, vast sprawling affairs which, of necessity, allowed considerable cultural autonomy to their heterogeneous array of ethnic societies, each, for the most part, occupying its own land base.[1] The feudal order, with its system of "estates" in which nobles and clergy dominated the vast peasant mass, emphasized identity with the semi-hereditary social class to which a man belonged, over and against the cross-cutting loyalties of ethnic background and budding nationhood. "Oh! you are an Englishman, are you?" Shaw has his nobleman twit the Chaplain in *Saint Joan*. "Certainly not, my lord: I am a gentleman," the cleric hastens to reply.

The momentous schism which we call the Protestant Reformation, and the rise of the nation-state, usher us into the modern era where national boundaries and concepts of statehood began to enclose groups of widely different ancestral heritages and variant and, initially, sharply conflicting, religious affiliations. The discovery and conquest of the Western hemisphere by the white-skinned Europeans brought them into contact with a new racial group, the Indian aborigines, and created the demand for cheap and heavy labor which caused the slave trade with Africa to flourish and resulted in the forced transportation to the New World of thousands of black men. The final developments of the modern era—the industrial revolution, which made both possible and necessary large-scale voluntary migration of peoples from Europe (and to a smaller extent Asia) to the Americas, the rapid growth of cities to the

[1] There are exceptions to this last point, to be sure. Spain, with its mixture of Christians, Moors, and Jews, is a conspicuous example. The Jews, of course, constituted small enclaves throughout Europe at this time.

point where Western life is predominantly and increasingly urban life, and the substantial widening of the channels for social mobility under free private enterprise capitalism so that a man could well change his social class position during his own lifetime—provide the setting for our contemporary inquiry. What now was a man to say when asked, Who are you?

THE ETHNIC GROUP

Before we endeavor to wrestle decisively with this question, let us look back at the brief historical survey with which we have opened this discussion and extract its relevant conceptual points. First and foremost, we note that early man identified himself as a member of a group, his "people," and that this "peoplehood" was, roughly, coterminous with a given rural land space, political government, no matter how rudimentary, a common culture in which a principal element was a set of religious beliefs and values shared more or less uniformly by all members of the group, and a common racial background ensuring an absence of wide differences in physical type. These are elements of the classic model of the "folk society," to use Robert Redfield's term,[2] a type of society which produces the characterological configuration described by David Riesman as fitting the "tradition-directed" person.[3] For my somewhat different purposes here, I wish to focus attention on the sense of "people-

[2] Robert Redfield, "The Folk Society," American Journal of Sociology, Vol. 52, No. 4 (January 1947), 293-308; Tepoztlan, A Mexican Village, Chicago, University of Chicago Press, 1930; and The Primitive World and Its Transformations, Ithaca, N.Y., Cornell University Press, 1953. Of course, there are other elements contained in the "folk society" model as discussed by Redfield and others; important among them are the absence of literacy and relative isolation from other groups.

[3] David Riesman, with the collaboration of Nathan Glazer and Reuel Denney, The Lonely Crowd: A Study of the Changing American Character, New Haven, Yale University Press, 1950.

hood" which, under the circumstances described, is unitary and uncomplicated. A convenient term for this sense of peoplehood is "ethnicity" (from the Greek word "ethnos," meaning "people" or "nation"), and we shall refer to a group with a shared feeling of peoplehood as an "ethnic group."[4]

The subsequent march of civilization, with its population increases, stimulation to social class formation, wars, migrations, creation of cities, proliferation of religious variation, and grouping in progressively larger political units has, in accelerating tempo, shattered and fragmented this sense of peoplehood—this ethnicity—detaching one by one each of the elements which composed the once unified whole, and isolating each element from the other. Accompanying these changes there have grown up ideologies which correspond to them. In the modern industrialized urban state, such an ideological model, stemming from classic eighteenth and nineteenth century liberalism blended with nationalism, views the huge nation as "the people"; the remnants of former types of ethnicity are then regarded as inconvenient vestiges—to be tolerated, if the state is democratic—but not to be encouraged. In the more extreme rationalist-liberal "one-world" or "federation of nations," "world government" ideological system, the ultimate point is reached: even nations are regarded as outmoded socio-political entities and the projected ideal sense of peoplehood is one which embraces the entire population of the world—the "brotherhood of man," knowing no boundaries, national or otherwise. Ethnicity, as representing a sense of special ancestral identification with some *portion* of mankind has, in this conception, disappeared entirely.

It is not my purpose at this point in the discussion to pass judgment on the desirability or undesirability of ethnicity or to evaluate its various forms, but rather to attempt to ascertain the realities as they exist. My essential thesis here is that the sense of ethnicity has

[4] Cf. E. K. Francis, "The Nature of The Ethnic Group," *American Journal of Sociology*, Vol. 52, No. 5 (March 1947), 393-400.

proved to be hardy. As though with a wily cunning of its own, as though there were some essential element in man's nature that demanded it—something that compelled him to merge his lonely individual identity in some ancestral group of fellows smaller by far than the whole human race, smaller often than the nation—the sense of ethnic belonging has survived. It has survived in various forms and with various names, but it has not perished, and twentieth-century urban man is closer to his stone-age ancestors than he knows.

Here we must digress for a moment to point out that the fragmentation of ethnicity left competing models of the sense of peoplehood, so that men were forced either to choose among them or to integrate them in some fashion—to arrange them, perhaps, in a series of concentric circles each a step farther removed from the core of personality and self-identification. Our knowledge of the social psychology of historical populations is not extensive, but we may speculate that the feudal peasant of the later Middle Ages, for instance, thought of himself as a member of Christendom, and that within this outer layer of group self-identification there were slight —probably very slight—overtones of identification as a Burgundian or a Sussexman, perhaps even as a Frenchman or an Englishman, but that closer to the core of his personality was his self-identification as a serf or a villein who lived in this particular village or as a part of the peasant group who served this particular lord of the manor. Peasant life in all ages is notoriously isolated and self-contained and relatively unaware of the larger world around it. The course and boundaries of empire, state, and nation might swirl and change above him, but what was this to the humble tiller of the soil? Life went on much as it did before—the oxen must be harnessed to the plough at dawn and driven over to the liege lord's acres regardless of whether the Anglo-Saxon Edward or the Norman William wielded the royal scepter.

In the above example, the sense of social class identity, which I wish to keep conceptually separate from ethnic identity, bulks larger than ethnicity itself, although it is still a social class contained within the white race, within Christendom, and more immediately, fused with the local village and manorial group all of whose members spoke the same dialect.

In the twentieth-century nation-state, and particularly in the United States, the competing models of ethnicity are the nation-state itself, race, religion, and national origin or nationality background. By the last term I mean the nation which our ancestors who first came to this country came *from*. The American who answers Who He Is, answers, then, from an ethnic point of view, as follows: I am an American, I am of the White or Negro or Mongoloid race, I am a Protestant, Catholic, or Jew, and I have a German, or Italian, or Irish, or English, or whatever, national background. While we can only speculate as to the order in which these layers of ethnic identity are arranged around the self, it is convenient to diagram the situation as in Figure 1.

In practice, it is probable that these discrete categories are attached to the self not separately or serially but in combination. Our conventional language of ethnic identification within the nation suggests as much. This American is a white Protestant Anglo-Saxon; that one is an Irish Catholic (white race understood), this one is a Negro Protestant (African background understood), that one is a Russian Jew (white race understood). This is the way we identify each other and ourselves when we think, ethnically, about Who We Are within the national boundaries. These are the labels of grouphood which history made sure would eventually be attached to our psychological self as we arrived in the world within the confines of this family rather than that one. "John Doe," rhapsodizes the newspaper editorial somewhat patronizingly about the American Negro who has gained respectable fame or fortune, "is a credit to his people." What "people" does the editorialist refer to? Not, we know, to his country, but to his race.

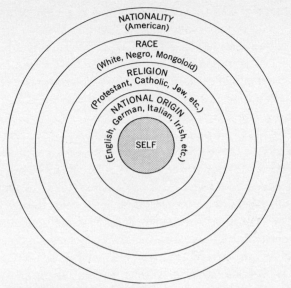

FIG. 1 ETHNIC IDENTITY OF AN AMERICAN

When I use the term "ethnic group," then, to refer to a type of group contained within the national boundaries of America, I shall mean by it any group which is defined or set off by race, religion, or national origin, or some combination of these categories. I do not mean to imply that these three concepts mean the same thing. They do not. Race, technically, refers to differential concentrations of gene frequencies responsible for traits which, so far as we know, are confined to physical manifestations such as skin color or hair form; it has no intrinsic connection with cultural patterns and institutions. Religion and national origins, while both cultural phenomena, are distinctly different institutions which do not necessarily vary concomitantly. However, all of these categories have a common social-psychological referent, in that all of them serve to create, through historical circumstances, a sense of peoplehood for

groups within the United States, and this common referent of peoplehood is recognized in the American public's usage of these three
terms, frequently in interchangeable fashion. Our point, then, is
not that we wish to legitimize confusion by giving it a name, but
that there is a common social-psychological core to the categories
"race," "religion," and "national origin"—the sense of peoplehood
—and the term "ethnic group" is a useful one for designation of
this common element.[5]

This "sense of peoplehood" itself deserves further examination.
Of what does it consist? What are its component elements? To a
member of a stone-age society—the man of prehistory—such a
question would have been incomprehensible since, for him, all the
potential elements of peoplehood were joined together in a unitary
whole. The members of the small band of which his family was a
part lived together on the land, worshipped in the same manner,
had roughly similar views of right and wrong, hunted, fished, or
planted in the same way, looked very much alike, and governed
themselves. While there were individual differences in personality
type or physical prowess, or skill, these differences remained on an
individual basis; they did not mark off groups beyond kinship lines.
Ethnicity, then, was simply the human environment in which one
breathed and functioned.

The man who has entered history, however, the man of cities,
occupational specialization, war, conquest, migration, and religious
variation, while clinging tenaciously to the sense of ethnicity, is
literally forced to mould its nebulous shape more narrowly in accordance with the vagaries of the history of which he is a part. At

---

[5] Some sociologists use the term "ethnic group" to refer to a national origins
group—thus the Italian or Polish ethnic group. I prefer the broader use of the
term because we have a specific phrase, "national origin" or "nationality background" and we need the broader term because of the common sense of peoplehood running through race, religion, or national origin—the common social-
psychological referent. It is thus simply a matter of semantic convenience. My
usage is in accord with that of E. K. Francis in the work cited above.

one time he may feel his peoplehood on the basis of present or past national grouping, at another on the basis of common religious adherence, and at still another, on the basis of common racial identity. Common to all these objective bases, however, is the social-psychological element of a special sense of both ancestral and future-oriented identification with the group. These are the "people" of my ancestors, therefore they are my people, and they will be the people of my children and their children. With members of other groups I may share political participation, occupational relationships, common civic enterprise, perhaps even an occasional warm friendship. But in a very special way which history has decreed, I share a sense of indissoluble and intimate identity with *this group* and *not that one* within the larger society and the world.

Once these attitudes of special ethnic group identity develop, it is obvious that they reinforce each other through the system of mutual expectations that grow up. As Will Herberg has pointed out, it is *expected* in American society that we *be* either a Protestant, a Catholic, or a Jew, whether we are formally connected with a church or synagogue or not.[6] And the "status" of being a Negro or a White or a Mongoloid Oriental is not one from which one may voluntarily resign. The occasional individual who may have determined independently that he will wear none of these labels— religious or racial—finds that the institutional structure of the society and the set of built-in social and psychological categories with which most Americans are equipped to place him—to give him a "name"—are loaded against him. Group categorization, then, has its own social momentum once it is set in motion and is by no means purely a matter of individual volitions acting in concert. Herberg put it this way: "The way in which one identifies and locates oneself ('Who, what, am I?') is closely related to how one is identified and located in the larger community ('Who, what, is he?'). Normally they reflect, sustain, and illumine each other; it is only in

[6] Herberg, op. cit., Chapter 3.

abnormal situations that they diverge and conflict."[7] It was the perception of this sociological fact and its implications that underlay the social psychologist Kurt Lewin's suggestion that "interdependence of fate" rather than similarity or dissimilarity in characteristics of individuals was the basic component of group constitution.[8] Considering it further, we may say that the similarities and dissimilarities of the past, which certainly played some role in group formation at any given time, both persuade and force us through the social grouping precipitations of history and the social-psychological expectations concerning group identity which these precipitations have created in the present, to take on group identifications which may or may not be congenial to our individual interests, preferences, and idiosyncracies.

SOCIAL STRUCTURE AND CULTURE

The ethnic group, besides being based on a social-psychological sense of peoplehood stemming from history, has another major characteristic which distinguishes it from all "small groups" and from most other "large groups." This is the nature of its relationship to the various phenomena which may be subsumed under the term "social structure." I have used this term in the previous chapter and suggested its meaning there, but I propose now to define it more closely since its elucidation is crucial to the entire argument of the book. By the social structure of a society I mean the set of crystallized social relationships which its members have with each other which places them in groups, large or small, permanent or temporary, formally organized or unorganized, and which relates them to the major institutional activities of the society, such as

[7] Herberg, op. cit. p. 25.
[8] Kurt Lewin, *Resolving Social Conflicts*, New York, Harper and Brothers, 1948, pp. 163-6; 183-5.

economic and occupational life, religion, marriage and the family, education, government, and recreation. To study a society's social structure is to study the nature of its family groups, its age and sex distribution and the social groupings based on these categories, its social cliques, its formal and informal organizations, its divisions on the basis of race, religion, and national origin, its social classes, its urban and rural groups, and the pattern of social relationships in school and college, on the job, in the church, in voting behavior and political participation, and in leisure time activities. It is a large definition but a consistent one in that it focuses on *social relationships*, and social relationships that are *crystallized*—that is, which are not simply occasional and capricious but have a pattern of some repetition and can to some degree be predicted, and are based, at least to some extent, on a set of shared expectations.

Of the various ways of classifying the groups which represent the crystallization of social relationships there is one which is of particular interest to us here. It is based on the concept of the "primary group," suggested by the pioneer American sociologist, Charles Horton Cooley,[9] and in its extended form includes the obverse concept of the "secondary group." The primary group is a group in which contact is personal, informal, intimate, and usually face-to-face, and which involves the entire personality, not just a segmentalized part of it. The family, the child's play group, and the social clique are all examples of a primary group. They are primary in that they are first both from the point of view of time in the "socialization" process—that is, the process by which the growing child is indoctrinated into the values of his culture—and first from the standpoint of their importance in moulding human personality.

[9] Charles Horton Cooley, *Social Organization*, New York, Charles Scribner's Sons, 1909, Chapter 3. See also, Leonard Broom and Philip Selznick, *Sociology: A Text with Adapted Readings*, Evanston, Ill., Row, Peterson and Co., 1955, Chapter 5.

In direct contrast, the secondary group is a group in which contacts tend to be impersonal, formal or casual, non-intimate, and segmentalized; in some cases they are face-to-face, in others not. We belong to many an "interest" organization, for instance, in American society, most of whose other members we never see, but whose annual bill for dues arrives promptly. The intimate friends we invite to our house regularly for dinner and to whose parties we are invited in return constitute a primary group. The civic committee for the preservation of the community's parks to which we belong and which meets twice a year is a secondary group. And, obviously, there will be groups which will be hard to classify but which will appear to have both primary and secondary aspects—to fall somewhere in the middle of a scale built on this dimension. To put the matter in another way, we may speak of *primary relationships* with other persons, which are personal, intimate, emotionally affective, and which bring into play the whole personality, as contrasted with *secondary relationships*, which are impersonal, formal, and segmentalized, and tend not to come very close to the core of personality.

Social structure, man's crystallized social relationships, is one side of the coin of human life, the other side of which is *culture*. Culture, as the social scientist uses the term, refers to the social heritage of man—the ways of acting and the ways of doing things which are passed down from one generation to the next, not through genetic inheritance but by formal and informal methods of teaching and demonstration. The classic definition of culture is that of the early anthropologist, E. B. Tylor, who described it as "that complex whole which includes knowledge, belief, art, morals, law, custom, and any other capabilities and habits acquired by man as a member of society."[10] Culture, in other words, is the way of life of a society, and if analyzed further is seen to consist of prescribed ways of behaving or norms of conduct, beliefs, values, and skills, along with

[10] E. B. Tylor, *Primitive Culture*, London, John Murray, 1891 (third edition), Vol. I, p. 1. The first edition appeared in 1871.

the behavioral patterns and uniformities based on these categories
—all this we call "non-material culture"—plus, in an extension of
the term, the artifacts created by these skills and values, which we
call "material culture."

Culture and social structure are obviously closely related and in
a constant state of dynamic interaction, for it is the norms and
values of the society which, for the most part, determine the nature
of the social groupings and social relationships which its members
will create; and, conversely, frequently it is through the action of
men in social groups that cultures undergo change and modification. To illustrate the first point we need only think of the adult
organizations so characteristic of American life (and which we take
for granted) composed of adults of both sexes, married and un-
married, who come together because of some common interest. An
example would be a municipal choral society, a poetry club, or a
chapter of the American Civil Liberties Union. An organization
composed in this fashion would be unthinkable in a traditional
Moslem society. To illustrate the second point, we may note that
it was an organization, the Bolshevik Party under Lenin, which
provided the dynamic thrust that produced the vast cultural
changes that constitute the enormous behavioral gap between Czar-
ist Russia during World War I and the Soviet Union of the 1960's.

When used in the general sense, the term "culture" refers to the
sum of man's social heritage existing over the world at any given
time. More frequently, however, the term is used specifically to
refer to the social heritage or way of life of a particular human
society at a particular time. Thus one speaks of American culture
in the twentieth century, as differentiated, for instance, from French
culture in the eighteenth century, or from contemporary Chinese
culture. It is obvious, then, that the term may be applied to human
groupings of various dimensions, whenever these groupings involve
shared behavioral norms and patterns that differ somewhat from
those of other groups. Thus in one sense, America, France, and
Italy are all a part of Western culture because of certain behavioral

values shared by Americans, Frenchmen, and Italians as the result
of their common social heritage of European life—values which
they do not share with peoples of Oriental or African cultural background. By the same token, groups *within* a national society may
differ somewhat in their cultural values since in a large, modern,
complex, multigroup nation, cultural uniformity of the type approximated in a primitive society is impossible of attainment. Thus
we may speak of the culture of a group smaller than the national
society.

THE SUBSOCIETY AND THE SUBCULTURE

With these concepts of "social structure" and "culture" in mind,
we may now go on to develop the argument. The ethnic group, I
have said, bears a special relationship to the social structure of a
modern complex society which distinguishes it from all small
groups and most other large groups. It is this: *within the ethnic
group there develops a network of organizations and informal social
relationships which permits and encourages the members of the
ethnic group to remain within the confines of the group for all of
their primary relationships and some of their secondary relationships throughout all the stages of the life-cycle.* From the cradle in
the sectarian hospital to the child's play group, to the social clique
in high school, the fraternity and religious center in college, the
dating group within which he searches for a spouse, the marriage
partner, the neighborhood of residence, the church affiliation and
the church clubs, the men's and the women's social and service
clubs, the adult clique of "marrieds," the vacation resort, and then
as the age-cycle nears completion, the rest home for the elderly and,
finally, the sectarian cemetery—in all of these activities and relationships which are close to the core of personality and selfhood—
the member of the ethnic group may, if he wishes, and will in fact
in many cases, follow a path which never takes him across the
boundaries of his ethnic subsocietal network.

In addition, some of the basic institutional activities of the larger society become either completely or in part ethnically enclosed. Family life and religion are, virtually by definition, contained within the ethnic boundaries. Education becomes ethnically enclosed to the extent that "parochial" school systems are utilized. Even within public and nonsectarian private schools and colleges, a system of social cliques and voluntary religious organizations set up for educational and social purposes may effectively separate the students from each other in all but formal classroom instruction. Economic and occupational activities, based as they are on impersonal market relationships, defy ethnic enclosure in the United States more than any institution except the political or governmental, but even here a considerable degree of ethnic enclosure is by no means a rarity. The white Christian who works for an all-white Christian business concern, or the Jew who is employed by an all-Jewish firm, labors at the points of intersection of the economic institution and ethnicity. Even in the "all-ethnic" business concern, impersonal secondary relationships across ethnic group lines may take place in wholesale purchasing or in sales. However, if the clientele of the concern is also of the same ethnic group— examples would be the kosher butcher shop or the retail store whose only merchandise is religious objects for Catholic consumption— then the isolation from inter-ethnic contacts even on the job is virtually complete.

Governmental relationships to the larger society are, by definition, non-ethnically oriented. That is, barring the exceptions noted earlier, the politico-legal system of the United States recognizes no distinctions on the basis of race, religion, or national origin, and a citizen's obligations, responsibilities, and relationships to the laws of the state are not ethnically qualified.[11] Active work in political

[11] A further exception should be noted here: the federal government's recognition of religious belief and background as relevant in the case of the conscientious objector to war and military service. Even here, the exemption is not absolute; "alternative service" of a non-military nature is required.

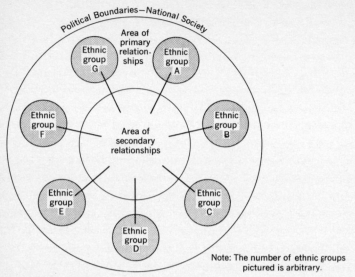

FIG. 2 AMERICAN SOCIETY

parties, if it is above the local neighborhood level (and frequently even there), takes one across ethnic group lines. "Bloc voting" on an ethnic basis has, of course, played an important part in American political affairs, and although the day of herding masses of unknowing immigrants to the polls is past, ethnic background still influences voting preferences in substantial fashion,[12] even though it is a reasonable guess that, over the long run, time and increasing socio-economic differentiation within each ethnic group will grad-

[12] See Paul F. Lazarsfeld, Bernard Berelson, and Hazel Gaudet, *The People's Choice*, New York, Columbia University Press, 1948 (second edition); Bernard R. Berelson, Paul F. Lazarsfeld, and William N. McPhee, *Voting*, Chicago, University of Chicago Press, 1954; Angus Campbell, Gerald Gurin, and Warren E. Miller, *The Voter Decides*, Evanston, Ill., Row, Peterson and Company, 1954; and Samuel Lubell, *The Future of American Politics*, New York, Doubleday and Co. (Second edition, Doubleday Anchor Books), 1956.

ually dilute the ethnic impact on politics. Military service, since the banishment of racial segregation from the armed forces, mixes people of varying ethnic backgrounds indiscriminately.

I shall return to this subject in greater detail later and discuss exceptions, individual and patterned, to the "model" of American society which I am presenting, but here my purpose is to paint the picture in broad strokes. In these terms, as far as we have gone, the American social structure may be seen, then, as a national society which contains within its political boundaries a series of *subsocieties* based on ethnic identity. The network of organizations, informal social relationships, and institutional activities which makes up the ethnic subsociety tends to pre-empt most or all primary group relationships, while secondary relationships across ethnic group lines are carried out in the "larger society," principally in the spheres of economic and occupational life, civic and political activity, public and private nonparochial education, and mass entertainment. All of these relationships, primary and secondary, are contained within the boundaries of common political allegiance and responsibility to the politico-legal demands and expectations of American nationality. The structure is shown in Figure 2. Table 2 presents the relationship of ethnicity to institutional functioning in America in summary form.

TABLE 2. ETHNICITY AND INSTITUTIONAL ACTIVITY

Institution	Ethnicity
Political	Mostly mixed
Economic	Mostly mixed, with significant exceptions
Education	Partly mixed—parochial schools and some segregation in social activities qualify mixing influence of formal structure of public and private non-parochial school systems
Religion	Ethnically enclosed
Family	Ethnically enclosed
Recreation	Ethnically enclosed in participation, except for impersonal relationships at mass entertainment functions

Thus far we have called attention to two functional characteristics of the ethnic group or subsociety. First, it serves psychologically as a source of group self-identification—the locus of the sense of intimate peoplehood—and second, it provides a patterned network of groups and institutions which allows an individual to confine his primary group relationships to his own ethnic group throughout all the stages of the life cycle. Its third functional characteristic is that it refracts the national cultural patterns of behavior and values through the prism of its own cultural heritage. This unique subnational heritage may consist of cultural norms brought over from the country of recent emigration, it may rest on different religious values, or on the cumulative domestic experiences of enforced segregation as a group within American borders over a number of generations, or on some combination of these sources of cultural diversity. It is this phenomenon which is patently the basis for the term "cultural pluralism," used to describe the model of American society as a composite of groups which have preserved their own cultural identity.[13] The question of the actual extent of this cultural diversity in contemporary American society I wish to leave for later discussion. My purpose here is simply to point out that provision for the possibility of cultural diversity within the larger national society is the third major functional characteristic of the ethnic subsociety. In this sense, then, just as we speak of the national culture as representing the cultural way of life or cultural patterns of the national society, one may think of the ethnic subsociety as having its own cultural patterns, these patterns consisting of the national cultural patterns blended with or refracted through the particular cultural heritage of the ethnic group; this blend or amalgam we may call, in preliminary fashion, the *subculture* of the ethnic subsociety.

The term "subculture" has been used by a number of sociologists to refer to the cultural patterns of any subgroup or type of sub-

[13] The historical development of this concept will be traced in Chapter 6.

group within the national society. One may speak of the subculture of a gang, a neighborhood, a factory, a hospital, etc. Albert K. Cohen's excellent study of delinquency in which he analyzes the cultural patterns of the delinquent gang is based on such a use of the term.[14] We prefer, however, to reserve the term "subculture" to stand for the cultural patterns of a subsociety which contains both sexes, all ages, and family groups, and which parallels the larger society in that it provides for a network of groups and institutions extending throughout the individual's entire life cycle. For the cultural patterns of a group more restricted in scope than an entire subsociety we suggest the term "groupculture."[15] The distinction allows us to isolate and distinguish from each other phenomena of different scope and import. It is summarized briefly in the paradigm presented in Table 3.

Thus far I have spoken of the subsociety as though it were equivalent to the ethnic group. However, if we stop to consider the functional characteristics of the subsociety—its salience as a locus of group identification, its network of groups and institutions which allow primary group relationships to be confined within its borders throughout the life cycle, and its role as a carrier of particular cultural patterns, then it becomes clear that other sociological categories, in addition to the ethnic group, demand consideration. The rise of the city created differences between the urban dweller and

[14] Albert K. Cohen, *Delinquent Boys*, Glencoe, Ill., The Free Press, 1955. See, also, for such a use of the term, several papers by Alfred McClung Lee: "Levels of Culture as Levels of Social Generalization," *American Sociological Review*, Vol. 10, No. 4 (August, 1945), pp. 485-95; "Social Determinants of Public Opinions," *International Journal of Opinion and Attitude Research*, Vol. 1, No. 1 (March 1947), pp. 12-29; and "A Sociological Discussion of Consistency and Inconsistency in Intergroup Relations," *Journal of Social Issues*, Vol. 5, No. 3, pp. 12-18.

[15] Cf. use of this term in Alfred McClung Lee, "Attitudinal Multivalence in Relation to Culture and Personality," *American Journal of Sociology*, Vol. 60, No. 3 (November 1954) pp. 294-9. Lee uses the term to refer to the particularized culture of any group, regardless of scope.

the farmer which were also reflected in the areas of group identification, social relationships, and cultural behavior. The eventual creation of the large nation meant that people living in areas widely distant from one another would develop regional differences in behavior and self-identification, as well as regionally contained social systems. But most important of all in this connection was the rise of *social classes*, to which we referred in our historical summary.

TABLE 3. SOCIAL UNITS AND THEIR CULTURES

Social Unit	Cultural Term
The National Society (or The Society): (the nation with its political boundaries)	The National Culture (or The Culture)
The Subsociety (the social unit, smaller than the national society, which contains a large network of groups and institutions extending through the entire life cycle of the individual)	The Subculture
The Group (groups of segmental import; for example, the gang, the play-group, the factory, the hospital, the office)	The Groupculture

Social class phenomena refer to hierarchical arrangements of persons in a society based on differences in economic power, political power, or social status.[16] (I have defined "social status" elsewhere as "a psychological system of attitudes in which superiority and inferiority are reciprocally ascribed.")[17] Usually these three categories or "variables" of class hierarchy vary together to a con-

[16] For general analyses of social class research and theory in the recent sociological literature, see Bernard Barber, *Social Stratification*, New York, Harcourt Brace and Co., 1957; Milton M. Gordon, *Social Class in American Sociology*, Durham, N.C., Duke University Press, 1958; Joseph A. Kahl, *The American Class Structure*, New York, Rinehart and Co., 1957; Leonard Reissman, *Class in American Society*, Glencoe, Ill., Free Press, 1960; and Kurt B. Mayer, *Class and Society*, New York, Doubleday and Co., 1955. For a popular account with emphasis on social status, see *The Status Seekers*, by Vance Packard (New York, David McKay Co., 1959).

[17] Gordon, op. cit., p. 245.

siderable extent—that is, those who are high in economic power tend to be high in political power and in social status, and so on. Each of the variables, in other words, "converts" easily to the other, and there is a process of constant interaction in which greater economic power allows one to secure higher social status, while higher social status, in turn, makes it easier to secure additional economic power. However, the variables do not vary together perfectly and there is always some overlapping or lack of synchronization when large numbers of people are being considered. For instance, the average clergyman has higher social status than he has economic power. Consequently, it is necessary to decide which of the variables or dimensions we will demarcate in order to designate groups in American life to which we attach the term "social classes." There is some reason to believe that the social status dimension is the most closely related to the variables of sense of group identification, confinement of intimate social relationships, and particularized cultural behavior—all criteria of the subsociety. Accordingly, we will use social status as our direct basis for social class division. When we speak of social classes, then, we shall mean the hierarchy of social status groups in American society, and it will be understood that these differences in social status also imply, on the average, differences in wealth and income—i.e. economic power —and differences in political power in the community and the nation.

The precise number of hierarchical status groups on the American scene has been a matter of dispute among sociologists, and there are a few who even describe the American status system as one vast hierarchical continuum without any groupings at all but simply individual differences in position on the continuum. My own view is that the idea of broadly conceived status groups gives a better fit to the realities of the American status system than the unbroken continuum theory.[18] These groups do not have hard and

18 For my reasons, see Gordon, op. cit., Chapters 6 and 8.

fixed boundaries but shade off imperceptibly into each other. As Vance Packard has well put it: "While there is a continuum, it is also true that people will tend to cluster so that the continuum is actually a series of bulges and contractions. The major bulges might be called the major class groupings."[19] The existence of these groups is based on the social-psychological constructs or categories in people's minds as they think about their own and other people's social status directly or obliquely, and on the social relationships and types of cultural behavior that develop in conjunction with these subjective categories. Some subgroupings of status are probably made within the major social classes so that there are internal status differentiations of lesser magnitude within each class. It is possible, provided the correct steps are taken, to move up in the class system, and this is what is referred to as upward social mobility. Downward mobility may also take place under certain circumstances.

While there will be variations depending on the type of community, the general social status structure in the United States may, in the present stage of our knowledge, most satisfactorily be described, with certain qualifications, as one made up of six classes. I follow the terminology of W. Lloyd Warner, a pioneer student of the American social status structure, and his associates in designating these classes as the upper-upper, lower-upper, upper-middle, lower-middle, upper-lower, and lower-lower.[20]

I shall discuss the American class system, and particularly its relationship to ethnicity, in more detail later; at this point it will be sufficient for our purposes to characterize these classes briefly. The upper-uppers are the "old family" aristocrats, to be found especially in the class systems of the larger cities of the eastern seaboard where

[19] Packard, op. cit., p. 30.
[20] See W. Lloyd Warner and Paul S. Lunt, *The Social Life of a Modern Community* (Yankee City Series, Vol. 1), New Haven, Yale University Press, 1941. For a detailed criticism and evaluation of the Warner method of studying social classes and of his findings, see Gordon, op. cit., Chapter 4.

long histories of settlement have made their claims to ancestral prestige possible. They are usually wealthy, but more importantly, they can point to a family tradition of wealth and leading social position in the community. This background of wealth and position transmitted over a number of generations has resulted in the development of cultural patterns of behavior in dress, clothes, and manner which mark them subtly as having been born and reared in the world of power, privilege, and "good taste." The men are bankers, owners and directors of important businesses, or work in high prestige professions such as medicine, law, and architecture. The families are listed in the city's *Social Register* or its equivalent, and they have been so listed since these compilations of the names, addresses, and schools of the elite began to appear in the late nineteenth century. They are the unostentatious but firmly established leaders of the "society" world of their city.

More and more, however, the upper-uppers find themselves sharing power, privilege, and social relationships with the families who have amassed substantial wealth and power more recently. These are the "newly rich," the lower-uppers, whose fortunes date from the post-Civil War industrial expansion of America or the even more recent industrial and military developments of the twentieth century and thus have not yet received the ultimate accolade of gentility which time, in sufficient quantity, will doubtless eventually bestow. The lower-uppers, however, although coolly received at first, gradually make their way into the organizations, social cliques, and institutions of the upper-uppers, this infiltration gradually being reflected for many in *Social Register* listing. Intermarriage and the passage of time establish many of the "newer" families securely in the upper class as the still later developments of American industrial life cast up a fresh lower-upper group. Time, then, tends to blur the distinction between the upper-upper and the lower-upper groups, and many communities outside of the East, because of their foreshortened history, have never had an upper-upper class in the terms described, and can best be characterized as possessing a five-class system headed by a relatively undifferentiated and unseparated upper class.[21]

The upper-middle class in American communities may best be described as the "solid substantial citizens," who, for the most part, are comfortably well off or have reasonably adequate incomes but are not wealthy or "social." If they are below forty-five years of age, they have probably been to college. Increasingly, a college education is the passport to upper-middle class status. They are the community's business executives and professionals—owners of middle-sized business concerns, middle-level executives of the large corporations, doctors, lawyers, architects, engineers, scientists, clergymen, college professors (the last two groups being among the relatively low-paid members of the class), and executives of the various service and civic bureaucracies that are becoming more and more numerous. This is only a partial occupational listing for the good-sized corps of largely (and increasingly) college-trained men who "run things" at the middle levels of power and decision-making in American communities of various sizes and who, in the metropolitan areas, ride the commuting trains home to their nightly refuge in the Scarsdales, Montclairs, and Ardmores of the nation.

Below the upper class and the upper-middle class, which W. Lloyd Warner groups together as "the Level Above the Common Man" and Vance Packard refers to collectively as "the Diploma

[21] Thus W. Lloyd Warner and his associates and August B. Hollingshead, in separate studies of the same small midwestern community carried out in the early 1940's, each divided the community into five classes, the upper class being undifferentiated into subclasses. See W. Lloyd Warner and Associates, *Democracy in Jonesville*, New York, Harper and Brothers, 1949; and August B. Hollingshead, *Elmtown's Youth*, New York, John Wiley and Sons, 1949. For an excellent study of a metropolitan upper class, see E. Digby Baltzell, *Philadelphia Gentlemen*, Glencoe, Ill., The Free Press, 1958. For a stimulating general discussion of the upper class in American life, with emphasis on the power rather than the status dimension, see C. Wright Mills, *The Power Elite*, New York, Oxford University Press, 1956.

Elite," are the lower-middle class and the two lower classes. The line between the lower-middle and the upper-lower class (these two constituting Warner's "Level of the Common Man") is becoming increasingly blurred as blue-collar workers in the huge production industries, organized into powerful labor unions, increasingly surpass lower-level white-collar workers in income and the material possessions which income can buy. Perhaps the matter can be put in this way. Historically, the lower-middle class was predominantly a class made up of white-collar people of the lower ranks—clerks, salespersons, secretaries, owners of small businesses, and the like—together with a few "aristocrats" of the blue-collar world doing highly skilled work. The upper-lower class was then solidly composed of the bulk of skilled and semi-skilled manual workers, plus those unskilled workers who maintained minimum standards in life-style. The income gains of the blue-collar workers under powerful post-World War II unions, at the expense of the largely unorganized white-collar workers, raise questions about the subsequent interplay of income, power, status, and style of life at these class levels—questions which are as yet largely unanswered by sociological research. The issues are doubtless still in the process of resolution. In terms of status all we can safely say is that traditionally the bulk of the blue-collar workers have been classified in the upper-lower or "working" class and that social class dynamics currently at work may modify this situation eventually for the reasons mentioned—to what degree, we can only speculate.

The lower-lower class is composed of the unskilled manual laborers and the frequently unemployed who inhabit the slums of the nation's cities, towns, and rural areas. Their living standards are low, they are looked upon with either contempt or pity by the rest of the community, and their way of life rarely breeds ambition in either themselves or their children. Family desertion by the male is common in this class, and frequently public relief is called upon to maintain the mother and her children.

Farm owners may be thought of as belonging to either the lower-middle, upper-lower, or in some cases upper-middle class, depending on the size and scope of their farm operation and the way of life they and their families engage in.

The significance of social class analysis for our argument is that social classes, though not as precisely bounded as ethnic groups, also become sources of group identification, social areas of confinement for primary group relations, and bearers of particular cultural patterns of behavior. This, in fact, from one point of view, is the most important set of findings which has emerged from the vast accumulation of research and inquiry into social class phenomena in America which social scientists, which accelerating tempo, have been carrying out during the past thirty years. The social class, in other words, while not formally delineated, tends to have its own network of characteristic organizations, institutional activities, and social cliques. These are created because people who are approximately in the same social class have similar interests and tastes, have a common educational background, and work at occupations which bring them in touch with one another in various ways and which involve common types of experience. Thus they feel "comfortable" with each other. These reasons are probably more compelling than sheer "social snobbery" or status consciousness itself in keeping people of widely separated social classes apart from each other in primary group relationships, although doubtless all these reasons interact with one another to produce social separation.

The child, then, grows up in a particular family which is part of a particular class and learns the cultural values of that class as those values are brought home to him in family training, neighborhood play groups, and class-oriented educational patterns. Men of the same social class will thus share certain cultural values and patterns which distinguish them from Americans of other class backgrounds. Upward social mobility, then, involves the need for learning and adopting values and behavior in accordance with the standards of the class into which the upwardly mobile person is moving.

We have now isolated four factors or social categories which play a part in creating subsocieties within the national society that is America. They are ethnic group, social class, rural or urban residence, and region of country lived in. In the original form in which I first published this theory in 1947, my essential thesis was that these four factors do not function in isolation, or serially, but *combine or intersect* to form the basic large social units which make up American society and which bear and transmit the subcultures of America.[22] While the factors are theoretically discrete, they tend to form in their combination *"a functioning unity which has an integrated impact on the participating individual."*[23] Thus a person is not simply a white Protestant. He is simultaneously a lower-middle class white Protestant living in a small town in the South, or he is an upper-middle class white Catholic living in a metropolitan area in the Northeast, or a lower-class Negro living in the rural South, and so on. To put it in another way, the stratifications based on ethnicity are intersected at right angles by the stratifications based on social class, and the social units or blocks of bounded social space created by their intersection are contained in an urban or a rural setting in a particular region of the country. The analytical scheme is summarized in Table 4.

Central to this type of analysis is, of course, the relationship of the ethnic group stratification system to the social class stratifica-

---

[22] See Milton M. Gordon, "The Concept of the Sub-Culture and Its Application," *Social Forces*, Vol. 26, No. 1 (October 1947), pp. 40-42. See, also, "A System of Social Class Analysis," *Drew University Studies*, No. 2 (August 1951) pp. 15-18; *Social Class in American Sociology, cit. supra*, pp. 252-6; and for a fuller exposition, "Social Structure and Goals in Group Relations," in *Freedom and Control in Modern Society*, Morroe Berger, Theodore Abel, and Charles H. Page (eds.), New York, D. Van Nostrand Co., 1954. In these publications I used the term "subculture" to stand elliptically for both the subsociety and the subculture as defined here.

[23] Gordon, ibid. p. 40 (italics as in original).

TABLE 4. THE SUBSOCIETY AND THE SUBCULTURE

Factors Combining to Form
the Subsociety

Ethnic Group
    race
    religion
    national origins   The Subsociety
                                         with its particular
Social Class   Subculture

Rural-Urban Residence

Regional Residence

Examples of particular subsocieties characterized by particular subcultures:

Upper-middle class white Protestant, southern urban
Lower-middle class white Catholic, northern urban
Lower-lower class Negro Protestant, southern rural
Upper-middle class Negro Protestant, northern urban
Lower-middle class white Jewish, western urban
Upper class white Jewish, northern urban

---

tion system. In 1951 I wrote: "American society is 'criss-crossed' by two sets of stratification structures, one based on social status, economic power, and political power differences, regardless of ethnic background, the other a set of status and power relationships based precisely on division of the population by racial, nationality background, and religious categories into 'Old Americans,' Negroes, Jews, Catholics, Japanese-Americans, Italians, French-Canadians, etc."[24] In effect, this means that each ethnic group may be thought of as being divided into subgroups on the basis of social class, and that theoretically each ethnic group might conceivably have the whole spectrum of classes within it, although in practice, some ethnic groups will be found to contain only a partial distribution of social class subgroups.

In the meantime, sociologists August B. Hollingshead and Jerome K. Myers, at Yale University, had been studying the social struc-

[24] Gordon, "A System of Social Class Analysis," op. cit., pp. 15-16; see also, *Social Class in American Sociology*, op. cit., p. 252.

ture of the city of New Haven and had come to a similar conclusion about the relationship of the ethnic group and the social class systems in American communities. In 1952, in a paper reporting on this research, Hollingshead stated:

The data indicate that the community's current social structure is differentiated *vertically* along racial, ethnic, and religious lines, and each of these vertical cleavages, in turn, is differentiated horizontally by a series of strata or classes that are encompassed within it. Around the socio-biological axis of race two social worlds have evolved—a Negro world and a white world. The white world is divided by ethnic origin and religion into Catholic, Protestant, and Jewish contingents. Within these divisions there are numerous ethnic schisms. The Irish hold aloof from the Italians, and the Italians move in different circles from the Poles. The Jews maintain a religious and social life separate from the Gentiles. The horizontal strata that transect each of these vertical structures are based upon the social values that are attached to occupation, education, place of residence in the community, and associations. Thus ethnic origin, occupation, education, and residence are combined into a complicated status system.

The vertically differentiating factors of race, religion, and ethnic origin, when combined with the horizontally differentiating ones of occupation, education, place of residence and so on, produce a social structure that is highly compartmentalized.[25]

Reviewing the evidence dealing with the nature of institutional and organizational life within some of the bounded strata created by this system, Hollingshead referred to "the development of *parallel class structures* within the limits of race, ethnic origin, and religion."[26]

[25] August B. Hollingshead, "Trends in Social Stratification: A Case Study," *American Sociological Review*, Vol. 17, No. 6 (December 1952), p. 685 (italics as in original). See also, August B. Hollingshead and Frederick C. Redlich, *Social Class and Mental Illness*, New York, John Wiley and Sons, 1958; and Jerome K. Myers and Bertram H. Roberts, *Family and Class Dynamics in Mental Illness*, New York, John Wiley and Sons, 1959.
[26] Hollingshead, "Trends in Social Stratification: A Case Study," op. cit., p. 686 (italics as in original). The term "ethnic" is obviously used here in the narrower sense of "national origin."

The role of regional and rural-urban factors in contributing to the differential nature of the subsocieties of America is doubtless decreasing with each passing decade, yet they cannot be ruled out entirely in a discussion of this topic even today. The vast differences in the cultural system of white attitudes and behavior toward the Negro which exist between North and South constitute an effective reminder that diversities of geography, climate, and historical experience have placed their respective marks on Americans of various regional localities. At least since the days of the great historian, Frederick Jackson Turner, these diversities and their effects have been matters of considerable concern to historians, social scientists, and literary critics.[27] As Robin Williams has put it, "Not only are there systematic regional differences in overt patterns of behavior, but there are different 'historical memories' and collectivity sentiments that persist with a strength sometimes disconcerting to makers of national policy. . . ."[28]

However, these regional differences, along with the differences in way of life between a shrinking rural America and an expanding urban America, are subject to the accelerating onslaught of rapid transportation, mass communications, and the increasing mechanization of a vast array of productive enterprises, including farming.[29] These forces continually narrow the cultural gap between farm and country or Midwest and Far West. Perhaps we can put it this way. In attempting to predict the cultural behavior patterns of any given persons on the basis of the factors making up his subsocietal participation, to know his "region" and whether he is rural or urban

[27] See Merrill Jensen (ed.), *Regionalism in America*, Madison, University of Wisconsin Press, 1951; and Howard W. Odum and Harry Estill Moore, *American Regionalism*, New York, Henry Holt and Co., 1938.
[28] Robin M. Williams, Jr., "Unity and Diversity in Modern America," *Social Forces*, Vol. 36, No. 1 (October 1957), p. 2.
[29] For a discussion of recent changes in the rural way of life in the United States, see Charles P. Loomis and J. Allan Beegle, *Rural Sociology: The Strategy of Change*, Englewood Cliffs, N.J., Prentice-Hall, 1957, especially Chapter 14.

(or his position on a scale representing the rural-urban dimension), along with his ethnic group and social class, increases the accuracy of the prediction of his subcultural behavior. However, after one has ascertained his ethnic group and social class, the increase in accuracy of prediction obtained by adding his region and his position on the rural-urban scale is probably not now great, and this increment of predictive accuracy is decreasing with the years. Thus, ethnic group and social class will become increasingly important as the principal background factors making up the subsociety with its subculture in American life.

THE ETHCLASS

If the portion of social space created by the intersection of the ethnic group with the social class is fast becoming the essential form of the subsociety in America, then we need a name for convenient reference to this subsocietal type. I have no great affection for neologisms and am pleased to do without them whenever possible; moreover, the one I am about to suggest has a quality about it which faintly calls to mind the Newspeak of Orwell's society of 1984. Nevertheless, I have thus tried to disarm my potential critics in advance because the need for some term of reference is great and because the term I am proposing has, at least, the virtues of simplicity and clarity of origin. I propose, then, that we refer to the subsociety created by the intersection of the vertical stratifications of ethnicity with the horizontal stratifications of social class as the *ethclass*. Thus a person's *ethclass* might be upper-middle class white Protestant, or lower-middle class white Irish Catholic, or upper-lower class Negro Protestant, and so on.

We must now inquire into what happens to the three crucial variables of group identity, social participation, and cultural behavior as they pertain to the subsociety of the ethclass, and thus discern how the ethclass functions differentially from the ethnic group itself. I shall offer the following remarks as a set of hypotheses which will be considered in a later chapter in relation to such empirical evidence as is available. These hypotheses apply to American society at mid-century.

1) With regard to cultural behavior, differences of social class are more important and decisive than differences of ethnic group. This means that people of the same social class tend to act alike and to have the same values even if they have different ethnic backgrounds. People of different social classes tend to act differently and have different values even if they have the same ethnic background.

2) With regard to social participation in primary groups and primary relationships, people tend to confine these to their own social class segment within their own ethnic group—that is, to the ethclass.

3) The question of group identification must be dealt with by distinguishing two types of such identification from one another— one the sense of peoplehood to which we referred earlier, the other a sense of being truly congenial with only a social class segment of that "people." I can best articulate the distinction by quoting in full from one of my previous writings: "The matter of psychological orientations, that is, group identification and patterns of 'in-grouping' and 'out-grouping,' is complicated by the fact that we are dealing here with more than one dimension. Although a person may participate largely in a social field circumscribed by both ethnic group and social class borders, the attribution of ethnic group membership *by itself* is a powerful pattern in our culture— a pattern generated both by pressure from within the ethnic group and from without. Rare is the Negro, or the Jew, for instance, who can fail to respond affectively to events or to evaluative allegations which concern, respectively, Negroes or Jews as a group. Nevertheless, the participation field and the field of close behavioral similarities are likely to be class-confined, as well as ethnic-confined.

Thus we may distinguish two types of psychological constellations corresponding to these respective experience patterns. 'I am ultimately bound up with the fate of these people' is the type of constellation attached to the ethnic group as a whole [See Kurt Lewin's concept of "interdependence of fate," referred to above]. We may call this *historical identification* since it is a function of the unfolding of past and current historic events. On the other hand, 'These are the people I feel at home with and can relax with' is the type of constellation attached to those persons with whom one participates frequently and shares close behavioral similarities. According to the subcultural hypothesis, these persons are likely to be of the same ethnic group *and* social class (and regional and rural-urban categories). This constellation we may call *participational identification*. To sum up: in terms of psychological orientations, the ethnic group is likely to be the group of historical identification, whereas the subculture [read "ethclass"] will be, in the majority of cases, the group of participational identification. It should be pointed out that identification with larger units—that is, American society as a whole, 'Western society,' 'all humanity,' are likely to be present at different levels of structuring."[30]

Succinctly, then, one may say that the ethnic group is the locus of a sense of *historical identification*, while the ethclass is the locus of a sense of *participational identification*. With a person of the same social class but of a different ethnic group, one shares behavioral similarities but not a sense of peoplehood. With those of the same ethnic group but of a different social class, one shares the sense of peoplehood but not behavioral similarities. The only group which meets both of these criteria are people of the same ethnic group *and* same social class. With these "birds of our feather" we truly share a sense of what the early sociologist, Franklin Giddings, called "consciousness of kind"—with these particular members of

[30] Gordon, "Social Structure and Goals in Group Relations," op. cit., pp. 146-7 (italics as in original).

the human race and no others we can really relax and participate
with ease and without strain.[31]

DEVIANCE AND MARGINALITY

I have stated this last hypothesis in unqualified fashion only for
the sake of conceptual clarity. At most, it is true, of course, only in
degree—something which may be said for all the hypotheses (depending on the method of statement) which constitute the theory
of subsocietal and subcultural life in America. Any theory of this
kind must include categories and concepts which allow for the inevitable exceptions to the main pattern. Such exceptions to the pattern of primary group relationships postulated by the theory of
American subsocieties and subcultures may be rather simply cross
classified under two dimensions; their degree of frequency and
whether they involve participation in primary relationships across
class lines or across ethnicity lines. On the frequency dimension,
such primary group contacts across subsocietal lines may be conveniently divided into two categories: exceptional and systematic.
The resulting typology of exceptions, then, gives us four dimensions: 1) Exceptional—across class lines; 2) Exceptional—across
ethnic lines; 3) Systematic—across class lines; and 4) Systematic—
across ethnic lines.

[31] E. K. Francis describes the ethnic group as a "secondary community" to
which, by a process of abstraction and transposition, the qualities of primary
group relationships have been attached. (See E. K. Francis, "The Nature of the
Ethnic Group," op. cit., p. 399). This puts the matter rather well except that
we would add two qualifications: 1) it is the ethclass rather than the ethnic
group itself to which primary group qualities are transposed; and 2) in the strict
sense the ethclass does not have primary group qualities itself—it is too large for
that. Rather it becomes the psychologically recognized *potential source*, or
population pool, for whatever primary groups and primary group relationships
are to be formed.

Let us look at these types separately. "Exceptional" or occasional primary group contacts across either social class or ethnic group lines occur in American life because of its multiplicity of opportunities for initial secondary contacts on the job, in the school, in the civic organization, and so on, and because of factors of individual congeniality and attraction which may come to the fore on such occasions. Thus we have the white Protestant who has one close Jewish friend, or one close Negro friend—or the small-town lawyer who plays poker once a month with a group of cronies which include a factory worker who had gone to high school with him. Such occasional forays across the lines which divide primary group life in America are only exceptions to the general pattern—for the person participating in them they do not involve breaking ties with his ethnic group or his social class or threaten his general immersion in the subsocietal life of either his ethnic group or his social class. Resting comfortably and securely in the subsocietal network of groups and institutions of his ethclass, as it were, this person simply ventures across group lines as an interesting and perhaps flavorful exception to the usual pattern of his social movement. His exceptions are those that "prove the rule."

By "systematic" contacts across social class and ethnic group lines in primary relationships, I mean those that are frequent and persistent and that make up a significant portion of the person's total primary group contacts. The two subtypes here demand individual and separate discussion.

Systematic primary group contacts across social class lines usually are an indication of vertical social mobility. That is, the person whose contacts are largely, or in a major way, with persons of the adjoining class above him in the hierarchy of social classes is probably engaged in the process of consolidating his position in the class of higher rank. This is a routine step in social mobility as educational, occupational, and economic changes are reflected in changes in interests, tastes, and values, and eventually the formation of relationships with those who occupy the superior and more powerful positions in the class structure and display the newly favored cultural patterns. Downward vertical mobility similarly involves changes in primary group relationships. Since upward mobility in social class position is a well-recognized and generally approved phenomenon as a result of the American value system's emphasis on "bettering oneself," the "rags to riches" theme, the triumph of "individual merit," and so on, it is probable that problems of changing social relationships in upward social class mobility, while they are not entirely absent by any means, are not of the same magnitude as the problems involved in frequent inter-ethnic primary group relationships. The more formidable problems of "marginality" (we shall discuss this term below) are found in substantial primary relationships across ethnic group lines.

The individual who engages in frequent and sustained primary contacts across ethnic group lines, particularly racial and religious, runs the risk of becoming what, in standard sociological parlance, has been called "the marginal man."[32] The marginal man is the person who stands on the borders or margins of two cultural worlds but is fully a member of neither. He may be the offspring of a racially mixed or interfaith marriage, or he may have ventured away from the security of the cultural group of his ancestors because of

[32] The concept was first presented by Robert E. Park in "Human Migration and the Marginal Man," *American Journal of Sociology*, Vol. 33, No. 6 (May 1928), pp. 881-93. It was developed and elaborated by Everett V. Stonequist in "The Problem of the Marginal Man," *American Journal of Sociology*, Vol. 41, No. 1 (July 1935), pp. 1-12; and *The Marginal Man*, New York, Charles Scribner's Sons, 1937. Some later discussions are Arnold W. Green, "A Re-examination of the Marginal Man Concept," *Social Forces*, Vol. 26, No. 2 (December 1947), pp. 167-71; Everett C. Hughes, "Social Change and Status Protest: An Essay on the Marginal Man," *Phylon*, Vol. 10, No. 1 (First Quarter, 1949), pp. 58-65; David Riesman, *Individualism Reconsidered*, Glencoe, Ill., The Free Press, 1954, pp. 153-78; David I. Golovensky, "The Marginal Man Concept; an Analysis and Critique," *Social Forces*, Vol. 30, No. 3 (March, 1952), pp. 333-9; and Aaron Antonovsky, "Toward a Refinement of the 'Marginal Man' Concept," *Social Forces*, Vol. 35, No. 1 (October 1956), pp. 57-62.

individual personality and experience factors which predisposed him to seek wider contacts and entry into social worlds which appeared more alluring. In the latter case, most frequently he is a member of a minority group attracted by the subsociety and subculture of the dominant or majority group in the national society of which he is a part. Frustrated and not fully accepted by the broader social world he wishes to enter, ambivalent in his attitude toward the more restricted social world to which he has ancestral rights, and beset by conflicting cultural standards, he develops, according to the classic conception, personality traits of insecurity, moodiness, hypersensitivity, excessive self-consciousness, and nervous strain. While the personality consequences of marginality have never been decisively proven, and while at least one acute observer of the contemporary American scene has pointed to the possible desirable personality results of marginality, such as greater insight, self-understanding, and creativity,[33] the sociological *position* of marginality may certainly be discerned. In the type most pertinent for our discussion, it is the position occupied by the social deviant from standard ethnic behavior—the person who ventures across the subsocietal lines of ethnicity in substantial fashion to seek the friendships, social cliques, and organizational affiliations that make up the world of his primary group relationships.

In some cases the marginal man may remain in his marginal position for an indefinite period; in others, he may eventually retreat to the comfort and familiarity of the ethnic group from which he originally ventured with high hopes. We must not overlook still a third possibility, however, and that is the gradual formation of a subsociety composed precisely of marginal men as here defined.[34] It is my contention that, to some degree, this eventuality is taking

[33] See David Riesman, *Individualism Reconsidered*, op. cit., pp. 153-78.
[34] See Everett C. Hughes, "Social Change and Status Protest: An Essay on the Marginal Man," op. cit.; Milton M. Gordon, "Social Structure and Goals in Group Relations," op. cit., and "Social Class and American Intellectuals," *American Association of University Professors Bulletin*, Vol. 40, No. 4 (Winter, 1954-55), pp. 517-28.

place in American society today, in one area particularly—the social world or worlds of "the intellectual" and the creative and performing artist, whether literary, musical, theatrical, or visual. I shall devote more consideration to this thesis in a later chapter; suffice it here to point out that in the situation of men and women coming together because of an overriding common interest in ideas, the creative arts, and mutual professional concerns, we find the classic sociological enemy of ethnic parochialism. The forces interested in maintaining ethnic communality recognize the danger and attempt to counter it by providing for the satisfaction of intellectual, artistic, and professional concerns within the boundaries of the ethnic group. This counterattack is only partially successful, however, since the main currents of intellectual and artistic activity flow unconcernedly on in the broader world beyond ethnicity. The marginality thus created and the kind of social world created by the interaction of marginal intellectuals constitute topics of considerable interest.

With this discussion of marginality we conclude the presentation of the theory of the subsociety and the subculture. We began with the sense of peoplehood, simple, unitary, and unfragmented in the life of stone-age man. We saw how the development of cities, occupational specialization, social classes, conquest, migration, industrialization, and the huge nation-state transformed the sense of peoplehood but did not destroy it, and we speculated on its survival in the racial, religious, and national background collectivities which compose the larger American society. We observed the outlines of a powerful system of horizontal stratification—the social class system—which transects the ethnic groups, and, now that rural-urban and regional differences are becoming increasingly minimized, leaves the social unit which we have called the "ethclass" as the effective model of the subsociety with its characteristic subculture in America—the social unit which allows for the maintenance of primary group relationships through the life cycle within its network of social organizations, cliques, and institutions, and which carries its characteristic system of cultural behavior. We discussed the differences between the ethnic group and the ethclass in the several dimensions of identification, social participation, and cultural behavior. And, finally, we took into consideration the deviant, or marginal man, who defies or ignores the conventional boundaries and behavior of subsocietal life. The theory has been painted in broad strokes as a set of hypotheses concerning the nature of American social life. In later chapters we shall fill in certain details and discuss the theory in relation to such empirical evidence for its validity as may be found. In the meantime, perhaps the foregoing exposition has brought us, if not to the answer, at least farther along the road of appreciation of the necessary complexity of the answer to the question of social identity which opened our inquiry, this complexity itself constituting a significant measure of the vast distances of social history which stand between our Pleistocene hunter and the man of the modern world.

3

The Nature of Assimilation

What happens "when peoples meet," as the phrase goes?[1] Such
meetings in the modern world are likely to take place under a variety of circumstances: colonial conquest, military occupation, re-
drawing of national boundaries to include diverse ethnic groups,
large-scale trade and missionary activity, technical assistance to
underdeveloped countries, displacement of an aboriginal population, and voluntary immigration which increases the ethnic diversity of the host country. In the American continental experience,
the last two types have been the decisive ones. The displacement
and attempted incorporation of the American Indian on the white
conqueror's terms, and the massive immigration into this land of
over 41 million people, largely from Europe but also from the other
Americas and to a smaller extent from the Orient, from the days
of the thinly populated and, even then, ethnically varied seaboard
republic to the continent-spanning nation of the present, constitute
the setting for the "meeting of peoples" in the American context.

[1] A collection of articles on racial and cultural contacts bears this title. See Alain
Locke and Bernhard J. Stern (eds.), *When Peoples Meet*, New York, Hinds,
Hayden and Eldridge, revised edition, 1946.

Sociologists and cultural anthropologists have described the processes and results of ethnic "meetings" under such terms as "assimilation" and "acculturation." Sometimes these terms have been used
to mean the same thing; in other usages their meanings, rather than
being identical, have overlapped. (Sociologists are more likely to
use "assimilation"; anthropologists have favored "acculturation"
and have given it a narrower but generally consistent meaning.)
With regard to the term "assimilation," particularly, there is a certain amount of confusion, and there is, further, a compelling need
for a rigorous and systematic analysis of the concept of assimilation
which would "break it down" into all the possible relevant factors
or variables which could conceivably be included under its rubric.
Such an analysis, based in part on the discussion in the preceding
chapter, will be attempted here. But first it would be helpful to
examine some of the existing definitions of the concepts which
social scientists have used to describe the coming together of
"peoples."

An authoritative definition of "acculturation" was provided by
a Subcommittee on Acculturation appointed by the Social Science
Research Council in the middle 1930's to analyze and chart the
dimensions of this field of study, so crucial to the field of cultural
anthropology. This special group, consisting of the distinguished
anthropologists Robert Redfield, Ralph Linton, and Melville J.
Herskovits, declared that acculturation

comprehends those phenomena which result when groups of individuals having different cultures come into continuous first-hand contact, with subsequent changes in the original cultural patterns of either
or both groups.[2]

[2] Robert Redfield, Ralph Linton, and Melville J. Herskovits, "Memorandum
for the Study of Acculturation," *American Anthropologist*, Vol. 38, No. 1
(January-March 1936), p. 149. For further anthropological discussion of the
term see Melville J. Herskovits, *Acculturation: The Study of Culture Contact*,
New York, J. J. Augustin, 1938; and Ralph Linton (ed.), *Acculturation in
Seven American Indian Tribes*, New York, D. Appleton-Century Co., 1940.

We note here that the term is used to designate one factor or dimension in the meeting of peoples: cultural behavior. The changes may take place in the cultures of either one of the two groups or there may be a reciprocal influence whereby the cultures of both groups are modified. Nothing is said about the social relationships of the two groups, the degree or nature of "structural" intermingling, if any, the question of group self-identification, or any other possible variable in the situation.

An early and influential definition of "assimilation" by the two sociologists Robert E. Park and Ernest W. Burgess reads as follows:

Assimilation is a process of interpenetration and fusion in which persons and groups acquire the memories, sentiments, and attitudes of other persons or groups, and, by sharing their experience and history, are incorporated with them in a common cultural life.[3]

What the Social Science Research Subcommittee referred to as "acculturation" is certainly included in this definition, and the phrases "sharing their experience" and "incorporated with them in a common cultural life" seem to suggest the additional criterion of social structural relationships. This is further suggested and specified in the later remarks:

As social contact initiates interaction, assimilation is its final perfect product. The nature of the social contacts is decisive in the process. Assimilation naturally takes place most rapidly where contacts are primary, that is, where they are the most intimate and intense, as in the area of touch relationship, in the family circle and in intimate congenial groups. Secondary contacts facilitate accommodations, but do not greatly promote assimilation. The contacts here are external and too remote.[4]

In a later definition of assimilation, solus, for the *Encyclopedia of the Social Sciences*, Park, one of the most prolific germinal think-

---

[3] Robert E. Park and Ernest W. Burgess, *Introduction to the Science of Sociology*, Chicago, University of Chicago Press, 1921, p. 735.
[4] Ibid., pp. 736-7.

THE NATURE OF ASSIMILATION

ers that American sociology has produced, appears to confine the referents of the term to the realm of cultural behavior (with political overtones), and, by implication, to secondary relationships. Assimilation (called here "social assimilation"), according to this definition, is

the name given to the process or processes by which peoples of diverse racial origins and different cultural heritages, occupying a common territory, achieve a cultural solidarity sufficient at least to sustain a national existence.

He goes on to add:

In the United States an immigrant is ordinarily considered assimilated as soon as he has acquired the language and the social ritual of the native community and can participate, without encountering prejudice, in the common life, economic and political. The common sense view of the matter is that an immigrant is assimilated as soon as he has shown that he can "get on in the country." This implies among other things that in all the ordinary affairs of life he is able to find a place in the community on the basis of his individual merits without invidious or qualifying reference to his racial origin or to his cultural inheritance.[5]

Here another variable—actually two, if a rightful distinction is made between prejudice and discrimination—is suggested. Assimilation has not taken place, it is asserted, until the immigrant is able to function in the host community without encountering prejudiced attitudes or discriminatory behavior.

Another process, "amalgamation," is distinguished by Park and Burgess. This is

a biological process, the fusion of races by interbreeding and intermarriage. Assimilation, on the other hand, is limited to the fusion of cultures. [What has happened to "social structure" here?]

[5] Robert E. Park, "Assimilation, Social," in *Encyclopedia of the Social Sciences*, Edwin R. A. Seligman and Alvin Johnson, (eds.), New York, The Macmillan Co., 1930, Vol. 2, p. 281.

However, it is pointed out that there is a relationship between the
two processes:

Amalgamation, while it is limited to the crossing of racial traits through
intermarriage, naturally promotes assimilation or the cross-fertilization
of social heritages.[6]

Two essays at a "dictionary" of sociological terms were made in
the early 1940's. In one, "social assimilation" is defined as

the process by which persons who are unlike in their social heritages
come to share the same body of sentiments, traditions, and loyalties.[7]

Here the emphasis is on changes in cultural values and behavior.
The use of the term "loyalties" suggests, also, a psychological variable of some sort, but in the absence of further comment, it is not
possible to describe precisely the nature of the author's conception
of this variable. In the other "dictionary," social assimilation is said
to be

the process by which different cultures, or individuals or groups representing different cultures, are merged into a homogeneous unit.

After comparison with the biological process of bodily assimilation
and reference to the resulting complex of differentiated but harmonious cell units, it is stated that

likewise, social assimilation does not require the complete identification
of all the units, but such modifications as eliminate the characteristics
of foreign origin, and enable them all to fit smoothly into the typical
structure and functioning of the new cultural unit. . . . [and later]
In essence, assimilation is the substitution of one nationality pattern
for another. Ordinarily, the modifications must be made by the weaker
or numerically inferior group.[8]

6 Park and Burgess, op. cit., p. 737.
7 Edward Byron Reuter, *Handbook of Sociology*, New York, Dryden Press,
1941, p. 84.
8 Henry Pratt Fairchild (ed.), *Dictionary of Sociology*, New York, Philosophical Library, 1944, pp. 276-7.

This definition contains a number of ambiguities. What does "merged into a homogeneous unit" mean? Is cultural behavior only being referred to here, or are social interrelationships envisaged also? And if the latter, what kind? What is the nature of the "new cultural unit"? The later summary sentence, we note, which refers to "substitution of one nationality pattern for another," appears to center the definition on changes in cultural patterns alone.

In recent writings, a number of sociologists have simply equated "assimilation" with "acculturation," or defined it as an extreme form of acculturation. Thus Brewton Berry declares that

By assimilation we mean *the process whereby groups with different cultures come to have a common culture*. This means, of course, not merely such items of the culture as dress, knives and forks, language, food, sports, and automobiles, which are relatively easy to appreciate and acquire, but also those less tangible items such as values, memories, sentiments, ideas, and attitudes. Assimilation refers thus to the fusion of cultural heritages, and must be distinguished from *amalgamation*, which denotes the biological mixture of originally distinct racial strains.[9]

Joseph Fichter defines assimilation as

a social process through which two or more persons or groups accept and perform one another's patterns of behavior. We commonly talk about a person, or a minority category, being assimilated into a group or a society, but here again this must not be interpreted as a "one-sided" process. It is a relation of interaction in which both parties behave reciprocally even though one may be much more affected than the other.[10]

Arnold Rose defines "acculturation" as "the adoption by a person or group of the culture of another social group. *Or*, the process

[9] Brewton Berry, *Race Relations*, Boston, Houghton Mifflin Co., 1951, p. 217 (italics as in original).
[10] Joseph H. Fichter, *Sociology*, Chicago, University of Chicago Press, 1957, p. 229.

leading to this adoption." He then goes on to characterize "assimilation" as

the adoption by a person or group of the culture of another social
group to such a complete extent that the person or group no longer
has any characteristics identifying him with his former culture and no
longer has any particular loyalties to his former culture. Or, the process
leading to this adoption.[11]

And John Cuber adds the variable of group rivalry and its diminu-
tion to his brief definition of "assimilation."

Assimilation may be defined, then, as the *gradual process whereby
cultural differences (and rivalries) tend to disappear*.[12]

Arnold Green, in his discussion of assimilation, quotes the Park
and Burgess definition, and then, in commenting on it, goes on to
make a perceptive differentiation between cultural behavior and
social structural participation:

Persons and groups may "acquire the memories, sentiments, and attitudes of other persons or groups," and at the same time be excluded
from "sharing their experience" and find themselves indefinitely delayed in being "incorporated with them in a common cultural life."
Why? Because many of the memories, sentiments, and attitudes of
the receiving group are common property; the inclusive ones in America—such as patriotism, Christianity, respect for private property, and
veneration for legendary heroes—are vested in the total society, and
they are readily accessible to all. On the other hand, the matter of sharing experience and incorporation in a common life is limited, first, by
a willingness on the part of the receiving group, and second by a desire on the part of the new arrivals to foster social participation.

Although it is usually the receiving group which erects barriers to
social participation, the immigrant group, or segments of it, may likewise wish to do so.[13]

[11] Arnold M. Rose, *Sociology: The Study of Human Relations*, New York,
Alfred A. Knopf, 1956, pp. 557-8.
[12] John F. Cuber, *Sociology: A Synopsis of Principles*, New York, Appleton-
Century-Crofts, 3rd ed., 1955, p. 609 (italics as in original).
[13] Arnold Green, *Sociology: An Analysis of Life in Modern Society*, New York,
McGraw-Hill Book Co., 1st ed., 1952, p. 66.

This differentiation, it seems to us, is crucial, since in the careful distinction between cultural behavior and social structure lies one of the major keys to the understanding of what the assimilation process has actually been like in the American experience. Such a distinction was conceptualized by the present writer in a discussion of the nature of the American pluralist society as the difference between "behavioral assimilation" and "structural assimilation,"[14] a distinction which we shall discuss further below.

Two recent monographs dealing with the process of immigrant-native interaction have emphasized the possibility of a cultural pluralist framework and have preferred the terms, respectively, "absorption" and "integration" of immigrants. Eisenstadt's study of immigrants in Palestine and the state of Israel is highly sensitive to the function of primary groups, elites, and structural and psychological contacts between immigrants and natives of the receiving society, and also makes good use of role analysis in considering the process of immigrant adjustment.[15] His concept of "institutional dispersion," that is, "the extent of the immigrants' dispersion or concentration within the various institutional spheres of the society"[16] pinpoints a significant dimension of the assimilation process. The survey by Borrie and others, based on the papers and pro-

---

[14] Milton M. Gordon, "Social Structure and Goals in Group Relations," in Morroe Berger, Theodore Abel, and Charles H. Page (eds.), *Freedom and Control in Modern Society*, New York, D. Van Nostrand Co., 1954, p. 151.

[15] S. N. Eisenstadt, *The Absorption of Immigrants*, London, Routledge and Kegan Paul, 1954. See also, his "The Place of Elites and Primary Groups in the Absorption of New Immigrants in Israel," *American Journal of Sociology*, Vol. 57, No. 3 (November 1951), pp. 222-31; "The Process of Absorption of New Immigrants in Israel," *Human Relations*, Vol. 5, No. 3 (August 1952), pp. 223-46; "Institutionalization of Immigrant Behaviour," *Human Relations*, Vol. 5, No. 4 (November 1952), pp. 373-95; "Communication Processes Among Immigrants in Israel," *Public Opinion Quarterly*, Vol. 16, No. 1 (Spring, 1952), pp. 42-58; "Analysis of Patterns of Immigration and Absorption of Immigrants," *Population Studies*, Vol. 7, Part 2 (November 1953), pp. 167-80.

[16] Eisenstadt, *The Absorption of Immigrants*, p. 13.

ceedings of a Unesco conference,[17] leans heavily on the idea of "integration," which in a paper by Bernard prepared for the conference is defined and discussed as follows:

The fact of the matter is that the United States has not assimilated the newcomer nor absorbed him. Our immigrant stock and our so-called "native" stock have each integrated with the other. That is to say that each element has been changed by association with the other, without complete loss of its own cultural identity, and with a change in the resultant cultural amalgam, or civilization if you will, that is vital, vigorous, and an advance beyond its previous level. Without becoming metaphysical let us say that the whole is greater than the sum of its parts, and the parts, while affected by interaction with each other, nevertheless remain complementary but individual.

It will be apparent that this concept of integration rests upon a belief in the importance of cultural differentiation within a framework of social unity. It recognizes the right of groups and individuals to be different so long as the differences do not lead to domination or disunity.[18]

Now that we have surveyed a sample of the accumulated usages and meanings of the terms used to describe the processes and results of the meeting of peoples, and have noted many of the variables which, with a greater or lesser degree of clarity, have already been distinguished, let us return to the task which we proposed to undertake at the outset of the chapter: a rigorous analysis of the assimilation process which would isolate and specify the major variables or factors and suggest their characteristic relationships. In part we shall build on the usage and nomenclature just reviewed. Illustrations from actual situations will be drawn largely from American life.

Let us, first of all, imagine a hypothetical situation in which a host country, to which we shall give the fictitious name of "Syl-

[17] W. D. Borrie, *The Cultural Integration of Immigrants*, (together with case studies by M. Diégues, Jr., J. Isaac, A. H. Neiva, C. A. Price, and J. Zubrzycki), Paris, Unesco, 1959.
[18] William S. Bernard, "The Integration of Immigrants in the United States," Unesco (mimeo.), 1956, p. 2; also quoted in Borrie, op. cit., pp. 93-4.

vania," is made up of a population all members of which are of the same race, religion, and previous national extraction. Cultural behavior is relatively uniform except for social class divisions. Similarly, the groups and institutions, i.e., the "social structure," of Sylvanian society are divided and differentiated only on a social class basis. Into this country, through immigration, comes a group of people who differ in previous national background and in religion and who thus have different cultural patterns from those of the host society. We shall call them the Mundovians. Let us further imagine that within the span of another generation, this population group of Mundovian national origin (now composed largely of the second generation, born in Sylvania) has taken on completely the cultural patterns of the Sylvanians, has thrown off any sense of peoplehood based on Mundovian nationality, has changed its religion to that of the Sylvanians, has eschewed the formation of any communal organizations made up principally or exclusively of Mundovians, has entered and been hospitably accepted into the social cliques, clubs, and institutions of the Sylvanians at various class levels, has intermarried freely and frequently with the Sylvanians, encounters no prejudice or discrimination (one reason being that they are no longer distinguishable culturally or structurally from the rest of the Sylvanian population), and raises no value conflict issues in Sylvanian public life. Such a situation would represent the ultimate form of assimilation—complete assimilation to the culture and society of the host country. Note that we are making no judgment here of either the sociological desirability, feasibility, or moral rightness of such a goal. We are simply setting it up as a convenient abstraction—an "ideal type"—ideal not in the value sense of being most desirable but in the sense of representing the various elements of the concept and their interrelationships in "pure," or unqualified, fashion (the methodological device of the "ideal type" was developed and named by the German sociologist, Max Weber).

Looking at this example, we may discern that seven major variables are involved in the process discussed—in other words, seven basic subprocesses have taken place in the assimilation of the Mundovians to Sylvanian society. These may be listed in the following manner. We may say that the Mundovians have

1) changed their cultural patterns (including religious belief and observance) to those of the Sylvanians;

2) taken on large-scale primary group relationships with the Sylvanians, i.e., have entered fully into the societal network of groups and institutions, or societal structure, of the Sylvanians;

3) have intermarried and interbred fully with the Sylvanians;

4) have developed a Sylvanian, in place of a Mundovian, sense of peoplehood, or ethnicity;

5) have reached a point where they encounter no discriminatory behavior;

6) have reached a point where they encounter no prejudiced attitudes;

7) do not raise by their demands concerning the nature of Sylvanian public or civic life any issues involving value and power conflict with the original Sylvanians (for example, the issue of birth control).

Each of these steps or subprocesses may be thought of as constituting a particular stage or aspect of the assimilation process. Thus we may, in shorthand fashion, consider them as types of assimilation and characterize them accordingly. We may, then, speak, for instance, of "structural assimilation" to refer to the entrance of Mundovians into primary group relationships with the Sylvanians, or "identificational assimilation" to describe the taking on of a sense of Sylvanian peoplehood. For some of the particular assimilation subprocesses there are existing special terms, already reviewed. For instance, cultural or behavioral assimilation is what has already been defined as "acculturation." The full list of assimilation subprocesses or variables with their general names, and special names, if any, is given in Table 5.

TABLE 5. THE ASSIMILATION VARIABLES

Subprocess or Condition	Type or Stage of Assimilation	Special Term
Change of cultural patterns to those of host society	Cultural or behavioral assimilation	Acculturation[19]
Large-scale entrance into cliques, clubs, and institutions of host society, on primary group level	Structural assimilation	None
Large-scale intermarriage	Marital assimilation	Amalgamation[20]
Development of sense of peoplehood based exclusively on host society	Identificational assimilation	None
Absence of prejudice	Attitude receptional assimilation	None
Absence of discrimination	Behavior receptional assimilation	None
Absence of value and power conflict	Civic assimilation	None

Not only is the assimilation process mainly a matter of degree, but, obviously, each of the stages or subprocesses distinguished above may take place in varying degrees.

In the example just used there has been assimilation in all respects to the society and culture which had exclusively occupied the nation up to the time of the immigrants' arrival. In other instances there may be other subsocieties and subcultures already on the

[19] The question of reciprocal cultural influence will be considered later.

[20] My use of the term here is not predicated on the diversity in race of the two population groups which are intermarrying and interbreeding. With increasing understanding of the meaning of "race" and its thoroughly relative and arbitrary nature as a scientific term, this criterion becomes progressively less important. We may speak of the "amalgamation" or intermixture of the two "gene pools" which the two populations represent, regardless of how similar or divergent these two gene pools may be.

scene when the new group arrives but one of these subsocieties and its way of life is dominant by virtue of original settlement, the preemption of power, or overwhelming predominance in numbers. In both cases we need a term to stand for the dominant subsociety which provides the standard to which other groups adjust or measure their relative degree of adjustment. We have tentatively used the term "host society"; however, a more neutral designation would be desirable. A. B. Hollingshead, in describing the class structure of New Haven, has used the term "core group" to refer to the Old Yankee families of colonial, largely Anglo-Saxon ancestry who have traditionally dominated the power and status system of the community, and who provide the "master cultural mould" for the class system of the other groups in the city.[21] Joshua Fishman has referred to the "core society" and the "core culture" in American life, this core being "made up essentially of White Protestant, middle-class clay, to which all other particles are attracted."[22] If there is anything in American life which can be described as an over-all American culture which serves as a reference point for immigrants and their children, it can best be described, it seems to us, as the middle-class cultural patterns of, largely, white Protestant, Anglo-Saxon origins, leaving aside for the moment the question of minor

[21] See August B. Hollingshead, "Trends in Social Stratification: A Case Study," op. cit., p. 686; and August B. Hollingshead and Frederick C. Redlich, *Social Class and Mental Illness*, op. cit., Chapters 3 and 4. It is not entirely clear to me whether Hollingshead reserves the term "core group" for "old family" Yankees in the upper class and upper-middle class only, or for Yankees throughout the class structure.

[22] Joshua A. Fishman, "Childhood Indoctrination for Minority-Group Membership and the Quest for Minority-Group Biculturism in America," (mimeo); a revised version of this paper was published under the title "Childhood Indoctrination for Minority-Group Membership," in "Ethnic Groups in American Life," *Daedalus: The Journal of the American Academy of Arts and Sciences*, Spring, 1961. See also, Jurgen Ruesch, "Social Technique, Social Status, and Social Change in Illness," in Clyde Kluckhohn and Henry A. Murray (eds.), *Personality in Nature, Society, and Culture*, New York, Alfred A. Knopf, 1948, for a use of the term "core culture" to refer to lower-middle class culture in America.

reciprocal influences on this culture exercised by the cultures of later entry into the United States, and ignoring also, for this purpose, the distinction between the upper-middle class and the lower-middle class cultural worlds.

There is a point on which I particularly do not wish to be misunderstood. I am not for one moment implying that the contribution of the non-Anglo-Saxon stock to the nature of American civilization has been minimal or slight. Quite the contrary. The qualitative record of achievement in industry, business, the professions, and the arts by Americans whose ancestors came from countries and traditions which are not British, or in many cases not even closely similar to British, is an overwhelmingly favorable one, and with reference to many individuals, a thoroughly brilliant one. Taken together with the substantial quantitative impact of these non-Anglo-Saxon groups on American industrial and agricultural development and on the demographic dimensions of the society, this record reveals an America in mid-twentieth century whose greatness rests on the contributions of many races, religions, and national backgrounds.[23] My point, however, is that, with some exceptions, as the immigrants and their children have become Americans, their contributions, as laborers, farmers, doctors, lawyers, scientists, artists, etc., have been made *by way* of cultural patterns that have taken their major impress from the mould of the overwhelmingly English character of the dominant Anglo-Saxon culture or subculture in America, whose dominion dates from colonial times and whose *cultural* domination in the United States has never been seriously threatened. One must make a distinction between influencing the cultural patterns themselves and contributing to the progress and development of the society. It is in the latter area that the influence of the immigrants and their children in the United States has been decisive.

Accordingly, I shall follow Fishman's usage in referring to mid-

[23] See Oscar and Mary F. Handlin, Chapter 1, "The United States," in *The Positive Contribution by Immigrants*, Paris, Unesco, 1955.

dle-class white Protestant Americans as constituting the "core society," or in my terms, the "core subsociety," and the cultural patterns of this group as the "core culture" or "core subculture." I shall use Hollingshead's term "core group" to refer to the white Protestant element at any social class level.

Let us now, for a moment, return to our fictitious land of Sylvania and imagine an immigration of Mundovians with a decidedly different outcome. In this case the Sylvanians accept many new behavior patterns and values from the Mundovians, just as the Mundovians change many of their ways in conformance with Sylvanian customs, this interchange taking place with appropriate modifications and compromises, and in this process a new cultural system evolves which is neither exclusively Sylvanian nor Mundovian but a mixture of both. This is a cultural blend, the result of the "melting pot," which has melted down the cultures of the two groups in the same societal container, as it were, and formed a new cultural product with standard consistency. This process has, of course, also involved thorough social mixing in primary as well as secondary groups and a large-scale process of intermarriage. The melting pot has melted the two groups into one, societally and culturally.

Whether such a process as just described is feasible or likely of occurrence is beside the point here. It, too, is an "ideal type," an abstraction against which we can measure the realities of what actually happens. Our point is that the seven variables of the assimilation process which we have isolated can be measured against the "melting pot" goal as well as against the "adaptation to the core society and culture" goal. That is, assuming the "melting pot" goal, we can then inquire how much acculturation of both groups has taken place to form such a blended culture, how much social structural mixture has taken place, and so on.[24] We now have a

[24] I am indebted to Professor Richard D. Lambert of the University of Pennsylvania for pointing out to me that my array of assimilation variables must be

model of assimilation with seven variables which can be used to analyze the assimilation process with reference to either of two variant goal-systems: 1) "adaptation to the core society and culture," and 2) the "melting pot." Theoretically, it would be possible to apply the analysis model of variables with reference to carrying out the goal-system of "cultural pluralism" as well. However, this would be rather premature at this point since the concept of cultural pluralism is itself so meagerly understood. In a later chapter, however, we shall investigate the relationship of these seven variables to the cultural pluralism concept. We shall also leave further discussion of the "melting pot" concept till later.

Let us now apply this model of assimilation analysis in tentative fashion to selected "minority" ethnic groups on the American scene. The applied paradigm presented in Table 6 allows us to record and summarize a great deal of information compactly and comparatively. We shall deal here, for illustrative purposes, with four groups: Negroes, Jews, Catholics (excluding Negro and Spanish-speaking Catholics), and Puerto Ricans. The basic goal-referent will be "adaptation to core society and culture." The entries in the table cells may be regarded, at this point, as hypotheses. Qualifying comments will be made in the footnotes to the table. The reader may wish to refer back to page 71 for definitions of each column heading.

One of the tasks of sociological theory is not only to identify the factors or variables present in any given social process or situation, but also to hypothesize how these variables may be related to each other. Let us look at the seven assimilation variables from this point of view. We note that in Table 6, of the four ethnic groups listed, only one, the Puerto Ricans, are designated as being substantially unassimilated culturally. The Puerto Ricans are the United States'

---

applied with reference to the basic assimilation goal. In my original scheme of presentation I had implicitly applied it only to the goal-system of "adaptation to the core society and culture."

TABLE 6. PARADIGM OF ASSIMILATION

Applied to Selected Groups in the United States—
Basic Goal Referent: Adaptation to Core Society and Culture

Group	Type of Assimilation						
	Cultural[25]	Structural	Marital	Identificational[27]	Attitude Receptional	Behavior Receptional	Civic
Negroes	Variation by class[26]	No	No	No	No	No	Yes
Jews	Substantially Yes	No	Substantially No	No	No	Partly	Mostly
Catholics (excluding Negro and Spanish-speaking)	Substantially Yes	Partly (variation by area)	Partly	No	Partly	Mostly	Partly[28]
Puerto Ricans	Mostly No	No	No	No	No	No	Partly

[25] Some reciprocal cultural influences have, of course, taken place. American language, diet, recreational patterns, art forms, and economic techniques have been modestly influenced by the cultures of non-Anglo-Saxon resident groups since the first contacts with the American Indians, and the American culture is definitely the richer for these influences. However, the reciprocal influences have not been great. See George R. Stewart, *American Ways of Life*, New York, Doubleday and Co., 1954, and our discussion in the following chapter. Furthermore, the minority ethnic groups have not given up all their pre-immigration cultural patterns. Particularly, they have preserved their non-Protestant religions. I have thus used the phrase "substantially Yes" to indicate this degree of adaptation.

[26] Although few, if any, African cultural survivals are to be found among American Negroes, lower-class Negro life with its derivations from slavery, post-Civil War discrimination, both rural and urban poverty, and enforced isolation from the middle-class white world, is still at a considerable distance from the American cultural norm. Middle and upper-class Negroes, on the other hand, are acculturated to American core culture.

newest immigrant group of major size. If we now examine the entries for the Negro, one of America's oldest minorities, we find that assimilation has not taken place in most of the other variables, but with allowance for social class factors, *has* taken place culturally. These two facts in juxtaposition should give us a clue to the relation of the cultural assimilation variable to all the others. This relationship may be stated as follows: 1) *cultural assimilation, or acculturation, is likely to be the first of the types of assimilation to occur when a minority group arrives on the scene; and* 2) *cultural assimilation, or acculturation, of the minority group may take place even when none of the other types of assimilation occurs simultaneously or later, and this condition of "acculturation only" may continue indefinitely.*

If we examine the history of immigration into the United States, both of these propositions are seen to be borne out. After the birth of the republic, as each succeeding wave of immigration, first from Northern and Western Europe, later from Southern and Eastern Europe and the Orient, has spread over America, the first process that has occurred has been the taking on of the English language and American behavior patterns, even while the creation of the immigrant colonies sealed off their members from extensive primary contacts with "core society" Americans and even when prejudice and discrimination against the minority have been at a high

27 As I pointed out earlier, ethnic identification in a modern complex society may contain several "layers." My point is not that Negroes, Jews, and Catholics in the United States do not think of themselves as Americans. They do. It is that they also have an "inner layer" sense of peoplehood which is Negro, Jewish, or Catholic, as the case may be, and not "white Protestant" or "white, Anglo-Saxon Protestant," which is the corresponding inner layer of ethnic identity of the core society.

28 Value and power conflict of Catholics with a large portion of the rest of the American population over such issues as birth control, divorce, therapeutic abortion, and church-state relationships constitute the reason for the entry of "Partly" here.

point. While this process is only partially completed in the immigrant generation itself, with the second and succeeding generations, exposed to the American public school system and speaking English as their native tongue, the impact of the American acculturation process has been overwhelming; the rest becomes a matter of social class mobility and the kind of acculturation that such mobility demands. On the other hand, the success of the acculturation process has by no means guaranteed entry of each minority into the primary groups and institutions—that is, the subsociety—of the white Protestant group. With the exception of white Protestant immigrant stock from Northern and Western Europe—I am thinking here particularly of the Scandinavians, Dutch, and Germans—by and large such structural mixture on the primary level has not taken place. Nor has such acculturation success eliminated prejudice and discrimination or in many cases led to large-scale intermarriage with the core society.

The only qualifications of my generalizations about the rapidity and success of the acculturation process that the American experience suggests are these: 1) If a minority group is spatially isolated and segregated (whether voluntarily or not) in a rural area, as is the case with the American Indians still on reservations, even the acculturation process will be very slow; and 2) Unusually marked discrimination, such as that which has been faced by the American Negro, if it succeeds in keeping vast numbers of the minority group deprived of educational and occupational opportunities and thus predestined to remain in a lower-class setting, may indefinitely retard the acculturation process for the group. Even in the case of the American Negro, however, from the long view or perspective of American history, this effect of discrimination will be seen to have been a delaying action only; the quantitatively significant emergence of the middle-class Negro is already well on its way.

Before we leave specific examination of the acculturation variable and its relationships, it would be well to distinguish between two types of cultural patterns and traits which may characterize any ethnic group. Some, like its religious beliefs and practices, its ethical values, its musical tastes, folk recreational patterns, literature, historical language, and sense of a common past, are essential and vital ingredients of the group's cultural heritage, and derive exactly from that heritage. We shall refer to these as *intrinsic* cultural traits or patterns. Others, such as dress, manner, patterns of emotional expression, and minor oddities in pronouncing and inflecting English, tend to be products of the historical vicissitudes of a group's adjustment to its local environment, including the present one (and also reflect social class experiences and values), and are in a real sense, external to the core of the group's ethnic cultural heritage. These may conveniently be referred to as *extrinsic* cultural traits or patterns.[29] To illustrate, the Catholicism or Judaism of the immigrant from Southern or Eastern Europe represent a difference in *intrinsic culture* from the American core society and its Protestant religious affiliation. However, the greater volatility of emotional expression of the Southern and Eastern European peasant or villager in comparison with the characteristically greater reserve of the upper-middle class American of the core society constitutes a difference in *extrinsic culture*. To take another example, the variant speech pattern, or argot, of the lower-class Negro of recent southern background, which is so widespread both in the South and in northern cities, is a product of external circumstances and is not something vital to Negro culture. It is thus an *extrinsic* cultural trait. Were this argot, which constitutes such a powerful handicap to social mobility and adjustment to the core culture, to disappear, nothing significant for Negro self-regard as a group or the Negro's sense of ethnic history and identity would be violated. While this distinction between intrinsic and extrinsic culture is a tentative

[29] Compare with the distinction in types of cultural traits made by William E. Vickery and Stewart G. Cole in *Intercultural Education in American Schools,* New York and London Harper and Brothers, 1943, pp. 43-4.

one, and cannot be uniformly applied to all cultural traits, it is still a useful one and may help cast further light on the acculturation process, particularly in its relationship to prejudice and discrimination.

As we examine the array of assimilation variables again, several other relationships suggest themselves. One is the indissoluble connection, in the time order indicated, between structural assimilation and marital assimilation. That is, entrance of the minority group into the social cliques, clubs, and institutions of the core society at the primary group level inevitably will lead to a substantial amount of intermarriage. If children of different ethnic backgrounds belong to the same play-group, later the same adolescent cliques, and at college the same fraternities and sororities; if the parents belong to the same country club and invite each other to their homes for dinner; it is completely unrealistic not to expect these children, now grown, to love and to marry each other, blithely oblivious to previous ethnic extraction. Communal leaders of religious and nationality groups that desire to maintain their ethnic identity are aware of this connection, which is one reason for the proliferation of youth groups, adult clubs, and communal institutions which tend to confine their members in their primary relationships safely within the ethnic fold.

If marital assimilation, an inevitable by-product of structural assimilation, takes place fully, the minority group loses its ethnic identity in the larger host or core society, and identificational assimilation takes place. Prejudice and discrimination are no longer a problem, since eventually the descendants of the original minority group become indistinguishable, and since primary group relationships tend to build up an "in-group" feeling which encloses all the members of the group. If assimilation has been complete in all intrinsic as well as extrinsic cultural traits, then no value conflicts on civic issues are likely to arise between the now dispersed descendants of the ethnic minority and members of the core society. Thus the remaining types of assimilation have all taken place like a row of tenpins bowled over in rapid succession by a well placed strike. We may state the emergent generalization, then, as follows: *Once structural assimilation has occurred, either simultaneously with or subsequent to acculturation, all of the other types of assimilation will naturally follow.* It need hardly be pointed out that while acculturation, as we have emphasized above, does not necessarily lead to structural assimilation, structural assimilation inevitably produces acculturation. Structural assimilation, then, rather than acculturation, is seen to be the keystone of the arch of assimilation. The price of such assimilation, however, is the disappearance of the ethnic group as a separate entity and the evaporation of its distinctive values.

There are a number of other crucial hypotheses and questions which can be phrased by the manipulation of these variables. One of the most important, of course, is whether "attitude receptional" and "behavior receptional" assimilation—that is, elimination of prejudice and discrimination—may take place when acculturation, *but not structural assimilation*, occurs. This can be shown to be one of the key questions in the application of our analytical model to "cultural pluralism," and thus we shall leave its discussion to a later chapter. Another interesting question is whether prejudice and discrimination are more closely related to differences between the core group and the ethnic minority in intrinsic culture traits or extrinsic culture traits. I would hypothesize that, at least in our era, differences in extrinsic culture are more crucial in the development of prejudice than those of an intrinsic nature.[30] Differences in religious belief, *per se*, are not the occasion for bitter acrimony in twentieth-century America,[31] particularly when these differences occur in middle-class Americans of native birth whose external ap-

[30] Cf. Vickery and Cole, op. cit., p. 45.
[31] Cf. R. M. MacIver's statement: "But we do not find sufficient reason to regard religion *by itself* as of crucial importance in provoking the tensions and cleavages manifested in the everyday relationships of American society." *The More Perfect Union*, New York, The Macmillan Co., 1948, p. 12 (italics as in original).

pearance, speech patterns, and manner are notably uniform. On the other hand, the gap in extrinsic cultural traits between the zoot-suited side-burned slum juvenile and the conservatively clothed and behaving middle-class American distinctly gives the signal for mutual suspicion and hostility. This is not to say that differences in intrinsic values among ethnic groups in America, particularly as these differences spill over into demands on the shaping of American public life, may not result in power conflict. But one must make a distinction between irrational ethnic prejudice, in what might be called the old-fashioned sense, and the conflict of groups in the civic arena over issues based on opposing value-premises, sincerely held in each case.

We shall forgo additional manipulation of the variables in the analytical model at this point[32] since the preceding discussion should have clarified its potential use. We now have an analytical

[32] The question, of great contemporary interest to social scientists and others concerned with problems of intergroup relations, of whether the objective behavioral phenomenon of discrimination can be reduced or eliminated prior to the reduction or elimination of the subjective attitudinal phenomenon of prejudice may be considered within this framework; thus, can "behavior receptional" assimilation take place prior to "attitude receptional" assimilation? The Supreme Court ban on racial segregation in the public schools, and state and municipal anti-discrimination legislation constitute, of course, a test of the hypothesis that legal curbs on discrimination may be successful even though prejudice still exists, and that such legal curbs may actually result in the reduction of prejudice. See Robert K. Merton, "Discrimination and the American Creed," in R. M. MacIver (ed.), *Discrimination and National Welfare*, New York, Harper and Brothers, 1949; David W. Petegorsky, "On Combating Racism," in Arnold M. Rose (ed.), *Race Prejudice and Discrimination*, New York, Alfred A. Knopf, 1951; Arnold M. Rose, "The Influence of Legislation on Prejudice," in Arnold M. Rose (ed.) *Race Prejudice and Discrimination*, op. cit.; John P. Roche and Milton M. Gordon, "Can Morality Be Legislated?", *The New York Times Magazine*, May 22, 1955, reprinted in Milton L. Barron (ed.), *American Minorities*, New York, Alfred A. Knopf, 1957; and National Community Relations Advisory Council, *The Uses of Law for the Advancement of Community Relations*, A Report of the Special Committee on Reassessment, June, 1955.

scheme—a set of conceptual categories—which allows us to appreciate the true complexity of the assimilation process, to note the varying directions it may take, and to discern the probable relationships of some of its parts. This set of analytical tools should serve us well as we consider the theories of assimilation and minority group life which have arisen historically in America.

4

Theories of Assimilation: Part I
Introduction and Anglo-Conformity

Although the relatively brief span of American history to date has been in the main a period whose story must be told within the setting of colonization and immigration, and although the 41 million immigrants who have come to America since the founding of the nation constitute the largest population transfer of its kind in the history of the world, remarkably little explicit attention has been given by the American people to devising or discussing theoretical models which either would formulate the preferred goals of adjustment to which this influx of diverse peoples might be expected to look for guidance, or would describe the processes of adjustment as they empirically have taken place. Furthermore, such discussion of this topic as may be found on the record is frequently embedded in a gilded frame of rhetoric not calculated to facilitate clarity or precise analytical distinctions. In some cases one must even make one's own guess as to whether the discussant is talking about "ideal goals" or historical processes which have already occurred, or both. Some inferences may be made, of course, from the concrete actions taken by the native American population with regard to immigrants and immigration. Articulation of the problem becomes more salient with the increasingly relevant and perplexing events of the twentieth century, but even so, the amount of theoretical attention focused on the problem of the assimilation of peoples of diverse social origins and cultures within the larger American society has been strikingly incommensurate with its magnitude and importance. Consequently, any description and classification of such theoretical attention to assimilation on the American scene throughout its history must come to terms with the paucity of material and, in some cases, ambiguities of meaning and incompleteness of analysis which the record reveals.

Over the course of the American experience, "philosophies," or goal-systems of assimilation, have grouped themselves around three main axes. These three central ideological tendencies may be referred to as "Anglo-conformity" (the phrase is the Coles's[1]), "the melting pot," and "cultural pluralism."[2] In preliminary fashion, we may say that the "Anglo-conformity" theory demanded the complete renunciation of the immigrant's ancestral culture in favor of the behavior and values of the Anglo-Saxon core group; the "melting pot" idea envisaged a biological merger of the Anglo-Saxon peoples with other immigrant groups and a blending of their respective cultures into a new indigenous American type; and "cultural pluralism" postulated the preservation of the communal life and significant portions of the culture of the later immigrant groups within the context of American citizenship and political and economic integration into American society. Various individual changes were rung on these three central themes by particular

[1] Stewart G. Cole and Mildred Wiese Cole, *Minorities and the American Promise*, New York, Harper and Brothers, 1954, Chapter 6.

[2] Cf. discussions in Isaac B. Berkson, *Theories of Americanization*, New York, Teachers College, Columbia University, 1920; Julius Drachsler, *Democracy and Assimilation*, New York, The Macmillan Co., 1920; William E. Vickery and Stewart G. Cole, *Intercultural Education in American Schools*, New York, Harper and Brothers, 1943; and Stewart G. Cole and Mildred Wiese Cole, op. cit.

proponents of assimilation goals, as we shall see, but the central tendencies remain.

"Cultural pluralism" as an articulated goal-system of assimilation is a relative late-comer on the American scene, being predominantly a development of the experiences and reflections of the twentieth century. Whatever the unconscious or unexpressed cultural goals of non-Anglo-Saxon immigrant groups may have been, and regardless of the factual existence of some degree of cultural pluralism in the colonial and nineteenth century experiences, these eras of American life are characterized by implicit or explicit adherence to theories which postulate either the Anglicization of the non-English portions of the population, or the forging of a new American cultural type out of the diverse heritages of Europe.

The white American population at the time of the Revolution was largely English and Protestant in origin, but had already absorbed substantial groups of Germans and Scotch-Irish and smaller contingents of Frenchmen, Dutchmen, Swedes, Swiss, South Irish, Poles, and a handful of immigrants from other European nations. Catholics were represented in modest numbers, particularly in the middle colonies, and a small number of Jews were residents of the incipient nation. With the exception of the Quakers and a few missionaries, the colonists had generally treated the Indians and their cultures with contempt and hostility, driving them from the coastal plains and making the western frontier a bloody battleground. (This had not prevented the transplanted Europeans, however, from taking over from the redman the cultivation of agricultural staples such as corn and tobacco, survival techniques for living in the wilderness, and some of his place names.) Although the Negro at this time made up nearly one-fifth of the total population, his predominantly slave status, together with racial and cultural prejudice, barred him from serious consideration as an assimilable element of the society. And while many of the groups of European national origin started out as determined ethnic enclaves (Germantown, Pennsylvania, was at first truly a German town, and the seventeenth-century Welsh immigrants had to be dissuaded by William Penn from setting up their own self-governing "barony" in Pennsylvania), eventually, most historians believe, considerable ethnic intermixture within the white population took place. "People of different blood [sic]—" write two eminent American historians about the colonial period, "English, Irish, German, Huguenot, Dutch, Swedish—mingled and intermarried with little thought of any difference."[3] In such a society, its people predominantly English, its white immigrants of other ethnic origins either English-speaking or having come largely from countries of Northern and Western Europe whose cultural divergences from the English were not great, and its dominant white population excluding by fiat the claims and considerations of welfare of the non-Caucasian minorities, the problem of assimilation understandably did not loom unduly large or complex.

The unfolding events of the next century and a half, with increasing momentum, shattered the complacency which rested upon the relative simplicity of colonial and immediate post-Revolutionary conditions. Large-scale immigration to America of the famine-fleeing Irish, the Germans, and the Scandinavians (along with additional Englishmen and other peoples of northern and western Europe) in the middle portion of the nineteenth century (the so-called "old immigration"), the emancipation of the Negro slaves and the problems created by post-Civil War Reconstruction, the placement of the conquered Indian with his broken culture on government Reservations, the arrival of the Oriental, attracted by the discovery of gold and other opportunities in the West, and finally, beginning in the last quarter of the nineteenth century and continuing to the early 1920's, the swelling to proportions hitherto unknown or unimagined of the tide of immigration from the peas-

[3] Allan Nevins and Henry Steele Commager, *America: The Story of a Free People*, Boston, Little, Brown and Co., 1942, p. 58.

antries and "pales" of Southern and Eastern Europe (the so-called "new immigration"), fleeing the persecutions and industrial dislocations of the day—all these events constitute the background against which we may consider the rise of the theories of assimilation which have been mentioned above.[4] We shall examine them serially.

ANGLO-CONFORMITY

"Anglo-conformity" is really a broad "umbrella" term which may be used to cover a variety of viewpoints about assimilation and immigration. All have as a central assumption the desirability of maintaining English institutions (as modified by the American Revolution), the English language, and English-oriented cultural patterns as dominant and standard in American life. However, bound up with this assumption are related attitudes which may range, on the one hand, from discredited notions about race and "Nordic" and "Aryan" racial superiority together with the Nativist political programs and exclusionist immigration policies which such notions entail, through an intermediate position of favoring immigration from Northern and Western Europe on amorphous, unreflective grounds ("They are more like us"), to, at the other end of the spectrum, a lack of opposition or animus toward any im-

---

[4] For surveys and discussions of the history of American immigration, see Marcus Lee Hansen, *The Atlantic Migration, 1607-1860*, Cambridge, Mass., Harvard University Press, 1940, and *The Immigrant in American History*, Cambridge, Mass., Harvard University Press, 1940; Oscar Handlin, *The Uprooted*, Boston, Little, Brown and Co., 1952; *Race and Nationality in American Life*, New York, Doubleday and Co. (Doubleday Anchor Book), 1957; and *The American People in the Twentieth Century*, Cambridge, Mass., Harvard University Press, 1954; Maurice R. Davie, *World Immigration*, New York, The Macmillan Co., 1936; and Donald R. Taft and Richard Robbins, *International Migrations: The Immigrant in the Modern World*, New York, The Ronald Press Co., 1955.

migration source as long as these immigrants and their descendants duly adopt the standard Anglo-Saxon cultural patterns.

It is quite likely that "Anglo-conformity" in its more moderate forms has been, however explicit its formulation, the most prevalent ideology of assimilation in America throughout the nation's history. During colonial times, suspicion of those who were "foreigners" either through religion or national background, or both, was not uncommon.[5] Concern was especially manifested in Pennsylvania, which had received the greatest quantity and variety of non-Anglo-Saxon immigrants, and, on the eve of the Revolution, was about one-third German in population. Benjamin Franklin, writes Maurice Davie, "had misgivings about the Germans because of their clannishness, their little knowledge of English, the German press, and the increasing need of interpreters. Speaking of the latter he said, 'I suppose in a few years they will also be necessary in the Assembly, to tell one-half of our legislators what the other half say.' Yet he was not for refusing them admission entirely; he urged better distribution and more mixture with the English."[6]

The founding fathers of the American nation were by no means men of unthinking prejudices. The disestablishment of religion and the separation of church and state so that no religious group—New England Congregationalists, Virginia Anglicans, or even all Protestants combined—could call upon the government for special favors or support, and so that man's religious conscience would be free, were cardinal points of the new national policy which they fostered. (George Washington had written the Jewish congregation of Newport during his first term as President, "The Government of

[5] See Roy L. Garis, *Immigration Restriction*, New York, The Macmillan Co., 1927, Chapters 1-2; and Maurice R. Davie, op. cit., Chapter 2.

[6] Maurice R. Davie, op. cit., p. 36. The Franklin quotation is cited therein as follows: "Letter of Benjamin Franklin to Peter Collinson, 9th May, 1753, on the condition and character of the Germans in Pennsylvania," in *The Works of Benjamin Franklin, with notes and a life of the author*, by Jared Sparks, Boston, 1828, Vol. VII, pp. 71-3.

the United States . . . gives to bigotry no sanction, to persecution
no assistance.") And their political differences with ancestral England had just been decided on the battlefield. But there is no reason
to suppose that they looked upon the fledgling country as an impartial melting pot for the merging of the various cultures of Europe,
or as a new "nation of nations," or as anything but a society in
which, with important political modifications, Anglo-Saxon speech
and institutional forms would be standard. Indeed, their newly won
victory for democracy and republicanism made them especially
anxious that these still precarious fruits of revolution should not be
threatened by a large influx of European peoples whose life experiences had accustomed them to bear the repressive bonds of des-
potic monarchy. Thus, although they explicitly conceived of the
new United States of America as a haven for those unfortunates of
Europe who were persecuted and oppressed and needed succor,
both Washington and Jefferson had characteristic reservations
about the effects of too free a policy. Washington had written to
John Adams in 1794, "My opinion, with respect to immigration,
is that except of useful mechanics and some particular descriptions
of men or professions, there is no need of encouragement, while
the policy or advantage of its taking place in a body (I mean the
settling of them in a body) may be much questioned; for, by so
doing, they retain the language, habits and principles (good or
bad) which they bring with them."[7] And Thomas Jefferson, whose
views on race and attitudes toward slavery were notably liberal and
advanced for his time, had doubts concerning the effects of mass
immigration on American institutions and, though conceding that
immigrants "if they come of themselves . . . are entitled to all the
rights of citizenship," could write in the early 1780's as follows:
"But are there no inconveniences to be thrown into the scale

[7] *The Writings of George Washington*, collected and edited by W. C. Ford,
New York, G. P. Putnam's Sons, 1889, Vol. XII, p. 489. Quoted in Maurice R.
Davie, op. cit., p. 38.

against the advantage expected from a multiplication of numbers by the importation of foreigners? It is for the happiness of those united in society to harmonize as much as possible in matters which they must of necessity transact together. Civil government being the sole object of forming societies, its administration must be conducted by common consent. Every species of government has its specific principles. Ours perhaps are more peculiar than those of any other in the universe. It is a composition of the freest principles of the English constitution, with others derived from natural right and natural reason. To these nothing can be more opposed than the maxims of absolute monarchies. Yet from such we are to expect the greatest number of emigrants. They will bring with them the principles of the governments they leave, imbibed in their early youth; or, if able to throw them off, it will be in exchange for an unbounded licentiousness, passing, as is usual, from one extreme to another. It would be a miracle were they to stop precisely at the point of temperate liberty. These principles, with their language, they will transmit to their children. In proportion to their numbers, they will share with us the legislation. They will infuse into it their spirit, warp and bias its directions, and render it a heterogeneous, incoherent, distracted mass."[8]

The attitudes of Americans toward foreign immigration in the first three quarters of the nineteenth century may correctly be described as ambiguous. On the one hand, immigrants were much desired to swell the population and importance of states and territories, to man the farms of expanding prairie settlement, to work the mines, build the railroads and canals, and take their place in expanding industry. This was a period in which no federal legislation of any consequence prevented the entry of aliens, and such state legislation as existed attempted to bar only on an individual

[8] Thomas Jefferson, *Notes on Virginia*, Query 8. Quoted in Saul K. Padover, (ed.), *Thomas Jefferson on Democracy*, New York, The New American Library (Mentor Books), 1946.

basis those who were likely to become a burden on the community, such as convicts and paupers. On the other hand, the arrival in an overwhelmingly Protestant society of large numbers of poverty-stricken Irish Catholics who settled in groups in the slums of eastern cities activated dormant fears of "Popery" and Rome. The substantial influx of Germans who made their way to the cities and farms of the Midwest, and whose different language, separate communal life, and freer ideas on temperance and sabbath observance brought them into conflict with the Anglo-Saxon bearers of the Puritan and Evangelical traditions, constituted another source of anxiety. Fear of foreign "radicals" and suspicion of economic demands of the occasionally aroused workingmen added fuel to the nativist fires.[9] To make matters worse, a number of European states and localities, particularly England and some of the German principalities, in fact conceived of the United States as a convenient place to dump a portion of their convicts and paupers and acted accordingly, the state laws to the contrary being largely ineffective. Add to all this the inhuman conditions of sanitation and sustenance on the passage over, and the consequent death and disease in the emigrant party, and the fears of many Americans may be understood, regardless of how they may be evaluated. Thus, even the immigration from England did not escape censure. Although many English immigrants of the period were skilled mechanics and farmers, the not infrequent boatloads of "undesirables" from the almshouses and prisons of the chief ancestral country aroused considerable concern. "Now, sir, is it just?" passionately protested Senator John Davis of Massachusetts to his colleagues on the Senate floor in 1836, "Is it morally right for Great Britain to attempt to throw upon us this oppressive burden of sustaining her poor? Shall she be permitted to legislate them out of the kingdom, and to impose on

[9] For an analysis of the elements in American nativism, see John Higham, *Strangers in the Land*, New Brunswick, N.J., Rutgers University Press, 1955, Chapter 1.

us a tax for their support, without an effort on our part to counter-vail such a policy? Would it not be wronging our own virtuous poor to divide their bread with those who have no just or natural claims upon us? And above all, sir, shall we fold our arms and see this moral pestilence sent among us to poison the public mind and do irremediable mischief?"[10] And the editorialist of *Niles' Weekly Register* bitingly commented in 1830 on the arrival of a ship at Norfolk with a group of elderly English paupers: "John Bull has squeezed the orange, but insolently casts the skins in our faces. . . ."[11]

The fruits of these fears in their extreme form were the Native American movement of the 1830's and 1840's and the "American" or "Know-Nothing" Party of the 1850's with their anti-Catholic campaigns and their demands for restrictive naturalization and im-migration laws and for keeping the foreign-born out of political office. While these movements scored local political successes and their turbulences rent the national social fabric in such a manner that the patches are not yet entirely invisible, they had no success in influencing national legislative policy toward immigration and immigrants. And their fulminations inevitably provoked the ex-pected reactions from thoughtful observers. Several years before he was to assume the Presidency, Abraham Lincoln wrote to his old friend, Joshua Speed: "Our progress in degeneracy appears to me to be pretty rapid. As a nation, we began by declaring that '*all men are created equal*.' We now practically read it 'all men are created equal, except *negroes*.' When the Know-Nothings get control, it will read 'all men are created equal, except negroes, *and foreigners and Catholics*.' When it comes to this I should prefer emigrating to some country where they make no pretense of loving liberty—

[10] Congressional Debates of 1835-6, Vol. XII, part 2, p. 1378. Quoted in Roy L. Garis, op. cit., p. 38.
[11] *Niles' Weekly Register*, Vol. XXXVIII (July 3, 1830), p. 335. Quoted in Roy L. Garis, op. cit., p. 39.

to Russia, for instance, where despotism can be taken pure, and without the base alloy of hypocracy [sic]."[12]

The flood of newcomers to the westward-expanding nation grew larger, reaching over one and two-thirds millions in the decade 1841-50, and over two and one-half millions in the decade prior to the Civil War.[13] Throughout the entire period, quite apart from the excesses of the Know-Nothings, the predominant conception of what the ideal immigrant adjustment should be was probably that which is summed up in a comment from a letter written in 1818 by John Quincy Adams, then Secretary of State, in answer to the inquiries of Baron von Fürstenwaerther: "They [immigrants to America] come to a life of independence, but to a life of labor— and, if they cannot accomodate themselves to the character, moral, political and physical, of this country with all its compensating balances of good and evil, the Atlantic is always open to them to return to the land of their nativity and their fathers.[14] To one thing they must make up their minds, or they will be disappointed in every expectation of happiness as Americans. They must cast off the European skin, never to resume it. They must look forward to their posterity rather than backward to their ancestors; they must be sure that whatever their own feelings may be, those of their children will cling to the prejudices of this country."[15] This conception of the nature of the young nation as already set in a predominantly English mould is well summed up in the remarks of

[12] Quoted in Benjamin P. Thomas, *Abraham Lincoln*, New York, Alfred A. Knopf, 1952, pp. 163-4 (italics as quoted).

[13] *Annual Report of the Commissioner General of Immigration*—1930, p. 200. Reproduced in Maurice R. Davie, op. cit., p. 53.

[14] An early and elegant version of "If they don't like it here, they can go back where they came from!"

[15] The letter is published in *Niles' Weekly Register*, Vol. XVIII, April 29, 1820, pp. 157-8, and excerpts from it appear in Jesse Chickering, *Immigration into the United States*, Boston, Charles C. Little and James Brown, 1848, pp. 79-80. See also, Marcus L. Hansen, *The Atlantic Migration, 1607-1860*, pp. 96-7.

a writer of one of the first general treatises on immigration, published in 1848:

The people of the United States, considered as a whole, are composed of immigrants and their descendants from almost every country. The principal portion of them, however, derived their origin from the British nation, comprehending by this term the English, the Scotch and the Irish. The English language is almost wholly used; the English manners, modified to be sure, predominate, and the spirit of English liberty and enterprise animates the energies of the whole people. English laws and institutions, adapted to the circumstances of the country, have been adopted here. . . .

The New England states, Virginia, Pennsylvania, Maryland and the Carolinas were principally settled by the English; New York and New Jersey by the Dutch; Mississippi and Louisiana by the French; Florida by the Spaniards. The new states have been settled mainly by emigrants from the older states, with large numbers from foreign countries, —Great Britain, Germany, Switzerland, &c. We have not the means at hand of determining the exact number that have been derived from these various sources. The tendency of things is to mould the whole into one people, whose leading characteristics are English, formed on American soil.[16]

Ethnic antagonisms tended to be submerged by the tidal wave of Civil War which swept over the divided nation, and, following the war, the era of wholesale industrial expansion began, which, together with the continued process of westward settlement, created a need for immigrants which guaranteed them a generally favorable reception. The national sources of the migrants from overseas were still predominantly the lands of Northern and Western Europe, with the Scandinavian countries assuming a more important role in this period as Swedes and Norwegians moved to take their place on the farm lands of the western prairie; also the French-Canadians began to spill down over the land border into the mill towns of New England. However, a mushrooming capital-

[16] Jesse Chickering, op. cit., p. 56.

ism eventually produced its own irritants of nativism, as sporadic
bursts of labor unrest rearoused fears of foreign radicalism. And
anti-Catholic feeling was not dead—only dormant.

In 1876 the United States Supreme Court declared state restrictions on immigration an infringement of the exclusive right of Congress to regulate foreign commerce, and six years later the first effective federal legislation dealing with immigration materialized.
It was a selective law which excluded, in its own terminology, luna-
tics, idiots, convicts (except those convicted of political offenses),
and persons likely to become a public charge. In the same year,
growing nativist pressures from the Pacific Coast led to the barring
of further immigration of Chinese laborers.

In fact, events of the 1880's inaugurated an era in American
nativism, which, while containing a number of ebbs and swells of
passion, was not to end until the quota laws of the 1920's were
passed.[17] In the earlier decade, the dislocations of growing class
cleavage and a new wave of industrial strikes culminated in the
explosive Haymarket Riot, which solidified general fear of the
foreign-born radical. Native-born workers pressed successfully for
a law excluding the bringing of contract laborers from abroad.
Municipal reformers began substantially to connect the problems
of political corruption, poverty, and crime in an urban setting with
the presence of the immigrant. Protestant fears of papal influence
revived, fed by the unmistakable signs of Catholic institutional
growth, particularly the parochial school system, and by Catholic
political prominence in some of the cities of the Northeast. Significantly, also, in 1882 nearly 800,000 migrants from other lands
entered the United States, the largest number by far up to that
time and a figure not to be reached again, or surpassed, until 1903.
Even more importantly, the decade of the 1880's brought with it
a portentous (though at the time little-recognized) change in the

[17] See Higham, op. cit. This section owes a substantial debt to Higham's book,
subtitled "Patterns of American Nativism, 1860-1925."

national origins of the newcomers, as the countries of Southern and Eastern Europe began to be represented in significant numbers for the first time. In the next decade immigrants from these sources became numerically dominant, and Italians, Jews, and Slavs began to outnumber the English, Irish, Germans, and Scandinavians.

The most salient nativist organization of the decade before the turn of the century was the American Protective Association, which was anti-Catholic and directed its animus particularly against the Irish. But already the new sources of foreign-born augmentation from the relatively unfamiliar lands and cultures of Italy, Russia, Austria-Hungary, and the Balkans were attracting unfavorable attention from many older Americans. Arriving at a time when the western frontier was rapidly closing and was soon closed, they huddled in the urban slums and took their economic places on the lowest rungs of the industrial ladder. And now the unfamiliar notes of a new, or at least hitherto unemphasized, chord from the nativist lyre began to sound—the ugly chord, or discord, of racism. Previously vague and romantic notions of Anglo-Saxon peoplehood were combined with general ethnocentrism, rudimentary wisps of genetics, selected tidbits of evolutionary theory, and naïve assumptions from an early and crude imported anthropology (later, other social sciences, at a similar stage of scientific development added their contributions) to produce the doctrine that the English, Germans, and others of the "old immigration" constituted a superior race of tall, blonde, blue-eyed "Nordics" or "Aryans," whereas the peoples of Eastern and Southern Europe made up the darker Alpines or Mediterraneans—both inferior breeds whose presence in America threatened, either by intermixture or supplementation, the traditional American stock and culture. These doctrines were given classic expression on this side of the Atlantic by the socialite, sportsman, and amateur zoologist, Madison Grant, in *The Passing of the Great Race*, published in 1916, but they were in the air a number of years before. Their obvious corollary was exclusion of the allegedly inferior breeds, but if the newer type of immigrant could not be excluded, at least all that could be done must be done to instill Anglo-Saxon virtues in these benighted creatures. Thus, one educator of the period, writing in 1909, could state routinely in one of his professional works: "These southern and eastern Europeans are of a very different type from the north Europeans who preceded them. Illiterate, docile, lacking in self-reliance and initiative, and not possessing the Anglo-Teutonic conceptions of law, order, and government, their coming has served to dilute tremendously our national stock, and to corrupt our civic life. The great bulk of these people have settled in the cities of the North Atlantic and North Central states, and the problems of proper housing and living, moral and sanitary conditions, honest and decent government, and proper education have everywhere been made more difficult by their presence. *Everywhere these people tend to settle in groups or settlements, and to set up here their national manners, customs, and observances. Our task is to break up these groups or settlements, to assimilate and amalgamate these people as a part of our American race, and to implant in their children, so far as can be done, the Anglo-Saxon conception of righteousness, law and order, and popular government, and to awaken in them a reverence for our democratic institutions and for those things in our national life which we as a people hold to be of abiding worth.*"[18]

Anglo-conformity received its fullest expression in the so-called Americanization movement, which gripped the nation like a fever during World War I.[19] While "Americanization" in its various stages had more than one emphasis, essentially it was a consciously

[18] Ellwood P. Cubberly, *Changing Conceptions of Education*, Boston, Houghton Mifflin Co., 1909, pp. 15-16 (italics mine).
[19] See Highham, op. cit., Chapter 9; Edward George Hartmann, *The Movement to Americanize the Immigrant*, New York, Columbia University Press, 1948; and Howard C. Hill, "The Americanization Movement," *American Journal of Sociology*, Vol. 24, No. 6 (May, 1919), pp. 609-42.

articulated movement to strip the immigrant of his native culture and attachments and make him over into an American along Anglo-Saxon lines—all this to be accomplished with great rapidity. To use an image of a later day, it was an attempt at "pressure-cooking assimilation." As far back as the 1890's the settlement houses had begun a gentler process of dealing with the adjustment of the hordes of impoverished newcomers from Southern and Eastern Europe, and some of them had shown an appreciation of the immigrant's own cultural heritage and its potential contribution to American life. Other private groups, notably the "lineage" patriotic societies, such as the Daughters of the American Revolution, the Society of Colonial Dames, and the Sons of the American Revolution, began to draw up and disseminate, in the decade or so before the war, educational programs designed to teach the foreign-born to understand American political institutions, to become naturalized, and to embrace patriotic sentiments. Another group concerned with "proper" education and indoctrination of the immigrant population during this period was the business and industrial community, aroused by continued labor unrest and the strike-fomenting and class war preachments of the Industrial Workers of the World; their concern took form in 1908 with the organization of the North American Civic League for Immigrants and its program of immigrant aid and adjustment. Also, some of the cities with large immigrant populations had initiated evening school classes designed to teach English to the foreign-born, and a few state and federal agencies had begun to concern themselves with the problem of the immigrant.

The repercussions of World War I, beginning with "preparedness" and culminating in America's entry in 1917, transformed the pressures on the immigrant to "Americanize" into an enormous force. Suspicion of the intent of the large German-American group produced in the minds of many citizens of the time the menace of the "hyphenated American," and hatred and persecution of Ger-

man cultural manifestations in this country were epidemic. This
suspicion bubbled over into a general concern for assuring the loyalty of all those who had come from other lands. The cry of the
hour was "100% Americanism," and now federal agencies in the
form of the Bureau of Education, the Bureau of Naturalization,
and the Committee on Public Information, state governments,
additional municipalities, and a veritable host of private organizations joined the effort to persuade the immigrant to learn English,
take out naturalization papers, buy war bonds, forget his former
origins, and give himself over to the full flush of patriotic hysteria.
In the words of John Higham, "By threat and rhetoric 100 per
cent Americanizers opened a frontal assault on foreign influence in
American life. They set about to stampede immigrants into citizenship, into adoption of the English language, and into an unques-
tioning reverence for existing American institutions. They bade
them abandon entirely their Old World loyalties, customs, and
memories. They used high-pressure, steam-roller tactics. They ca-
joled and they commanded."[20]

It is evident that several interwoven strands made up the cloth
of the Americanization program. The concern for political loyalty
and external manifestations of patriotism dominated the emotional
tone of the later stages, but running through the whole were more
prosaic instrumental programs of instruction in the use of the English language, elementary American history, the nature of American
government, and so on. Both the patriotic appeals and the instrumental materials, however, were embedded in a framework of either
explicit denigration or implicit disregard of the immigrant's own
native culture and the groups and institutions which, with his fellows, he had created on American soil. Thus the Superintendent of
the New York Public Schools could state in 1918: "Broadly speaking, we mean . . . [by Americanization] an appreciation of the
institutions of this country, absolute forgetfulness of all obligations

[20] Higham, op. cit., p. 247.

or connections with other countries because of descent or birth."[21] Samuel Rea, president of the Pennsylvania Railroad, expressed similar sentiments when he wrote in a leaflet published during this period by the National Americanization Committee that "they [the foreign-born] must be induced to give up the languages, customs, and methods of life which they have brought with them across the ocean, and adopt instead the language, habits, and customs of this country, and the general standards and ways of American living."[22] And in 1915 the President of the United States had informed an assemblage of naturalized citizens in Philadelphia that ethnic group identity was not compatible with being a "thorough American." "America does not consist of groups," Woodrow Wilson had stated. "A man who thinks of himself as belonging to a particular national group in America has not yet become an American."[23]

The winds of the Americanization crusade continued to blow strong after the Armistice, and even intensified, as a result of the breath of the Big Red Scare. However, by 1921 the crusade was over, and though homelier elements of it survived through the 1920's in routine programs of instruction for the foreign-born in English and civics, and in the augmentation of the adult education movement, the excesses of the preceding program of immigrant indoctrination evaporated. In its place, however, there arose a demand for restriction of the influx of new immigrants which had resumed after the hiatus of the war years. This new wave of restrictionist sentiment was based in considerable part on the racist as-

[21] Quoted in Berkson, op. cit., p. 59. Original source given as "The *Evening Post*, August 9, 1918."
[22] Quoted in Hill, op. cit., pp. 630-31. Original source given as "Samuel Rea, *Making Americans on the Railroad*, leaflet published by the National Americanization Committee." No date given.
[23] Woodrow Wilson, *President Wilson's Addresses* (G. M. Harper, ed.) New York, 1918. Quoted in Oscar Handlin, *The American People in the Twentieth Century*, p. 121.

sumption of the inherent inferiority and lack of assimilability of
the immigrants from Southern and Eastern Europe ("Americanization" had at least *implied* that the assimilation of these groups was
feasible), and its goal was not only to effect a decrease in the total
number of immigrants to the United States, but to set up a formula which would favor the entry of immigrants from Northern
and Western Europe and keep the number of the unfavored groups
to a minimum. The literacy requirement, instituted by an appre-
hensive Congress in 1917 over President Wilson's veto, had failed
to achieve this purpose. The goals of the restrictionists were thoroughly accomplished in a series of acts beginning in 1921 and culminating in the national origins formula which went into effect in
1929, restricting immigration from Europe and Africa to a total
of slightly over 150,000 per year and allotting quotas to the various
countries on the basis of an estimate of their respective contributions to the national origins of the white American population of
1920. Most Asiatics were banned entirely.

The great depression of the 1930's and the cataclysm of World
War II in the following decade produced no significant change in
American immigration policy, and the national origins formula was
reaffirmed, with minor modifications (token quotas were assigned
to the countries of Asia) in the McCarran-Walter Act of 1952.
Both racial assumptions and Anglo-conformity may be said to be
built-in implicit features of this policy. The currents of prejudice
signalized by the Ku Klux Klan of the 1920's, and the anti-Semitic
flurries of the 1930's, stimulated by economic hard times and events
in Nazi Germany, proved that nativism was not extinguished in
the America of this portion of the twentieth century, and the
wholesale internment of Japanese and Japanese-Americans during
World War II revealed that in times of acute stress racist premises could again direct the hand of official action. In the current
prosperous period, however, although problems of group adjustment remain endemic, noisy nativism of the traditional variety is

not conspicuous. In its place have come resistance to the long-forming bid of the Negro minority for equal treatment and civic integration, and the problems growing out of the migration to the United States of peoples from other parts of North America—the Spanish-speaking peoples of Mexico and Puerto Rico. The effect of the national origins formula on admission of migrants from outside the Western Hemisphere, however, assures that the day of large-scale immigrant colonies of white Europeans is over. The number of foreign-born Europeans in the United States continually shrinks as the ranks of the older generation are thinned by mortality and are replaced in only token amounts, and the problems of assimilation and group adjustment for these elements of the population must increasingly be placed in the context of the attitudes and aspirations of the second and third generations—native-born Americans. It is in the context of all the events described above that the doctrine of Anglo-conformity—probably still the dominant implicit theory of assimilation in America, though not unchallenged—must be evaluated. To such a preliminary evaluation let us now turn.

It is necessary, first of all, to emphasize that a belief in Anglo-conformity as the desirable goal of assimilation in America cannot automatically be equated with racism. While, as our historical survey has revealed, the two ideologies have intersected and reinforced each other at particular points in the American experience, such has not always been the case, and conceptually we may note that each can exist independently of the other. In actual fact, it would appear that all racists, in so far as they have conceded the right of any of their disfavored groups to be present in America, and notwithstanding their pessimism as to the success of the assimilation venture, have been Anglo-conformists; but the converse is not true —all upholders of Anglo-conformity have not been racists. The non-racist Anglo-conformists presumably are either convinced of the *cultural* superiority of Anglo-Saxon institutions as developed in the

United States, or believe simply that, regardless of superiority or inferiority, since English culture has constituted the dominant framework for the development of American institutions, newcomers should expect to adjust accordingly.

None of the spokesmen for Anglo-conformity, to my knowledge, has presented a careful delineation in sociological depth of what the process actually involves. If we examine their statements and pleas, however, in relation to the system of assimilation variables outlined in the previous chapter, we note that their most concerted explicit focus is on behavioral assimilation, or acculturation. That is, all of them demand with greater or lesser importunity, that the newcomers to America give up the cultural forms of their native lands and take on the behavior and attitudes of the dominant Anglo-Saxon mould of their adopted country. Less frequently explicit, but usually implicit, is the disapproval, except for non-white groups, of ethnic "colonies" and communal life. Although the Anglo-conformists are pleasantly vague as to the details of any alternative, the favored course would appear to be that the immigrants and their descendants eschew the development of their own institutions and organizations, and any sense of distinct ethnic identity, and enter the "general" American structure of institutional life. Presumably this would lead to extensive intermarriage. Put in our own terms, this amounts to a demand for structural assimilation, identificational assimilation, and marital assimilation. It is also expected that since the newcomers will have adopted "American" values and goals, they will have no "alien" demands on the body politic, and thus civic assimilation will have taken place. Prejudice and discrimination, the two remaining variables, are rarely brought to the level of articulation in these formulations, but the implicit assumption is that if the immigrant will conform in all the above respects, unfavorable attitudes and behavior toward him will disappear.

Leaving out for the time being considerations based on value premises, what can be said of the Anglo-conformity goal from the point of view of both the American historical experience thus far and the type of sociological analysis which we have suggested? Basically, our thesis is this: From the long-range point of view, the goal of Anglo-conformity has been substantially, although not completely, achieved with regard to *acculturation*. It has, in the main, not been achieved or only partly been achieved with regard to the other assimilation variables. This statement requires, of course, considerable explication and qualification.

Let us consider, first, the impact of the assimilation process on the immigrants themselves—those, at least, that came in sizable numbers after the original English settlements. All such groups, with the probable exception of the British in the nineteenth century, have initially flocked together in "colonies," urban or rural, and have developed a form of communal life oriented, in varying details, around their own burial and insurance societies, churches of their native faith with services conducted in their native language, organizations devoted to the defense of the group domestically and the memories or aspirations of the native land, recreational patterns involving native customs and tongue, and a network of personal friendships with their ethnic compatriots.[24] And why not? To have expected otherwise was absurd. The process of leaving one's native land to take up permanent residence in an alien society with an alien culture is difficult enough in the most propitious of circumstances. When we consider that the American immigration experience in the nineteenth and early twentieth centuries implicated, for the most part, peasants whose previous horizons rarely stretched beyond their native village, meagerly educated workmen and tradesmen, and refugees from medieval ghettoes, and that all of these immigrants were received by a society at best

[24] See Robert E. Park and Herbert A. Miller, *Old World Traits Transplanted*, New York, Harper and Brothers, 1921; and Handlin, *The Uprooted*, and *The American People in the Twentieth Century*.

largely indifferent, at worst hostile to them, and concerned only
with their instrumental economic skills in the context of a raw and
untempered expanding capitalism, then we must recognize how
fortunate it was that the immigrant groups were separately large
enough to provide the warmth, familiar ways, and sense of acceptance that prevented the saga of "uprooting" from becoming a dis-
locating horror.

The self-contained communal life of the immigrant colonies
served, then, as a kind of decompression chamber in which the
newcomers could, at their own pace, make a reasonable adjustment
to the new forces of a society vastly different from that which they
had known in the Old World. The semi-hysterical attempt at
pressure-cooking assimilation which was the Americanization crusade of World War I, while it contained worth-while instrumental
elements, was fundamentally misguided in its demand for a rapid
personal transformation and a draconic and abrupt detachment
from the cultural patterns and memories of the homeland. Instead
of building on the positive values of the immigrant's heritage, emphasizing the common denominator of understandings and aspirations which his native background shared with the American and
assuring him of the elementary right of self-respect, it flayed his
alienness with thinly veiled contempt, ignored his stabilizing ties
to the groups which made him a person in the sociological sense,
and widened the gap between himself and his children.[25] Under
these circumstances, it is hardly surprising that the Americanization
movement in its formal aspects, as is generally conceded, had small
success. The newcomers, in widely different ways and in varying
degrees gradually made suitable progress in acculturation to the
American patterns and integration into the civic (as distinguished
from the area of primary group relationships) life of the society,
but not in the forced march tempo demanded by "Americaniza-

[25] Cf. Berkson, op. cit., Chapter 2; Drachsler, op. cit., Chapter 7; and Cole and
Cole, op. cit., Chapter 6.

tion." As E. G. Hartmann, the historian of the movement, writes, ". . . The number of immigrants who become Americanized along the formal lines advocated by the Americanization groups must have been small, indeed, when compared with the great bulk of their fellows who never saw the inside of an American schoolroom or settlement house. The great majority of the latter became Americanized in time through the gradual process of assimilating American customs, attitudes, speech, and ideals from their native American neighbors and from their American-born children."[26] In this entire process, with respect to both concerted effort and *laissez faire*, it is worth emphasizing that the heartache, bewilderment, and tension of assimilation for the immigrant and his family could have been considerably decreased if American public opinion had been inclined and wise enough to build *onto* the newcomer's heritage rather than treating it with disdain.

This brings us to the children of the uprooted. Here is where the acculturation process has been overwhelmingly triumphant. While the lineaments of this triumph and the evidence for it will be reserved for consideration in a later chapter, we may note here that in whatever contest ensued between the behavior models of the parents' culture and those of the general American society, the latter pressed upon the new generation's sensibilities by the public school system and the mass media of communication, there was no question as to which would be the winner. In fact, the problem was that the forces were so unevenly balanced that the greater risk consisted in possible alienation from family ties and in status and role reversals of the generations which could easily subvert normal relationships of parent and child. It is true that the images of American behavior often came through curiously refracted and distorted by the social class background of the immediate environs, and sometimes the immigrant's offspring rejected the restrictions of the parental culture only to fail to take on the social restraints

[26] Hartmann, op. cit., p. 271.

inherent in the patterns of the broader society, a situation con-
ducive to delinquency. But, by and large, the massive forces of the
acculturation process transformed the seed of Ireland, Germany,
Italy, the Russian Pale, and other areas into aspiring Americans,
who were at home in the English language whatever the class ac-
cents and minor ancestral inflections that tinged their version, and,
with varying perspectives, eager to climb the ladder of social class
which they knew had rungs marked "made in the U.S.A."

There were exceptions to this generalization, to be sure. When
minorities were grouped in rural enclaves widely separated in distance from native American neighbors, or when, occasionally, parochial school systems emphasized the parental language rather
than English, the acculturation process was delayed. But usually
delayed only—not checked. Perhaps it waited upon a move to the
city with its broader horizons after childhood—or until the third
generation grew up. But its ultimate victory was inevitable.

As for the Negro, the Indian, and the Latin-American minorities,
additional factors entered the situation and have modified the outcome. The rural Negro of the South, under both slavery and post-
Reconstruction exploitation and discrimination, developed a set of
subcultural patterns considerably remote from those of the core
society of middle-class whites. As he moved in the twentieth century to the cities of the North and South, the acculturation process
was retarded because of the massive size and strength of the prejudice and consequent discrimination directed toward him. The Negro is developing a middle class indistinguishable in basic behavior
patterns from middle-class whites, at what is undoubtedly an accelerating rate since World War II, but there is still some distance to
go before his class distribution and appropriate modifications in
the lower-class subculture will signalize complete acculturation
to the American scene. For somewhat similar reasons, augmented by
the language difference, the Spanish-speaking people of Mexican
origin in the Southwest appear to be developing a middle class out

of the second generation rather slowly, an unmistakable sign of a retardation in the acculturation process. The Puerto Ricans of New York and a few other northern cities have been here such a short time that it has not been possible to observe acculturation over two full generations, although there are signs that the development of a strong middle-class contingent will not be as rapid as in the case of the European (and the Oriental),[27] probably because of the depth of the prejudice against them as well as indigenous cultural factors. The American Indians who still remain on the reservations, relatively isolated as they are in rural enclaves, still retaining a fierce pride in their ancestral cultures and group identity, and occupying a special legal status which reinforces their group separatism, have taken only a partial step towards acculturation to the patterns and values of the core society.

Was acculturation entirely a one-way process? Was the core culture entirely unaffected by the presence of the immigrants and the colored minorities? In suggesting the answer to this question, I must once again point to the distinction between the impact of the members of minority groups *as individuals* making their various contributions to agriculture, industry, the arts, and science in the context of the Anglo-Saxon version (as modified by peculiarly American factors) of the combination of Hebraic, Christian, and Classical influences which constitutes Western civilization, and the specific impact on the American culture of the minority cultures themselves. The impact of individuals has been so considerable that it is impossible to conceive of what American society or American life would have been like without it. The impact of minority group culture has been of modest dimensions, I would argue, in most areas, and significantly extensive in only one—the area of institutional religion. From a nation overwhelmingly and characteristically Protestant in the late eighteenth century, America has become a

[27] See Nathan Glazer, "New York's Puerto Ricans," *Commentary*, Vol. 26, No. 6 (December 1958), pp. 469-78.

national entity of Protestants, Catholics, and Jews—where membership in, or identificational allegiance to, one or the other of these three great faiths is the norm, and where the legitimacy of the institutional presence and ramifications of this presence of the three denominations is routinely honored in American public opinion.[28] In the course of taking root in American soil, Catholicism and Judaism have themselves undergone changes in form and expression in response to the forces and challenges of the American experience. For the rest, there have been minor modifications in cuisine, recreational patterns, place names, speech, residential architecture, sources of artistic inspiration, and perhaps a few other areas—all of which add flavor and piquancy to the totality of the American culture configuration but have scarcely obscured its essential English outlines and content.

Over the generations, then, the triumph of acculturation in America has been, if not complete, at least numerically and functionally overwhelming. It is with regard to the other assimilation variables that the assimilation process has refused to take the path which the Anglo-conformists, at least by implication, laid out for it. The key variable which unlocks the mystery of this deviation, both revealing it and suggesting its causes, is, as usual, the cluster of phenomena associated with participation in cliques, organizations, and institutions which we have called *structural assimilation*. Again, it is necessary to point out that the evidence for the statements to be made below, and their illustration, await later presentation. Here we shall merely delineate in brief the broad picture. It is a picture to which we have already referred in Chapter 2—an American society in which each racial and religious (and to a lesser extent, national origins) group has its own network of cliques, clubs, organizations, and institutions which tend to confine the primary group contacts of its members within the ethnic enclave, while interethnic contacts take place in considerable part

[28] See Herberg, op. cit.

only at the secondary group level of employment and the political and civic processes. Each ethnic group contains the usual class divisions, and the behavior patterns of members of the same class are very similar regardless of their race, religion, or national origin. But they do not go their similar ways together; separated by the invisible but powerful barriers of ancestral identification and belief, they carry out their intimate life in the separate compartments of ethnicity which make up the vertical dimensions of the American social structure. The only substantial exception to this picture of ethnic separation is the compartment marked "intellectuals and artists"— a social world we shall deal with later.

If structural assimilation in substantial fashion has not taken place in America, we must ask why. The answer lies in the attitudes of both the majority and the minority groups and in the way in which these attitudes have interacted. A folk saying of the current day is that "It takes two to tango." To utilize the analogy, there is no good reason to believe that white Protestant America ever extended a firm and cordial invitation to its minorities to dance. Furthermore, the attitudes of the minority group members themselves on the matter have been divided and ambiguous. Let us, again, examine the situation serially for the various types of minorities.

With regard to the immigrant, in his characteristic numbers and socio-economic background, structural assimilation was out of the question. He did not want it, and he had a positive need for the comfort of his own communal institutions. The native American, moreover, whatever the implications of his public pronouncements, had no intention of opening up his primary group life to entrance by these hordes of alien newcomers. The situation was a functionally complementary standoff.

The second generation found a much more complex situation. Many of them believed they heard the siren call of welcome to the social cliques, clubs, and institutions of white Protestant America.

After all, it was simply a matter of learning American ways, was it not, and had they not grown up as Americans and were they not culturally different from their parents, the greenhorns? Or perhaps an especially eager one reasoned, like the Jewish protagonist of Myron Kaufmann's novel, *Remember Me To God*, bucking for membership in the prestigous club system of Harvard undergraduate social life: If only I can go the last few steps in Ivy League manners and behavior, they will surely recognize that I am one of them and take me in.[29] But, Brooks Brothers suit notwithstanding, the doors of the fraternity house, the city men's club, and the country club were slammed in the face of the immigrant's offspring. That invitation wasn't really there in the first place; or, to the extent it was there, it was, in Joshua Fishman's telling phrase, a " 'look me over but don't touch me' invitation to the American minority group child."[30] And so the rebuffed one returned to the homelier but dependable comfort of the communal institutions of his ancestral group. There he found his fellows of the same generation who had never stirred from the home fires at all. Some of these had been too timid to stray; others were ethnic ideologists positively committed to the group's survival; still others had never really believed in the authenticity of the siren call or were simply too passive

[29] Cf. Joshua Fishman's statement: "The assumptions posit a compelling American core culture toward which the minority group child grows up with ambivalent feelings. He is attracted to it, surrenders willingly to it, desires full participating membership in it—as does 'every red-blooded American' child. Were it not for a lack of total congruence between his aspiration and the permissiveness of the core-in-action (not the core-in-theory), there would be no ambivalence and perhaps no retentionism either. Nevertheless, the minority group child is ever ready to 'swallow his pride' and to try once more. Like the ever hopeful suitor, he constantly rationalizes: 'Perhaps she will like me in new shoes, perhaps she will like me in a new hat.' The child's views of his own shoes and hat are, in comparison, devaluational." (Joshua A. Fishman, "Childhood Indoctrination for Minority-Group Membership and The Quest for Minority-Group Biculturism in America," *cit. supra.*
[30] Ibid.

to do more than go along the familiar way; all could now join in the task that was well within the realm of the sociologically possible—the build-up of social institutions and organizations within the ethnic enclave, manned increasingly by members of the second generation and suitably separated by social class.

Those who had for a time ventured out gingerly or confidently as the case may be, had been lured by the vision of an "American" social structure that was somehow larger than all subgroups and ethnically neutral. And were they, too, not Americans? But they found to their dismay that at the primary group level a neutral American social structure was a myth—a mirage. What at a distance seemed to be a quasi-public edifice flying only the all-inclusive flag of American nationality turned out, on closer inspection, to be the clubhouse of a particular ethnic group—the white Anglo-Saxon Protestants, its operation shot through with the premises and expectations of its parental ethnicity. In these terms, the desirability of whatever invitation was grudgingly extended could only become considerably attenuated to those of other ethnic backgrounds.

With the racial minorities there was not even the pretense of an invitation. Negroes, to take the most salient example, have for the most part been determinedly barred from the cliques, social clubs, and churches of white America. Consequently, with due allowance for internal class differences, they have constructed their own network of organizations and institutions—their own "social world." There are now many vested interests served by the preservation of this separate communal life, and doubtless many Negroes are psychologically comfortable in it, even though at the same time they keenly desire that discrimination in such areas as employment, education, housing, and public accommodations be eliminated. However, the ideological attachment of Negroes to their communal separation is, as we noted earlier, not conspicuous. Their sense of identification with ancestral African national cultures is virtually nonexistent, although Pan-Africanism engages the interest of some intellectuals and although "black nationalist" and "black racist" fringe groups have recently made an appearance at the other end of the communal spectrum. As for their religion, they are either Protestant or Catholic (overwhelmingly the former). Thus there are here no "logical" ideological reasons for separate communality; dual social structures are created solely by the dynamics of prejudice and discrimination rather than being reinforced by ideological commitments of the minority itself.

Structural assimilation, then, turned out to be the rock on which the ship of Anglo-conformity foundered. And if structural assimilation, to large degree, did not take place, then in similar measure amalgamation and identificational assimilation could not. It is a commonplace of empirical observation that prejudice and discrimination still remain on the American scene, though probably in slowly decreasing amounts, and the fact that value conflict arising out of varying religious adherences still occurs on public issues indicates that civic assimilation has not been complete. All this, while Anglo-conformity, with the exceptions and qualifications noted above, has substantially triumphed in the behavioral area. To understand, then, that acculturation without massive structural intermingling at primary group levels has been the dominant motif in the American experience of creating and developing a nation out of diverse peoples is to comprehend the most essential sociological fact of that experience.

5

Theories of Assimilation: Part II
The Melting Pot

While Anglo-conformity, in various guises, has probably been the most prevalent ideology of assimilation in the American historical experience, a competing viewpoint with more generous and idealistic overtones has had its adherents and exponents from the eighteenth century onward. Conditions in the virgin continent were modifying the institutions which the English colonists brought with them from the mother country. Immigrants from non-English homelands, such as Germany, Sweden, and France, were similarly exposed to this fresh environment. Was it not possible, then, to think of the evolving American society not simply as a slightly modified England but rather as a totally new blend, culturally and biologically, in which the stocks and folkways of Europe were, figuratively speaking, indiscriminately mixed in the political pot of the emerging nation and melted together by the fires of American influence and interaction into a distinctly new type?

Such, at any rate, was the conception of the new society which motivated that quietly romantic eighteenth century French-born writer and agriculturalist, J. Hector St. John Crèvecoeur, who had settled in New York and, after many years of American residence

and accumulated familiarity with the existing scene, issued in 1782
his various reflections and observations in a small volume entitled
Letters from an American Farmer. "What . . . ," asks Crèvecoeur, "is the American, this new man?' And he answers: "He is
either an European, or the descendant of an European, hence that
strange mixture of blood, which you will find in no other country.
I could point out to you a family whose grandfather was an Englishman, whose wife was Dutch, whose son married a French woman,
and whose present four sons have now four wives of different nations. *He* is an American, who leaving behind him all his ancient
prejudices and manners, receives new ones from the new mode of
life he has embraced, the new government he obeys, and the new
rank he holds. He becomes an American by being received in the
broad lap of our great *Alma Mater*. Here individuals of all nations
are melted into a new race of men, whose labours and posterity will
one day cause great changes in the world."[1] And in an earlier passage he had characterized the people of his adopted homeland as
"a mixture of English, Scotch, Irish, French, Dutch, Germans, and
Swedes." "From this promiscuous breed," he declared, "that race
now called Americans have [sic] arisen."[2]

Some observers have interpreted the open-door immigration policy of the first three-quarters of the nineteenth century as reflecting
an underlying native faith in the effectiveness of the American melting pot, in the belief, to quote Oscar Handlin, "that all could be
absorbed and that all could contribute to an emerging national
character."[3] No doubt many who observed the nativist agitation of
the times with dismay felt as did Ralph Waldo Emerson that such
conformity-demanding and immigrant-hating forces represented a

[1] J. Hector St. John Crèvecoeur, *Letters from an American Farmer*, New York,
Albert and Charles Boni, 1925 (reprinted from the original edition, London,
1782), pp. 54-5.
[2] Ibid., p. 51.
[3] Oscar Handlin (ed.), *Immigration as a Factor in American History*, Englewood Cliffs, N.J., Prentice-Hall, 1959, p. 146.

perversion of the best American ideals. In 1845, Emerson wrote in his Journal:

I hate the narrowness of the Native American Party. It is the dog in the manger. It is precisely opposite to all the dictates of love and magnanimity; and therefore, of course, opposite to true wisdom. . . . Man is the most composite of all creatures. . . . Well, as in the old burning of the Temple at Corinth, by the melting and intermixture of silver and gold and other metals a new compound more precious than any, called Corinthian brass, was formed; so in this continent,—asylum of all nations,—the energy of Irish, Germans, Swedes, Poles, and Cossacks, and all the European tribes,—of the Africans, and of the Polynesians,—will construct a new race, a new religion, a new state, a new literature, which will be as vigorous as the new Europe which came out of the smelting-pot of the Dark Ages, or that which earlier emerged from the Pelasgic and Etruscan barbarism. *La Nature aime les croisements.*[4]

Eventually, the melting pot hypothesis found its way into the rarefied air of historical scholarship and interpretation. While many American historians of the late nineteenth century, some of them fresh from graduate study at German universities, tended to adopt the view that American institutions derived in essence from Anglo-Saxon, and ultimately Teutonic, sources, others were not so sure.[5] One of these was Frederick Jackson Turner, a young historian from Wisconsin, who had taken his graduate training at Johns Hopkins. Turner presented a paper to the American Historical Association, meeting in Chicago in 1893. Called "The Significance of the Frontier in American History," this paper proved to be one of the most influential essays in the history of American scholarship. Its point of view, supported by Turner's subsequent writings and his teaching, pervaded the field of American historical interpretation for at

[4] Quoted in the Introduction by Stuart P. Sherman to *Essays and Poems of Emerson*, New York, Harcourt Brace and Co., 1921, p. xxxiv.
[5] See Edward N. Saveth, *American Historians and European Immigrants, 1875-1925*, New York, Columbia University Press, 1948.

least a generation.[6] Turner's thesis was, essentially, that the dominant influence in the shaping of American institutions and American democracy was not this nation's European heritage in any of its forms, or the forces emanating from the eastern seaboard cities, but rather the experiences created by a moving and variegated western frontier. Among the many effects attributed to the frontier environment and the challenges it presented was that it acted as a solvent for the national heritages and separatist tendencies of the many nationality groups which had joined the trek westward, including the Germans and Scotch-Irish of the eighteenth century and the Scandinavians and Germans of the nineteenth. "The frontier," asserted Turner, "promoted the formation of a composite nationality for the American people. . . . In the crucible of the frontier the immigrants were Americanized, liberated, and fused into a mixed race, English in neither nationality nor characteristics. The process has gone on from the early days to our own."[7] And later, in an essay on the role of the Mississippi Valley, he refers to "the tide of foreign immigration which has risen so steadily that it has made a composite American people whose amalgamation is destined to produce a new national stock."[8]

It was the special nature of midwestern democracy, according to Turner, to encourage mixing, not only biologically but culturally. "It is not merely that the section was growing rapidly and was made up of various stocks with many different cultures, sectional and European," he declared; "what is more significant is that these elements did not remain as separate strata underneath an estab-

---

[6] Since the 1930's the Turner frontier thesis has been subject to increasing criticism. For a collection of papers presenting views both supporting and countering the Turner position, see George Rogers Taylor (ed.), *The Turner Thesis Concerning the Role of the Frontier in American History*, Boston, D. C. Heath and Co., 1949 (Amherst College, Problems in American Civilization Series).

[7] Frederick Jackson Turner, *The Frontier in American History*, New York, Henry Holt and Co., 1920, pp. 22-3.

[8] Ibid., p. 190.

lished ruling order, as was the case particularly in New England. All were accepted and intermingling components of a forming society, plastic and absorptive." "Thus," he concluded, "the Middle West was teaching the lesson of national cross-fertilization instead of national enmities, the possibility of a newer and richer civilization, not by preserving unmodified or isolated the old component elements, but by breaking down the line-fences, by merging the individual life in the common product—a new product, which held the promise of world brotherhood."[9]

While Turner presented little or no empirical proof of his claim that the western frontier acted as a solvent for national heritages and stocks, or that it did so any more than did the eastern cities, the "frontier melting pot" thesis remained an important part of his larger influential theory of the role of the frontier in shaping the characteristic outlines of American society and character.

Thus far, the proponents of the melting pot idea had dealt largely with diversity produced by sizable immigration only from the countries of Northern and Western Europe—the so-called "old immigration," consisting of peoples with cultures and physical appearance not greatly different from those of the Anglo-Saxon stock. Emerson, it is true, had impartially included Africans, Polynesians, and Cossacks in his vision of elements of the mixture, but it was only in the last two decades of the nineteenth century that the rise of a large-scale influx of peoples from the countries of Southern and Eastern Europe—the so-called "new immigration"—imperiously posed the question of whether these uprooted newcomers who were crowding into the large cities of the nation and the industrial sector of the economy could also be successfully "melted." Would the "urban melting pot" work as well as the "frontier melting pot" of an essentially rural society was alleged to have done? Turner, it is interesting to note, was rather cool toward these later immigrants who settled in the urban slums (as the Irish had before them) to fill the

[9] Ibid., pp. 350-51.

demands of an expanding industrialization, and he failed to include them in his vision of the American melting process.[10]

It remained for an English Jewish writer with strong social convictions, moved by his observation of the role of the United States as a haven for the poor and oppressed of Europe, to give utterance to the broader view of the American melting pot in a way which attracted public attention. In 1908, Israel Zangwill's drama, *The Melting Pot*, was produced in this country and became a popular success. It is a play dominated by the vision of its protagonist, a young Russian Jewish immigrant to America, a composer whose goal is the completion of a vast "American" symphony which will express his deeply felt conception of his adopted country as a divinely inspired crucible in which all the ethnic divisions of mankind will divest themselves of their ancient animosities and differences and become fused into one group signifying the brotherhood of man. In the process he falls in love with a beautiful and cultured Gentile girl. The play ends with the completion and performance of the symphony and, after numerous vicissitudes and traditional family opposition from both sides, the approaching marriage of David Quixano and his beloved. During the course of these developments, David, in the rhetoric of the time, delivers himself of such sentiments as these:

America is God's crucible, the great Melting Pot where all the races of Europe are melting and re-forming!. Here you stand, good folk, think I, when I see them at Ellis Island, here you stand in your fifty groups, with your fifty languages and histories, and your fifty blood hatreds and rivalries. But you won't be long like that, brothers, for these are the fires of God you've come to—these are the fires of God. A fig for your feuds and vendettas! Germans and Frenchmen, Irishmen and Englishmen, Jews and Russians—into the Crucible with you all! God is making the American.

And later,

[10] See Saveth, op. cit., Chapter V, "Frontier and Urban Melting Pots."

Yes, East and West, and North and South, the palm and the pine, the pole and the equator, the crescent and the cross—how the great Alchemist melts and fuses them with his purging flame! Here shall they all unite to build the Republic of Man and the Kingdom of God. Ah, Vera, what is the glory of Rome and Jerusalem where all nations and races come to worship and look back, compared with the glory of America, where all races and nations come to labour and look forward.[11]

Here, then, we have a conception of a melting pot which admits of no exceptions or qualification with regard to the ethnic stocks which will fuse in the great crucible. Englishmen, Germans, Frenchmen, Slavs, Greeks, Syrians, Jews, Gentiles, even the black and yellow races, were specifically mentioned in Zangwill's rhapsodic enumeration. And this pot must patently boil in the great cities of America.

Thus, around the turn of the century, the melting pot idea was embedded in the rhetoric of the time as one response to the immigrant-receiving experience of the nation. It may be found, for instance, in the writing and speeches of two presidents: Theodore Roosevelt and Woodrow Wilson,[12] and, significantly enough, the published volume of Zangwill's play on the theme was dedicated to the first Roosevelt to lead the nation. However, as must now be apparent, a certain ambiguity surrounds the melting pot concept, allowing its adherents to interpret it in various ways. Neither Roosevelt nor the mature Wilson favored theories of racial superiority (although it is possible to detect a preference for the earlier immigration sources in their writings[13]), and both believed that the new immigrants from Southern and Eastern Europe were essentially capable of being absorbed into the American scene. However, Roosevelt, while viewing America as a nation in which "the repre-

11 Israel Zangwill, *The Melting Pot*, New York, The Macmillan Co., 1909, pp. 37, 199.
12 See Saveth, op. cit., pp. 112-21 and 137-49.
13 Ibid.

sentatives of many old-world races are being fused together into a
new type," maintained at the same time that "the crucible in which
all the new types are melted into one was shaped from 1776 to
1789, and our nationality was definitely fixed in all its essentials
by the men of Washington's day."[14] And a similar view, according
to a careful study of the matter, was shared by Wilson. In the
minds of both Roosevelt and Wilson, writes Edward Saveth, "unlike the frontier melting pot, which occurred earlier and was accepted as part of the process of nation making, the later mingling
of peoples was looked upon more as an assimilative process whereby
the peoples from southern and eastern Europe were indoctrinated
in canons of Americanism established by earlier arrivals."[15]

The melting pot idea was soon to be challenged by a new philosophy of group adjustment (to be discussed later), and was always
competing with the more pervasive adherence to Anglo-conformity.
However, it continued to draw a portion of such attention and discussion as was consciously directed to this aspect of the American
scene in the first half of the twentieth century. In the middle 1940's
a sociologist, Ruby Jo Reeves Kennedy, who had carried out an
investigation of intermarriage trends in New Haven, Connecticut,
described a revised conception of the melting process as it had
taken place in that city and suggested a basic modification of the
theory. In New Haven, Mrs. Kennedy reported, after a study of
intermarriage from 1870 to 1940, the rate of in-marriage, or endogamy, among the various national origins groups was high over
the whole period, although it had dropped from 91.20 per cent in
1870 to 65.80 per cent in 1930 to 63.64 per cent in 1940. But while
there was a decreasing emphasis on national origins lines in choosing a mate, there was still a considerable tendency to marry within

14 Quoted in Saveth, op. cit., p. 121; original source given as "Speech at the
unveiling of the Sheridan statue in Washington, cited in introduction to *The
Jews in Nazi Germany* (New York, 1935), p. viii."
15 Saveth, op. cit., p. 148.

one's own religious group. In 1940, 79.72 per cent of the British-Americans, Germans, and Scandinavians intermarried among themselves—that is, within a Protestant "pool"; 83.71 per cent of the Irish, Italians, and Poles intermarried among themselves—a Catholic "pool;" and 94.32 per cent of the Jews married other Jews. (The question of intermarriage between Jews of Central European origins and Jews of Eastern European origins was not studied.) Where Catholic-Protestant marriages took place—and it should be noted that in 1940 both the Irish and the Italians, when they did marry outside their own national group, preferred British-Americans to any other single national origins group—the majority of such marriages were sanctioned by Catholic nuptials, thus prescribing that the children would be brought up as Catholics. In other words, intermarriage was taking place across nationality background lines, but there was a strong tendency for it to stay confined within the basic influential field of one or the other of the three major religious groups: Protestants, Catholics, and Jews. Thus, declared Mrs. Kennedy, the picture in New Haven resembled a "triple melting pot" based on religious divisions, rather than a "single melting pot."[16] Her study indicated, she stated, that "while strict endogamy is loosening, religious endogamy is persisting and the future cleavages will be along religious lines rather than along nationality lines as in the past. If this is the case, then the traditional 'single-melting-pot' idea must be abandoned, and a new conception, which we term the 'triple-melting-pot' theory of American assimilation, will take its place as the true expression of what is happening to the various nationality groups in the United States."[17] The triple melting pot

[16] Ruby Jo Reeves Kennedy, "Single or Triple Melting-Pot? Intermarriage Trends in New Haven, 1870-1940," *American Journal of Sociology*, Vol. 49, No. 4 (January 1944), pp. 331-9; see also, her "Single or Triple Melting-Pot? Intermarriage in New Haven, 1870-1950," *American Journal of Sociology*, Vol. 58, No. 1 (July 1952), pp. 56-9.
[17] "Single or Triple Melting-Pot? Intermarriage Trends in New Haven, 1870-1940," p. 332 (Author's italics omitted).

thesis was later taken up by the theologian, Will Herberg, and formed an important sociological frame of reference for his analysis of religious trends in American society, published as *Protestant— Catholic—Jew*.[18]

Having now examined the rise and development of the melting pot idea, let us examine it with the aid of our analytical scheme, and against the background of the realities of American group life. We shall deal first with the "single melting pot" version, since this version is not only historically and logically prior but is the form in which this idea has captured the imagination of a number of articulate interpreters of American society for over a century and a half.

Partisans of the idea of America as one huge melting pot, like adherents of Anglo-conformity, have provided no systematic delineation of their views. Indeed, the concept is one which singularly lends itself to expression in vague rhetoric which, however noble its aims, gives minimal clues as to the exact implications of the term for the manifold spheres of societal organization and behavior. Nevertheless, certain logical inferences can be made, and one feature appears to be envisaged in all the statements of the idea: a complete mixture of the various stocks through intermarriage—in other words, marital assimilation, or amalgamation.

With regard to cultural behavior, the most characteristic implication is that the cultures of the various groups will mix and form a blend somewhat different from the cultures of any one of the groups separately. However, a neglected aspect of this model of cultural intermixture is whether all groups will make an equally influential contribution to the boiling pot, or whether there is to be a *proportionate* influence depending upon the size, power, and strategic location of the various groups. If, to illustrate hypothetically and simply, there are 100,000 Sylvanians occupying their own country, and 2000 Mundovians enter as immigrants, under the melting pot model of cultural interpenetration will the resulting

18 Op. cit.

blend—assuming some rough measurement were possible—consist of equal parts of Sylvanian and Mundovian culture, or will the Sylvania cultural contribution be fifty times as important and pervasive as the Mundovian contribution? The answer to this question obviously has significant consequences for the contributing societies, in relation to the questions of both objective cultural survival and group psychology.

Indeed, at one extreme of interpretation—a loose and illogical one, to be sure—the melting pot concept may envisage the culture of the immigrants as "melting" completely into the culture of the host society without leaving any cultural trace at all. It would appear that some exponents of the idea came close to feeling that this was the proper role for Southern and Eastern European immigrants to play in the American melting process. In this form, of course, the melting pot concept embraces a view of acculturation which is hardly distinguishable in nature from that of Anglo-conformity, except that the conformity is to be exacted toward a cultural blend to which the cultures of immigrant groups from Northern and Western Europe have been conceded an earlier contribution.

With regard to the remaining assimilation variables, the analysis may proceed as follows: If large-scale intermarriage is to have taken place, then obviously the immigrants must have entered the cliques, clubs, other primary groups, and institutions of the host society and, in addition, placed their own impress upon these social structures to some extent. Thus the process of structural assimilation must somehow reflect a blending effect, also. Identificational assimilation takes place in the form of all groups merging their previous sense of peoplehood into a new and larger ethnic identity which, in some fashion, honors its multiple origins at the same time that it constitutes an entity distinct from them all. Prejudice and discrimination must be absent since there are not even any identifiably separate groups to be their target, and "civic assimilation" will have taken place since disparate cultural values are assumed to have

merged and power conflict between groups would be neither necessary nor possible. This, then, is the "ideal-typical" model of the
melting pot process. With this analysis and the previous discussion
in mind, let us take a quick look at the American experience to see
how well the model applies. A fuller discussion of some of the issues
is reserved for later chapters.

While no exact figures on the subject are attainable, it is safe to
say that a substantial proportion of the descendants of the non-
English immigrants of colonial times and the first three-quarters
of the nineteenth century (with the exception of the Irish Catholics and the German Jews) have by now been absorbed into the
general white "sociological Protestant" sector of American life.
That is to say, they do not live in communal subsocieties which are
lineal descendants of those which their immigrant ancestors created, and so far as they understand it, are simply "Americans" who
may be vaguely conscious of an immigrant forebear here and there
from a non-English source but for whom this has little current
meaning. This would include many descendants of the Scotch-Irish,
German Protestants, Swedes, and Norwegians, among other groups
from Northern and Western Europe, as well as, in all probability,
a few with colonial Jewish ancestry whose early American progeni-
tors converted to Christianity (not to mention occasional individuals who have a mulatto ancestor who, at some time, "passed" into
the white group[19]). This does not mean that communal societies
with appropriate institutions representing most of these ancestral
groups do not still exist, but that, in relation to the total number
of ethnic descendants, they become increasingly thinly manned as

[19] Estimates of the number of very light Negroes who "pass" permanently into
the white group range from 2000 to 30,000 annually, although the practice is
obviously so shrouded in secrecy that even these limits may not include the true
figure. See Maurice R. Davie, *Negroes in American Society*, New York, McGraw-
Hill Book Co., 1949, pp. 401-7; also, Gunnar Myrdal, with the assistance of
Richard Sterner and Arnold Rose, *An American Dilemma*, New York, Harper
and Brothers, 1944, pp. 129-30, 683-8.

the third and fourth generation leave their rural or small town (occasionally urban) enclaves and venture forth into the broader social world.

The burden of our point should now be clear. Entrance by the descendants of these immigrants into the social structures of the existing white Protestant society, and the culmination of this process in intermarriage, has not led to the creation of new structures, new institutional forms, and a new sense of identity which draws impartially from all sources, but rather to immersion in a subsocietal network of groups and institutions which was already fixed in essential outline with an Anglo-Saxon, general Protestant stamp. The prior existence of Anglo-Saxon institutional forms as the norm, the pervasiveness of the English language, and the numerical dominance of the Anglo-Saxon population made this outcome inevitable.

If we turn to the cultural realm, we find much the same result. The tremendous contributions of non-English immigrants—of both the "Old" and "New" varieties—to American civilization collectively in the form of agricultural and industrial manpower, as sources of population growth, as bearers of strategic new crafts and skills, and as patrons of the developing fine arts is not here in question. Nor is the brilliant record achieved by countless individual immigrants and their descendants in the business, professional, scientific, and artistic life of the nation. All this has been mentioned before. The question at issue is rather the alteration of cultural forms. Here we would argue that, in great part, rather than an impartial melting of the divergent cultural patterns from all immigrant sources, what has actually taken place has been more of a transforming of the later immigrant's specific cultural contributions into the Anglo-Saxon mould. As George Stewart has put it, a more accurate figure of speech to describe the American experience would be that of a "transmuting pot" in which "as the foreign elements, a little at a time, were added to the pot, they were not

merely melted but were largely transmuted, and so did not affect
the original material as strikingly as might be expected."[20] Will
Herberg echoes this view. "The enthusiasts of the 'melting pot'
. . . ," he writes, "were wrong . . . in regard to the cultural aspect
of the assimilative process. They looked forward to a genuine blending of cultures, to which every ethnic strain would make its own
contribution and out of which would emerge a new cultural synthesis, no more English than German or Italian and yet in some
sense transcending and embracing them all. In certain respects this
has indeed become the case: our American cuisine includes anti-
pasto and spaghetti, frankfurters and pumpernickel, filet mignon
and french fried potatoes, borsch, sour cream, and gefüllte fish,
on a perfect equality with fried chicken, ham and eggs, and pork
and beans. But it would be a mistake to infer from this that the
American's image of himself—and that means the ethnic group
member's image of himself as he becomes American—is a composite or synthesis of the ethnic elements that have gone into the making of the American. It is nothing of the kind: the American's
image of himself is still the Anglo-American ideal it was at the beginning of our independent existence. The 'national type' as ideal
has always been, and remains, pretty well fixed. It is the *Mayflower*,
John Smith, Davy Crockett, George Washington, and Abraham
Lincoln that define the American's self-image, and this is true
whether the American in question is a descendant of the Pilgrims
or the grandson of an immigrant from southeastern Europe. . . .
Our cultural assimilation has taken place not in a 'melting pot,' but
rather in a [citing Stewart] 'transmuting pot' in which all ingredients have been transformed and assimilated to an idealized 'Anglo-
Saxon' model."[21]

[20] George R. Stewart, *American Ways of Life*, New York, Doubleday and Co.,
1954, p. 23. Stewart's views emphasize the similarities between the culture of the
early English settlers and those of other groups from Northern and Western
Europe.
[21] Will Herberg, op. cit., pp. 33-4.

Both structurally and culturally, then, the "single melting pot" vision of America has been something of an illusion—a generous and idealistic one, in one sense, since it held out the promise of a kind of psychological equality under the banner of an impartial symbol of America larger than the symbols of any of the constituent groups—but one which exhibited a considerable degree of sociological naïveté. Given the prior arrival time of the English colonists, the numerical dominance of the English stock, and the cultural dominance of Anglo-Saxon institutions, the invitation extended to non-English immigrants to "melt" could only result, if thoroughly accepted, in the latter's loss of group identity, the transformation of their cultural survivals into Anglo-Saxon patterns, and the development of their descendants in the image of the Anglo-Saxon American.

Culturally, this process of absorbing Anglo-Saxon patterns has moved massively and inexorably, with greater or lesser speed, among all ethnic groups. Structurally, however, the outcome has, so far, been somewhat different, depending on whether we are considering white Protestant descendants of the "Old" immigration, white Catholics and Jews of both periods of immigration, or the racial and quasi-racial minorities. Here, then, is where the "triple melting pot" hypothesis of Kennedy and others becomes applicable. While Protestant descendants of Germans and Scandinavians can, if they wish, merge structurally into the general white Protestant subsociety with relative ease, Jews, Irish Catholics, Italian Catholics, and Polish Catholics cannot do so without either formal religious conversion or a kind of sociological "passing"—neither process being likely to attract overwhelmingly large numbers. Negroes, Orientals, Mexican-Americans, and some Puerto Ricans are prevented by racial discrimination from participating meaningfully in either the white Protestant or the white Catholic communities. Nationality background differences within the white population, however, appear to be more amenable to dissolving influences, for reasons which we shall consider later. The passing of the "nationality" communities may be slower than Kennedy and Herberg intimate[22] and the rate of Catholic-Protestant intermarriage has been shown to be substantially higher in the country as a whole than in New Haven.[23] However, a vastly important and largely neglected sociological point about mixed marriages, racial, religious, or national, apart from the rate, is *in what social structures the intermarried couples and their children incorporate themselves.* If Catholic-Protestant intermarried couples live more or less completely within either the Catholic social community or the Protestant social community, the sociological fact of the existence of the particular religious community and its separation from other religious communities remains.

The result of these processes, structurally speaking, is that American society has come to be composed of a number of "pots," or subsocieties, three of which are the religious containers marked Protestant, Catholic, and Jew, which are in the process of melting down the white nationality background communities contained within them; others are racial groups which are not allowed to melt structurally; and still others are substantial remnants of the nationality background communities manned by those members who are either of the first generation, or who, while native born, choose to remain within the ethnic enclosure. All of these consti-

[22] See our discussion in Chapter 7.

[23] August B. Hollingshead's data on intermarriage in New Haven in 1948 support the Kennedy thesis. However, John L. Thomas's broader study of Catholic-Protestant intermarriage found that between 1940 and 1950, "mixed marriages sanctioned by Catholic nuptials approximated 30% of all Catholic marriages in the United States." To these must be added an unknown rate of mixed marriages involving one Catholic partner which are not sanctioned by Catholic nuptials. See August B. Hollingshead, "Cultural Factors in the Selection of Marriage Mates," *American Sociological Review*, Vol. 15, No. 5 (October 1950), pp. 619-27, and John L. Thomas, "The Factor of Religion in the Selection of Marriage Mates," *American Sociological Review*, Vol. 16, No. 4 (August 1951), pp. 487-91. The Thomas quotation above will be found on p. 488.

tute the ethnic subsocieties which we have described earlier, with their network of primary groups, organizations, and institutions within which a member's life may be comfortably enclosed except for secondary contacts with "outsiders" in the process of making a living and carrying out the minimal duties of political citizenship, if he so desires. Another pot besides the religious containers which is actually doing some structural melting is labeled "intellectuals." All these containers, as they bubble along in the fires of American life and experience are tending to produce, with somewhat differing speeds, products which are culturally very similar, while at the same time they remain structurally separate. The entire picture is one which, with the cultural qualifications already noted, may be called a "multiple melting pot." And so we arrive at the "pluralism" which characterizes the contemporary American scene.

6

Theories of Assimilation: Part III
Cultural Pluralism

Both the Anglo-conformity and the melting pot theories had envisaged the disappearance of the immigrants' group as a communal identity and the absorption of the later arrivals to America and their children, as individuals, into the existing "American" social structure. This goal, however, was not universally shared by the immigrants themselves. Coinciding with the nature of the American land base in the first century of the nation's life—large and thinly populated—early attempts by immigrants to establish communal societies were projected in the context of the group's occupying exclusively a particular territorial portion of its own. Probably the German migration to the American Midwest and to Texas in the 1830's, 40's, and 50's, led by liberal intellectuals fleeing an inhospitable political climate, was possessed of the greatest degree of national self-consciousness, and some of these leaders surely looked forward to the creation of an all-German state within the union, or even more hopefully, to the eventual formation of a separate German nation as soon as the expected dissolution of the union under the impact of the slavery controversy should take place.[1]

As early as 1818, the aid of the national government had been solicited in an attempt to associate ethnic communality with a given land base, and this aid had been refused. In that year certain Irish organizations of New York and Philadelphia petitioned the Congress for a piece of land in the West on which to settle Irish charity cases. Congress turned down the petition on the grounds that the formal assignment of a national group to a particular territory was unwise and could lead to a series of similar requests by other nationalities which would fragment the nation.[2] Marcus Hansen, the noted student of immigration to America, perceptively remarked that "probably no decision in the history of American immigration policy possesses more profound significance. By its terms the immigrant was to enjoy no special privileges to encourage his coming; also he was to suffer no special restrictions. His opportunities were those of the native, nothing more, nothing less."[3] Thus the principle was established that the formal agencies of American government could not be used to establish territorial ethnic enclaves throughout the nation. Whatever ethnic communality was to be achieved (the special situation of the American Indians excepted) must be achieved by voluntary action within a legal framework which was formally cognizant only of individuals.

While *de jure* communality could not be established, *de facto* ethnic societies developed in the first generation as the result of numerous natural factors: the settlement, in groups, of Germans

[1] Nathan Glazer, "Ethnic Groups in America: From National Culture to Ideology," in Morroe Berger, Theodore Abel, and Charles H. Page (eds.), *Freedom and Control in Modern Society*, New York, D. Van Nostrand Co., 1954, p. 161; Marcus Lee Hansen, *The Immigrant in American History*, Cambridge, Harvard University Press, 1940, pp. 129-40; John A. Hawgood, *The Tragedy of German-America*, New York, G. P. Putnam's Sons, 1940, *passim*.
[2] Hansen, *The Immigrant in American History*, p. 132.
[3] Ibid.

and, later, Norwegians and Swedes, on the sparsely settled farm-
lands of the interior plains of America, the later accretion of
friends, relatives, and countrymen seeking out oases of familiarity
in a strange land, the desire of the settlers to recreate, necessarily
in miniature, a society in which they could communicate in the
familiar tongue and maintain familiar institutions, and, finally, the
necessity to band together for mutual aid and mutual protection
against the uncertainties of a strange and sometimes hostile environment.

And so came into being the ethnic church, conducting services
in the native language, the ethnic school for appropriate indoctrination of the young, the newspaper published in the native tongue,
the mutual aid societies, the recreational groups, and, beneath the
formal structure, the informal network of ethnically enclosed
cliques and friendship patterns which guaranteed both comfortable
socializing and the confinement of marriage within the ancestral
group. "To a great extent," writes a careful student of one of the
ethnic movements to America, "the Germans used their language
as a weapon to ward off Americanization and assimilation, and
used every social milieu, the home, the church, the school, the
press, in the fight to preserve the German language, even among
their children and grandchildren."[4] And the Swedes and Norwegians, well isolated in their prairie farms and villages, were even
more successful in creating strong ethnic communality.[5] Even in
the cities, where physical separation from other groups was patently
more difficult, the sociological results were not greatly different. In
1850, the city of Milwaukee was composed of 6000 Germans and
4000 native-born Americans. Only six of the Germans were married to non-Germans.[6] And in the urban centers of the Northeast,

[4] Hawgood, op. cit., p. 39.
[5] Glazer, "Ethnic Groups in America: From National Culture to Ideology,"
pp. 163-4, in Berger, Abel, and Page (eds.), *Freedom and Control in Modern
Society, cit. supra.*
[6] Hawgood, op. cit., p. 38.

the Irish, segregated in the slums and cut off occupationally and culturally from their Anglo-Saxon neighbors, developed a distinct group consciousness and a separate institutional life: "Unable to participate in the normal associational affairs of the community," writes Oscar Handlin, "the Irish felt obliged to erect a society within a society, to act together in their own way. In every contact therefore the group, acting apart from other sections of the community, became intensely aware of its peculiar and exclusive identity."[7]

Thus cultural pluralism was a fact in American society before it became a theory—at least a theory with explicit relevance for the nation as a whole and articulated and discussed in the general English-speaking circles of American intellectual life.[8]

Eventually, the cultural enclaves of the Germans and the Scandinavians declined in scope and significance as succeeding generations of their native-born attended public schools, left the farms and villages to strike out as individuals for the Americanizing city, and generally became subject to the influences of a standardizing industrial civilization. The German-American community, too, was struck a sharp and powerful blow by the accumulated force of the passions generated by World War I—a blow from which it never fully recovered. And the Irish became the dominant and pervasive

[7] Oscar Handlin, Boston's Immigrants, Cambridge, Mass., Harvard University Press, 1959 (Rev. ed.), p. 176.

[8] Obviously, the specific attempts to create ethnic enclaves throughout the nineteenth century were predicated upon an implicit ideology of cultural pluralism. Occasionally, an attempt would be made by one or another ethnic apologist to construct an ideological model of what was happening with respect to his particular group. Thus Carl Rümelin, a prominent founder and first president of the Pionier Verein von Cincinnati, declared in 1869 in an address to the group: "We did not wish to establish here a mere New Germany, nor, on the other hand did we wish simply to disappear into America. . . . It is necessary for us to declare, with a bold consciousness of the fact, that we have succeeded in remaining honourably German without at the same time being untrue to our new Fatherland." (Quoted in Hawgood, op. cit., p. 274.)

element in the gradual emergence of a pan-Catholic subsociety in America. But the lineaments of these developments revealed themselves only in the twentieth century. In the meantime, in the last two decades of the 1800's, the influx of immigrants from Southern and Eastern Europe had begun. Now it was the Italians, the Jews, and the Slavs who made up the migrant hordes—all the more sociologically visible because the closing of the frontier, the occupational demands of an expanding industrial economy, and their own poverty combined to make it inevitable that they would remain in the crowded urban centers and urban portions of the nation. It was in the swirling fires of controversy and the steadier flame of experience created by these new events that the ideology of cultural pluralism as a philosophy for the nation was forged.

The arrival on American shores of these darker swarms of migrants—the so-called "new immigration"—was countered by the development of a new note in American nativism: the racist claim of ineluctable biological superiority for those with lighter skins, fairer hair, and earlier debarkation dates. Together with the older nativist themes of anti-Catholicism, fear of "foreign radicalism," attribution of responsibility for the city slum to the newcomer, and general xenophobia, this newer development in collective hatred, along with an awakening anti-Semitism, combined to produce the onslaught on the immigrant's culture, social organization, and self-regard known as the Americanization movement—a development which, as we have seen before, was brought to its highest pitch by the events of World War I and the immediate post-war period. It was as a reaction to the incessant demands of this movement on the immigrant—that he divest himself at once of the culture of his homeland, that he cease to speak its language, that he regard with the same suspicion and hostility as his attackers his familiar and psychologically satisfying ethnic institutions and organizations—to repeat, it was as a reaction to these essentially unreasonable and unfulfillable commands that a different doctrine began to evolve.

This doctrine was to oppose the assumptions and demands of the "Americanization" or Anglo-conformity viewpoint and in the process was to reject, also, the more kindly intended blueprint of the melting pot enthusiasts.

The first manifestations of an ideological counterattack against draconic Americanization came not from the beleaguered newcomers, who were, after all, more concerned with survival than with theories of adjustment, but from those idealistic members of the middle class who, in the decade or so before the turn of the century, had followed the example of their English predecessors and "settled" in the slums to "learn to sup sorrow with the poor."[9] Immediately, these workers in the "settlement houses" were forced to come to grips with the realities of immigrant life and adjustment. Not all of them reacted in the same way, but on the whole the settlements developed an approach to the immigrant which was sympathetic to his native cultural heritage and to his newly created ethnic institutions.[10] For one thing, their workers, necessarily in intimate contact with the lives of these often pathetic and bewildered newcomers and their daily problems, could see how unfortunate were the effects of those forces which demanded or impelled rapid Americanization in their impact on the immigrant's children, who not infrequently became alienated from their parents

[9] The phrase comes from a letter written in 1883 by Samuel A. Barnett, the moving spirit in the founding of Toynbee Hall, in London, the first social settlement, in answer to a request for advice sent him by a group of Oxford students who wished to be of service to those in need. Barnett answered, in part: "The men might hire a house, where they could come for short or long periods and, living in an industrial quarter, learn to sup sorrow with the poor." (Quoted in Arthur C. Holden, *The Settlement Idea*, New York, The Macmillan Co., 1922, p. 12.) It was through the efforts of this group that Toynbee Hall was established.

[10] Jane Addams, *Twenty Years at Hull-House*, New York, The Macmillan Co., 1914, pp. 231-58; Arthur C. Holden, op. cit., pp. 109-31, 182-9; John Higham, *Strangers in the Land*, New Brunswick, N.J., Rutgers University Press, 1955, p. 236.

and the restraining influence of family authority. Were not their
parents ignorant and uneducated "Hunkies," "Sheenies," or "Da-
goes," as that limited portion of the American environment in
which they moved defined the matter? Ethnic "self-hatred" with
its debilitating psychological consequences, family disorganization,
and juvenile delinquency were not unusual results. Furthermore,
the immigrants themselves were adversely affected by the incessant
attacks on their culture, their language, their institutions, their very
conception of themselves. How were they to maintain their self-
respect when all that they knew, felt, and dreamed, beyond their
sheer capacity for manual labor—in other words, all that they *were*
—was despised or scoffed at in America? And their own children
had begun to adopt the contemptuous attitude of the "Americans."
Jane Addams relates, in a moving chapter of her *Twenty Years at
Hull-House*, how, after coming to have some conception of the extent and depth of their problems, she created at the settlement a
"Labor Museum" in which the immigrant women of the various
nationalities crowded together in the slums of Chicago could illustrate their familiar native methods of spinning and weaving, and
the relation of these earlier techniques to contemporary factory
methods could be graphically shown. For the first time these peasant women were made to feel by some part of their American environment that they were possessed of valuable and interesting
skills—that they too had something to offer—and for the first time
the daughters of these women who, after a long day's work at their
dank "needletrade" sweatshops, came to Hull-House to observe,
could begin to appreciate the fact that their mothers, too, had a
"culture," that this culture possessed its own merit, and that it was
related to their own contemporary lives. Jane Addams concluded
her chapter with the hope that "our American citizenship might
be built without disturbing these foundations which were laid of
old time."[11]

[11] Jane Addams, op. cit., p. 258. See also, her *Newer Ideals of Peace*, New
York, The Macmillan Co., 1911.

This appreciative view of the immigrant's cultural heritage and of its distinctive usefulness both to himself and his adopted country received additional sustenance from another source: those intellectual currents of the time which, however overborne by their currently more powerful opposites, emphasized liberalism, internationalism, and tolerance. From time to time, an occasional educator or publicist protested against the sharp demands of the Americanizers, arguing that the immigrant, too, had an ancient and honorable culture, and that this culture had much of value to offer an America whose character and destiny were still in the process of formation and which must serve as an inspirational example of harmonious cooperation of various heritages to a world inflamed by nationalism and war. Thus the philosopher, John Dewey, in an address before the National Education Association in 1916, declared that "Such terms as Irish-American or Hebrew-American or German-American are false terms because they seem to assume something which is already in existence called America, to which the other factor may be externally hitcht [sic] on. The fact is, the genuine American, the typical American, is himself a hyphenated character. This does not mean that he is part American and that some foreign ingredient is then added. It means that, as I have said, he is international and interracial in his make-up. He is not American plus Pole or German. But the American is himself Pole-German-English-French-Spanish-Italian-Greek-Irish-Scandinavian-Bohemian-Jew-and so on. The point is to see to it that the hyphen connects instead of separates. And this means at least that our public schools shall teach each factor to respect every other, and shall take pains to enlighten all as to the great past contributions of every strain in our composite make-up. I wish our teaching of American history in the schools would take more account of the great waves of migration by which our land for over three centuries has been continuously built up, and made every pupil conscious of the rich breadth of our national make-up. When every pupil recognizes all the factors which have gone into our being, he will continue to prize and reverence that coming from his own past, but he will think of it as honored in being simply one factor in forming a whole, nobler and finer than itself."[12]

Was there anything more than the melting pot idea in this view of America by one of its foremost philosophers? It would be hard to say, although Dewey's appreciation of the cultural values in America's various heritages is clear enough. However, two observers of the contemporary scene writing in that same year sounded the note of separate group identity and its preservation more sharply. Norman Hapgood, prominent author and editor of the day, in an article addressed to a Jewish audience, advised his readers not to merge with the general population but to remain distinct, preserving their culture for the general benefit of American society. "Democracy will be more productive," he declared, "if it has a tendency to encourage differences. Our dream of the United States ought not to be a dream of monotony. We ought not to think of it as a place where all people are alike. If in a little town in Italy more geniuses could once be produced than are produced in all the world today, our hope should be to have in a country that occupies almost the whole continent twenty different kinds of civilization, all harmonious."[13] And in the pages of the *Atlantic Monthly*, Randolph Bourne, young literary critic and essayist, wrote of his vision of a "trans-national" America—a new type of nation in which the various national groups would preserve their identity and their cultures, uniting as a kind of "world federation in miniature." Attempts to melt the immigrant had failed, Bourne argued, as the outbreak of European war and its repercussions here in the nationalistic activi-

[12] John Dewey, "Nationalizing Education," National Education Association of the United States, *Addresses and Proceedings of the Fifty-fourth Annual Meeting*, 1916, pp. 185-6. Jane Addams writes of conversations with Dewey about the problem of immigrant adjustment at the time that she was considering establishment of her "Labor Museum." See *Twenty Years at Hull-House*, p. 237.
[13] Norman Hapgood, "The Jews and American Democracy," *The Menorah Journal*, Vol. II, No. 4 (October 1916), p. 202.

ties of various groups had revealed. What was needed was the realization that the immigrants' colonies, their cultures and their European attachments constituted a magnificent opportunity, not an occasion for despair. Here at last might be founded the type of nation which the conditions of modern life demanded—one in which many nationalities would live in concert, each maintaining the flavor of its original heritage and its interest in its original homeland, at the same time combining to form a richer, more cosmopolitan culture in America and providing a lesson in international amity for other countries. In this vision of the nation, the immigrants now become "threads of living and potent cultures, blindly striving to weave themselves into a novel international nation, the first the world has seen."[14]

The classic statement of the cultural pluralist position, however, had been made over a year before either Hapgood's or Bourne's essay was published. Early in 1915 there appeared in the pages of *The Nation* a series of two articles under the title "Democracy Versus the Melting-Pot." Their author was Horace Kallen, a Harvard educated philosopher with a decided concern for the application of philosophy to societal affairs, and as an American Jew, himself derivative of an ethnic background which was subject to the contemporary pressures for dissolution implicit in the "Americanization" or Anglo-conformity, and the melting pot theories. In these articles Kallen vigorously rejected the usefulness of these theories either as correct models of what was actually transpiring in American life or as worthy ideals for the future. Rather he was

[14] Randolph S. Bourne, "Trans-National America," *The Atlantic Monthly*, Vol. 118, July 1916, p. 95. Bourne's death at the age of 32, little more than two years after this essay was published, was a tragic loss to American life and letters. For a luminous appreciation of his life and work, see Van Wyck Brooks's Introduction to the collection, *The History of a Literary Radical and Other Papers by Randolph Bourne*, New York, S. A. Russell, 1956. For a more extended account see Louis Filler, *Randolph Bourne*, American Council on Public Affairs, Washington, D.C., 1943.

impressed by the way in which the various ethnic groups in America were coincident with particular areas and regions, and with the tendency for each group to preserve its own language, religion, communal institutions, and ancestral culture. All the while, he pointed out, the immigrant has learned to speak English as the language of general communication, and has participated in the over-all economic and political life of the nation. These developments, in which "the United States are in the process of becoming a federal state not merely as a union of geographical and administrative unities, but also as a cooperation of cultural diversities, as a federation or commonwealth of national cultures,"[15] the author argued, far from constituting a violation of historic American political principles, as the "Americanizers" claimed, actually represented the inevitable consequences of democratic ideals since individuals are implicated in groups, and democracy for the individual must, by extension, also mean democracy for his group.

The processes just described, however, as Kallen develops his argument, are far from having been thoroughly realized. They are menaced by "Americanization" programs, assumptions of Anglo-Saxon superiority, and misguided attempts to promote "racial" amalgamation. Thus America stands at a kind of cultural crossroads. It can attempt to impose by force an artificial Anglo-Saxon-oriented uniformity on its peoples, or it can consciously allow and encourage its ethnic groups to develop democratically, each emphasizing its particular deep-rooted cultural heritage. If the latter course is followed, then, as Kallen puts it in the closing paragraphs of his essay, "the outlines of a possible great and truly democratic commonwealth become discernible. Its form would be that of the federal republic; its substance a democracy of nationalities, coop-

---

[15] Horace M. Kallen, "Democracy *Versus* the Melting Pot," *The Nation*, February 18 and 25, 1915, reprinted in Horace M. Kallen, *Culture and Democracy in the United States*, New York, Boni and Liveright, 1924. The quotation is on page 116 of the book.

erating voluntarily and autonomously through common institutions
in the enterprise of self-realization through the perfection of men
according to their kind. The common language of the commonwealth, the language of its great tradition, would be English, but
each nationality would have for its emotional and involuntary life
its own peculiar dialect or speech, its own individual and inevitable
esthetic and intellectual forms. The political and economic life of
the commonwealth is a single unit and serves as the foundation and
background for the realization of the distinctive individuality of
each *natio* [sic] that composes it and of the pooling of these in a
harmony above them all. Thus 'American civilization' may come to
mean the perfection of the cooperative harmonies of 'European
civilization'—the waste, the squalor and the distress of Europe
being eliminated—a multiplicity in a unity, an orchestration of
mankind."[16]

Within the next decade, Kallen published in various periodicals
several more essays dealing with the theme of American multiple

[16] Kallen, *Culture and Democracy in the United States*, p. 124. Randolph
Bourne had read this two-part essay of Kallen's in *The Nation* and been
greatly influenced by it before writing his own article on "trans-national America." This is clearly specified in another article of Bourne's; "The Jew and
Trans-National America," *The Menorah Journal*, Vol. II, No. 5 (December
1916), p. 280. Whether Hapgood had seen Kallen's articles before coming to
his own point of view, described above, I do not know. It seems unlikely that,
as a practicing journalist of the day, he would not have read them.
As to those forces which consciously influenced Kallen himself, Kallen writes:
". . . the commingling of [William] James's lectures and [Barrett] Wendell's
history [at Harvard] crystallized in my mind into a new outlook, the results of
which were: first, discovery of the meaning of 'equal' as used in the Declaration;
second, recognition of the social role of freedom and of individual and group differences, later to be expounded at length in my own philosophy; and finally, such
a reappraisal of my Jewish affiliations as required an acquiescence in my Jewish
inheritance and heritage, an expanding exploration into the content and history
of both, and a progressively greater participation in Jewish communal enterprises.
Among the latter, the Zionist movement was then the most intellectually relevant and practically comprehensive." ("The Promise of the Menorah Idea,"
The Menorah Journal, Vol. XLIX, Nos. 1 & 2, Autumn-Winter, 1962, p. 11).

144 ASSIMILATION IN AMERICAN LIFE

group life, which were collected in a volume of his papers entitled *Culture and Democracy in the United States*, published in 1924.[17] It was in the introductory note to this volume that he used in print for the first time the term "cultural pluralism" to refer to his position. All of these essays reflect both his increasingly sharp rejection of the onslaughts on the immigrant and his culture which the coming of World War I and its attendant fears, the "Red Scare," the projection of themes of racial superiority, continued economic exploitation of the newçomers, and the rise of the Ku Klux Klan served to increase in intensity, and his emphasis on cultural pluralism as the democratic antidote to these ills of the national social organism. In the succeeding years, occasional essays have appeared from his prolific pen, elaborating or annotating the theme of cultural pluralism.[18] Thus, for at least forty-five years, most of them spent as a teacher at the New School for Social Research, Kallen has been acknowledged as the originator and leading philosophical exponent of the cultural pluralism idea. In his accumulated explorations of the concept beyond the first *Nation* articles, at least three themes have received special emphasis.

One relates to the nature of the ethnic group itself in its relation to the individual. All other groups, according to Kallen—the social club, the fraternal order, the educational institution, the political party, even the state itself—are groups with which the individual affiliates voluntarily; they are based on contractual relationships.

[17] Kallen, op. cit.
[18] See, particularly, "National Solidarity and the Jewish Minority," *The Annals of The American Academy of Political and Social Science*, Vol. 223, September 1942, pp. 17-28; "*Americanism and Its Makers*, Bureau of Jewish Education, 1944; *Cultural Pluralism and the American Idea*, Philadelphia, University of Pennsylvania Press, 1956 (with comments by Stanley H. Chapman, Stewart G. Cole, Elisabeth F. Flower, Frank P. Graham, R. H. Henle, S.J., Herold C. Hunt, Milton R. Konvitz, Leo Pfeffer, and Goodwin Watson); "American Jews, What Now?" *Jewish Social Service Quarterly*, Vol. XXXII, No. 1 (Fall, 1955), pp. 12-29; "On 'Americanizing' the American Indian," *Social Research*, Winter, 1958, pp. 469-73.

The ethnic group, however, rests on ancestry and family connections and is involuntary: "For each man or woman is the intersection of a line of ancestry and a line of social and cultural patterns and institutions, and it is what we are by heredity and early family influence that comes nearest to being inalienable and unalterable."[19] Or, as he had put it even more succinctly in his early essay: "Men may change their clothes, their politics, their wives, their religions, their philosophies, to a greater or lesser extent: they cannot change their grandfathers."[20] Not only is the individual related to his ethnic group involuntarily and indissolubly, but in a positive sense the individual realizes himself and his potentialities through membership in this group. It is "the efficacious natural *milieu* or habitat of his temperament . . . , the center at which he stands, the point of his most intimate social reactions, therefore of his intensest emotional life."[21] Thus, while Kallen favors and encourages participation for the individual in a wide variety of types of associational groups, he attaches to ethnic group membership and participation special significance for personality satisfaction and development.

A second theme which highlights Kallen's development of the cultural pluralism position is that his position is entirely in harmony with the traditional ideals of American political and social life, and that, indeed, any attempt to impose Anglo-Saxon conformity constitutes a violation of those ideals. The Declaration of Independence and the Preamble and Amendments to the Constitution are declared to be the central documents of "the American Idea," and their support for the doctrine of equality is interpreted to mean support for the concept of "difference" as well. " 'Equal,' in the intent of the Declaration," Kallen states, "is an affirmation of the right to be different: of the parity of every human being and every

19 Kallen, *Culture and Democracy in the United States*, p. 60.
20 Ibid., p. 122.
21 Ibid., p. 200.

association of human beings according to their kinds, in the rights of life, liberty, and the pursuit of happiness."[22] Differences of various sorts among human beings are inevitable, and in all other countries these differences had served as the occasion for hereditary privilege and power. However, "to all this the Declaration said, No. Female and male, Indian, Negro and white, Irishman, Scotchman and Englishman, German and Spaniard and Frenchman, Italian and Swede and Pole, Hindu and Chinaman, butcher, baker and candlestick maker, workingman and gentleman, rich man and poor man, Jew and Quaker and Unitarian and Congregationalist and Presbyterian and Catholic—they are all different from each other, and different as they are, all equal to each other."[23] As one item of evidence that the Founding Fathers were conscious of the ethnic diversity of the nation and wished to legitimize it, Kallen points out that the initial recommendation for the form of the Great Seal of the United States, suggested by a committee composed of Thomas Jefferson, John Adams, and Benjamin Franklin, contained a symbolism which reflected not only the political diversity being united in the new nation, but the ethnic diversity as well. It was proposed that the seal be engraved on one side with a shield divided into six parts reflecting the then six major cultural sources of the American people: England, Scotland, Ireland, France, Germany, and Holland. While this portion of the proposal was subsequently not adopted, Kallen regards its salience as indicative of his point.[24]

The third major theme in Kallen's exposition runs like a leitmotif through his entire body of work on the subject of pluralism. It asserts the positive value to the nation as a whole which derives from the existence of various ethnic cultures and their interaction within the framework of a democratic society. This value accrues in two ways: directly, as the ethnic groups contribute elements

[22] Kallen, *Americanism and Its Makers*, p. 8.
[23] Ibid., p. 8.
[24] Kallen, *Cultural Pluralism and the American Idea*, pp. 68-9.

from their cultural heritage to the total national culture, making it richer and more varied; and indirectly, as the end-product of the competition, interaction, and creative relationship of the later arrived ethnic cultures with the Anglo-Saxon culture and with each other. Surveying the history and state of American arts and letters in the mid 1920's and noting the substantial contributions made by men and women of various ethnic heritages, Kallen attributes this contribution to the principle that "creation comes from the impact of diversities." "Cultural values," he goes on to state, "arise upon the confrontation, impact, and consequent disintegration and readjustment of different orders, with the emergence therefrom of new harmonies carrying unprecedented things in their heart."[25] Particularly in his later writings, this emphasis on the creativity of the process of diversified group interaction comes to include reference to other types of groups, besides those of an ethnic nature. Writing on the meaning of Americanism in 1944, Kallen implicates these groups in his favorite image: "The American way," he declares, "is the way of orchestration. As in an orchestra, the different instruments, each with its own characteristic timbre and theme, contribute distinct and recognizable parts to the composition, so in the life and culture of a nation, the different regional, ethnic, occupational, religious and other communities compound their different activities to make up the national spirit. The national spirit is constituted by this union of the different. It is sustained, not by mutual exclusions, nor by the rule of one over others, but by their equality and by the free trade between these different equals in every good thing the community's life and culture produce. This is the relation that the Constitution establishes between the States of the Union; this is the relation that develops between the regions within the States and the communities within the regions. In all directions there obtains . . . a mutual give and take in equal liberty on equal terms. The result is a strength and a rich-

25 Kallen, *Culture and Democracy in the United States,* pp. 209-10.

ness in the arts and sciences which nations of a more homogeneous strain and an imposed culture . . . do not attain."[26]

If one inquires, however, as to the specific nature of the communication and interaction which is to exist between the various ethnic communities and between the individuals who compose them in the "ideal" cultural pluralistic society, the answer does not emerge clearly from Kallen's descriptions. On the one hand, he is opposed to "ghetto" existence and group isolation and favors creative interaction. On the other hand, he is against the dissolution of the communities. The nature of the types and varieties of interaction and communication which will obviate the former alternative and ensure the latter is a question of considerable complexity which demands careful social and psychological analysis. Is "middle ground" interaction possible, and, if so, what are its lineaments and implications, and under what conditions does it flourish? These questions serve to underscore the absence of a system of sociological analysis in Kallen's constructions which might place the subject of cultural pluralism in a framework where its sociological nature might be more clearly understood and where researchable hypotheses might be set up concerning its feasibility and viability.

This is not to say that the pre-eminent philosopher of cultural pluralism has ignored sociological considerations altogether in his writings on the subject. Even apart from the emphasis on processes of cultural interaction, quite a number of relevant sociological forces and consequences are adumbrated in his analysis. For instance, he correctly points to the role of industrial technology and mass communications techniques in producing tendencies toward cultural uniformity which militate against the ethnic cultural variability which he favors, although he is less sensitive to the consequences for social structure of these developments. His occasional references to the economic and political orders, as the institutional areas where ethnic communality does not apply, significantly foreshadow a

[26] Kallen, *Americanism and Its Makers*, pp. 13-14.

major analytical distinction of the present analysis. He is aware of some of the implications of socio-economic stratification for his problem. And his discussion of the sociological alternatives open to intermarried couples, wherein he points out that they must either identify with one or the other of the ethnic groups, or form still a third group, is an analytical point of the first importance.[27] But these occasional forays into some of the "hard" questions about cultural pluralism remain as rather isolated adumbrations. Their implications, for the most part, are not developed; they are not co-ordinated and extended into a system of analysis which subjects the cultural pluralism idea to rigorous scientific scrutiny; and they tend to be subordinated to the much larger weight of attention given to the arguments concerning the cultural fruitfulness of the position and its philosophical justification in terms of the American value system. Thus Kallen's body of work on the cultural pluralism idea, remarkable and germinal as it is, tends to be embodied in a general framework of rhetoric and philosophical analysis which has not pushed to the fore that kind of rigorous sociological inquiry which the crucial importance of the idea ultimately demands.

Five years after the appearance of Kallen's original series of articles in *The Nation*, two educators published, separately, full-length appraisals of the problem of immigrant assimilation in which the idea of cultural pluralism was upheld, although Kallen's specific formulation of the goal was sharply criticized.[28] Both Isaac Berkson and Julius Drachsler postulated the desirability of promoting the preservation of the communal institutions of the ethnic groups and their various cultures, but both argued for greater flexibility and alternatives of choice than the Kallen presentation allegedly allowed for, and both were less optimistic about the long-term possibilities

[27] Kallen, *Culture and Democracy in the United States*, pp. 186-90.
[28] Isaac B. Berkson, *Theories of Americanization: A Critical Study, with Special Reference to the Jewish Group*, New York, Teachers College, Columbia University, 1920; Julius Drachsler, *Democracy and Assimilation: The Blending of Immigrant Heritages in America*, New York, The Macmillan Co., 1920.

for the preservation of the ethnic groups and cultures under American conditions than was Kallen. In addition, Berkson and Drachsler differed between themselves on a number of interpretive issues and emphases.

Berkson's discussion is directed specifically toward formulating a rationale for the preservation of the Jewish group as a communal group in the United States, although he posits the applicability of his presentation to other ethnic groups as well. Kallen's "federation of nationalities" theory, as it was then called, is rejected on three grounds: 1) that it is based on assumptions about the existence of powerful hereditary racial qualities, to which Berkson gives little credence; 2) that it rests on the identification of ethnic enclaves with particular areas of the country, a condition which hardly obtains in the United States; and 3) that it violates democratic principles since it attempts to predetermine the individual's fate by his ethnic group membership, subordinates all his other relationships to groups and individuals to the ethnic criterion, and fails to allow for the free play of multitudinous forces which, alone, should determine what the individual's destiny will be.

The first two of these charges may be dealt with briefly, since the themes which they indict, although they may be discerned in the earlier writings of Kallen on cultural pluralism, later disappear. At one time Kallen evidently believed in the existence of hereditary racial characteristics which expressed themselves in the personalities of the members of an ethnic group and in the culture which the group produced.[29] There is no attribution of superiority or inferiority in these racial references—simply difference. In these earlier writings, also, his emphasis on the implications of the ethnic group for personality development could also be interpreted in a racial framework. Moreover, in conformity with the usage of the time, nationality groups and a religio-culture group, the Jews, are indiscrimi-

[29] See, particularly, Kallen, *Culture and Democracy in the United States*, pp. 172-90.

nately, at times, placed under the racial rubric. This racial theme does not appear in his writings on cultural pluralism after the mid 1920's, and one might well conclude that later scientific findings about the nature and meaning of "race" disabused him of his earlier views.[30]

The emphasis on ethnic groups occupying their own locality, which is particularly apparent in *The Nation* essays on cultural pluralism, and is exemplified by Kallen's reference to Great Britain and Switzerland as models for the preferred American development, also is not discernible in his later discussions. Here, of course, the facts of the matter have changed over the course of American history and have always existed as a matter of degree, and thus called forth varying interpretations. America's ethnic groups were, at one time, concentrated in particular areas of the country, but this area concentration has diminished with growing industrialization, urbanization, internal migration, and the appearance of successive generations. Area dispersion, however, does not necessarily mean the disintegration of ethnic communality. The amplification of this generalization and the question of the interrelationships between these two variables will concern us later.

Berkson's third criticism of Kallen's formulation of goals for America raises a most important issue which is as alive today as it was a generation and more ago, when Berkson wrote. While the doctrine of cultural pluralism claims to be truly democratic because it allows each ethnic group to maintain its communality and culture, how democratic is it if it is presented in such a categorical fashion that each *individual* must remain within the structural and cultural confines of his "birthright" ethnic group regardless of his

[30] In 1955, Kallen writes: "It is by now a commonplace of observation and study that what is Jewish in the Jewish being is not biological heredity but social heritage"; and "Hebraism is no more than Hellenism or any other *ism* a spirit that an individual is born with, but a culture which he grows up in, and learns and believes in. Becoming a Jew is a process of acculturation." From "American Jews, What Now?" op. cit., pp. 13, 14.

wishes in the matter? To put the issue more succinctly, while cultural pluralism may be democratic for groups, how democratic is it for individuals? In a society of advanced industrialization, mass communications, a high degree of urbanization, heterogeneous contacts, and virtually unlimited mobility, many interests and influences besides those of an ethnic nature will play upon the individual. Many of these will tend to pull him away from ethnic communality. While some persons will be able to effect a satisfactory integration of ethnic values and those of the larger society, others may not. Are these latter individuals to be compelled, or to feel compelled, to subordinate their broader interests to the overriding goal of immersion in their ethnic group? Berkson recognizes this point, and in discussing the role of intermarriage as a threat to ethnic communality—a threat which he readily perceives—he makes the following concession. "Our theory . . . ," he states, "does not propose absolute non-intermarriage either as possible or as desirable. Wherever the ethnic affiliation has lost its significance, either because the individual is too gross to appreciate it or because a universal cause, such as science, music or art has become a religious enthusiasm and displaced other loyalties, intermarriage may take place without social detriment. In the one case, no cultural value exists anyway; in the other case, we may console ourselves that new spiritual values have been substituted."[31]

It is interesting to note that Kallen, in a paper published in 1955 dealing with the preservation of Jewish communality in America, makes a similar concession, albeit somewhat grudgingly. Once made, however, the concession is countered, not only with the usual argument about the positive values of ethnic affiliation, which is repeated and which we have met before, but with a new note of psychological analysis which reflects some of the considerations which the more sophisticated social psychology of a later age has brought to attention. "Aren't all the children of Adam human be-

[31] Berkson, op. cit., p. 108.

ings before they are Jews or Christians or Moslems or what have you?" asks Kallen, stating the position which would appear to follow from the principles of modern liberalism; "And is freedom freedom if it doesn't enable one to stay a human being by ceasing to be a Jew or whatever else is an impediment in one's struggle for existence? Where remembrance is crippling pain and knowledge is sorrow, doesn't freedom mean exercising the right to ignorance and forgetting?" Then he replies to this series of questions whose implications he rightly recognizes as posing a threat to ethnic group survival: "Abstractly, correct answers to these questions would, I judge, be such as Jewish 'assimilationists' and other escapists desire for themselves. And of course, they could in no way modify the equal liberty of those who are odd like God and choose the Jews, to make their choice. But no confirmation of a Jew's right to disengage himself from his Jewish being can in fairness to him be unconditional. If he is directing his disengagement toward what he imagines as a life more abundant and safe, he must needs see to it that his choice is informed, enlightened and brave, not anxious, ignorant, afraid and blind. The consensus of scientific students of the human person—whatever their branch or school of thought—appraises personality as a continuing growth whose any present moment is its living past participating somehow in the formation of its unformed future. Not remembering any phase of this past is not the same as extirpating or annihilating it; rather is forgetting a sort of ghettoizing, a segregation and suppression of a dynamic component of the forgetter's individuality that keeps pushing toward the light of consciousness and seeking its own free support and growth. The energy of suppression is a diversifying psychosomatic tension. It figures in consciousness as anxiety, feelings of insecurity or guilt, as self-conscious, unstable, searching and seeking. From all this the individual quests for relief via all sorts of aggressive projections and compensatory actions that tend only to perpetuate the questing condition. Persons in such a state are not whole, not truly in good health. Their unhappy psychosomatic stance is a center of infection. With the best will, they make neither good parents nor good neighbors. Having mistaken the matrix and conditions of the happiness they pursue, their eagerness avails only to contract the wholeness of growth and maturation which it postulates into little else than anxious animal survival."[32]

Thus the question of the meaning of ethnic group affiliation and disaffiliation as it may be interpreted through the insights of depth psychology is raised for its pertinence to the problem of ethnic group integration on the American scene. We shall return to this crucial question later.

Berkson's positive program, which he calls the "Community" theory, emphasizes the desirability of a goal by which each ethnic group which desires to do so should be permitted to create its own communal life, preserving and developing its cultural heritage while at the same time participating effectively in the broader life of the nation as a whole. The central agency of this communal life is to be the complementary school, which members of the younger generation would attend after public school hours, and which would serve also as a kind of communal center for ethnic activities generally. The author regards maintenance and development of an ethnic culture under modern conditions as a task requiring a high degree of effort and dedication and he does not predict that great numbers will be attracted to it in a significant way. But he believes the goal to be a most worthy one and, as he puts it, "on the other hand, if the ethnic group finally disintegrates, the 'Community' theory really resolves itself into the 'Melting Pot' theory, accomplishing the fusion without the evils of hasty assimilation. Its essential merit is that it rejects the doctrine of predestination; it conceives the life of the individual to be formed not in accordance with some preconceived theory but as a result of the interaction of his own nature with the richest environment. In this it satisfies the basic notion of

[32] Kallen, "American Jews, What Now?" pp. 20-21.

democracy that the individual must be left free to develop through forces selected by the laws of his own nature, not moulded by factors determined upon by others either in the interests of themselves or in accordance with an assumed good."[33]

Drachsler's discussion of assimilation goals rests in part on his own empirical study of intermarriage rates for various ethnic groups in New York City during a five-year period shortly before the outbreak of World War I. He found that, particularly for the European nationality groups, intermarriage across ethnic lines increased sharply in the second generation. The only groups which maintained consistently low rates were Negroes and Jews. On the basis of these findings, he predicts that the American melting pot will soon be effective, causing most of the separate ethnic communities to disappear. While he does not believe that this process can be halted, he argues that it is taking place too rapidly, producing the danger of demoralization for the ethnic group members themselves and depriving the descendants of immigrants of any substantial knowledge and experience of their ancestral culture, valuable elements of which might otherwise be "contributed" to the American culture as a whole when intermarriage did take place. Thus he favors efforts by the ethnic community to maintain its communal and cultural life, providing a rich and flavorful environment for its successive generations; at the same time he believes that the government should play a role by instituting in the public schools a program emphasizing knowledge and appreciation of the various ethnic cultural heritages. The cumulative effect of these efforts would be to prevent the melting process from proceeding at a precipitous speed and to ensure that when it did become effective, the resulting cultural amalgam would be truly enriched by what the immigrants have brought to America. Some groups, such as the Negroes and the Jews, would continue to maintain their separate communal existence, and this is to be considered a course legitimately sanc-

[33] Berkson, op. cit., p. 118.

tioned by democratic values, since the choice of whether to fuse or to remain separate, either for the group or the individual, should be a free one. The idea of the legitimization of numerous ethnic communities and their cultures is referred to as "cultural democracy," a concept which Drachsler asserts should be added to the older ideas of political and economic democracy.[34]

The rise of the Nazi movement in Germany with its demonic racist ideology and the eruption of World War II with its harsh overtones of conflict over the role of race in human affairs stimulated additional interest in the United States in problems of prejudice and thus in questions concerning the adjustment of ethnic groups to each other and to American society as a whole.

In the late 1930's and continuing into the '40's, Louis Adamic, the Yugoslavian immigrant who had become a prolific American writer, took up the theme of America's multicultural heritage and the role of these many groups and cultures in forging the country's national character. Borrowing Walt Whitman's phrase, he described America as "a nation of nations," and while his ultimate goal was closer to the melting pot idea than to cultural pluralism, he saw the immediate task as that of making America conscious of what it owed to all its ethnic groups, not just the Anglo-Saxon. The children and grandchildren of immigrants of non-English origins, he was convinced, must be taught to be proud of the cultural heritage of their ancestral ethnic group, and of its role in building the American nation; otherwise they would fail to lose the sense of ethnic inferiority and feeling of rootlessness which he claimed to find in them.[35]

Out of the background of "intercultural education," William Vickery, Stewart Cole, and Mildred Wiese Cole attempted to devise a philosophy of group adjustment which would reconcile the

[34] Drachsler, op. cit., *passim*.
[35] See Louis Adamic, *My America*, New York and London, Harper and Brothers, 1938, pp. 187-259; *From Many Lands*, New York and London, Harper and Brothers, 1940; *A Nation of Nations*, New York and London, Harper and Brothers, 1944.

right of America's racial, religious, and national origins groups to maintain a creative relationship to their diverse ethnic heritages with the need of a democratic society for unity and cooperation in matters essential to the society's functioning and progress.[36] Deserving particular mention here is Vickery and S. Cole's reiteration of the insight contributed earlier by Berkson, that democratic practice demands that individuals should have the right *either* to "preserve their group's corporate identity," or if they so desired, to reject their ethnic heritage and "lose themselves in the population as a whole."[37] Helpful as these discussions were on the philosophical level and in the area of potenial value conflict, they did not focus clearly on the structural variables inherent in the problem.

Thus, over the years of the twentieth century, and particularly since World War II, aided by the cumulative impact of the writings already reviewed, "cultural pluralism" became a term and a concept which worked its way into the vocabulary and imagery of professional intergroup relations specialists and leaders of ethnic communal groups. Careful sociological analyses of the nature and implications of a cultural pluralist society, however, hardly began to make their appearance until the 1950's. The work of Eisenstadt in Israel, Borrie, the Australian, and others for Unesco, and Gordon in the United States has already been alluded to in Chapter 3.[38] As shown in Chapter 1, however, there is little evidence that the insights of incipient sociological analyses of cultural pluralism have up to now made their way into the thinking of professional intergroup relations workers or the American public—even that segment of the public which is highly literate and keeps abreast of significant current events.

If we now apply the "assimilation variables" of our analytical

36 William E. Vickery and Stewart G. Cole, *Intercultural Education in American Schools*, New York and London, Harper and Brothers, 1943; Stewart G. Cole and Mildred Wiese Cole, *Minorities and the American Promise*, New York, Harper and Brothers, 1954.
37 Vickery and Cole, op. cit., p. 35.
38 See pp. 67-8.

model to the concept of cultural pluralism, the following picture emerges. The key variable, again, turns out to be structural assimilation. For, if plural cultures are to be maintained, they must be carried on by subsocieties which provide the framework for communal existence—their own networks of cliques, institutions, organizations, and informal friendship patterns—functioning not only for the first generation of immigrants but for the succeeding generations of American-born descendants as well. And here a crucial theoretical point must be recognized. While it is not possible for cultural pluralism to exist without the existence of separate subsocieties, the reverse is not the case. It *is* possible for separate subsocieties to continue their existence even while the cultural differences between them become progressively reduced and even in greater part eliminated.

The presumed goal of the cultural pluralists is to maintain enough subsocietal separation to guarantee the continuance of the ethnic cultural tradition and the existence of the group, without at the same time interfering with the carrying out of standard responsibilities to the general American civic life. In effect, this demands keeping primary group relations across ethnic lines sufficiently minimal to prevent a significant amount of intermarriage, while cooperating with other groups and individuals in the secondary relations areas of political action, economic life, and civic responsibility. Within this context the sense of ethnic peoplehood will remain as one important layer of group identity while, hopefully, prejudice and discrimination will disappear or become so slight in scope as to be barely noticeable. Value conflict, where it exists, is to be fought out in the arena of the ballot box and public opinion, but the goal is to keep such conflict at a minimum by emphasizing the areas of flexibility, permitted alternatives, and free choice in American life and by refraining from imposing one's own collective will as standards of enforced behavior for other groups. This, in brief, is the ideal model of the cultural pluralist society as inferred from its proponents' writings and as analyzed with the aid of the system of variables we have presented.

In actual fact, the American experience approximates some elements of this model and falls short of others. The most salient fact, as we have indicated before, is the maintenance of the structurally separate subsocieties of the three major religious and the racial and quasi-racial groups, and even vestiges of the nationality groupings, along with a massive trend toward acculturation of all groups—particularly their native-born—to American culture patterns. In our view, then, a more accurate term for the American situation is *structural pluralism* rather than cultural pluralism, although some of the latter also remains. Structural merging does take place to substantial degree among the nationality groups within each of the three major religions, and in the occupational areas of the intellectual and artistic world. In the latter instance, each ethnic group tends to lose, in any functional sense, a large percentage of its intellectually oriented young people to the newly forming subsociety composed of intellectuals.

Structural pluralism, then, is the major key to the understanding of the ethnic makeup of American society, while cultural pluralism is the minor one. The important residual theoretical question then becomes that of how ethnic prejudice and discrimination can be eliminated or reduced and value conflict kept within workable limits in a society where the existence of separate subsocieties keeps primary group relations among persons of different ethnic backgrounds (except in the intellectual world) at a minimum. This is a question to which we shall return in the final chapter. In the chapter which immediately follows we shall examine more closely and with some documentation the structural and cultural picture of American society which we have heretofore presented in categorical fashion.

7

The Subsociety and the Subculture
in America

We have hitherto described American society as a mosaic of ethnic groups based on race, religion, and, to a declining extent, national origins, criss-crossed by social class stratification to form the characteristic subsocietal unit, the ethclass. Some persons are marginal to these social units, and intellectuals and artists tend to form a loosely structured subsocietal collectivity of their own. Acculturation to dominant American values and behavior, a complex stemming largely from Western European civilization, Anglo-Saxon culture, and industrialization, meanwhile either proceeds apace or in some cases has been completed for these various subsocietal groups. This sociological picture of the American scene has, up to now, been presented as a series of hypotheses. In this chapter we shall examine the empirical evidence which relates to this view, whether confirming, qualifying, or invalidating it. Major attention will be devoted to four groups: Negroes, Jews, Catholics, and white Protestants, although occasional references will be made to other ethnic groups as well. The studies to be referred to range in date from the early 1930's to the present, and vary widely in scope and persuasiveness. However, in their accumulation we believe that a consistent pattern will emerge. From time to time, in areas where empirical studies do not exist (or have not come to our attention), I shall resort to my own observations, as a "participant observer" in American society, but will label such observations accordingly. Thus we are now ready to examine contemporary American society more closely than we have been able to do in the preceding discussion.

Many of the studies to which we shall have reference were carried out in particular city or town—that is, in a particular community. This would, then, be an appropriate occasion to comment, briefly and generally, on the relationship between spatial localization or concentration and our concept of the subsociety. Each subsociety—for instance, that of upper-middle-class Jews, or upper-class white Protestants—exists only as an abstraction, a reference group in the minds of its members. The tangible units of each subsociety are localized in space in particular cities or towns. Each community is composed of its subcommunities based on the intersection of ethnic group and social class factors.[1] Thus one might speak of the upper-middle-class Jews of Akron, Ohio, or the upper-class white Protestants of Philadelphia. These subcommunities in the various cities and towns of the land are connected with each other, in part by class and ethnic-typed institutions and organizations which are national in scope, and in part by class and ethnic-typed friendships across community lines, which, in view of the characteristic residential mobility of Americans[2] are considerable in

[1] Some students of society use the term "subcommunity" to refer to the ethnic group, alone, within a given community. We have already explained in Chapter 2 why we consider this formulation less valid.

[2] See Donald J. Bogue, The Population of the United States, Glencoe, Ill., The Free Press, 1959, Chapter 15, "Internal Migration and Residential Mobility," pp. 375-418. Bogue points out that "During the course of a single year between 19 and 22 percent of the nation's inhabitants move from one house or apartment to another, and about 5 to 7 percent of them move from one county to another in the process of changing their residence. Not more than 2 or 3 percent of the adult population has spent its entire life in one house or apartment, and perhaps not more than 10 to 15 percent live their entire lives within the same county." p. 375.

number. But even more importantly, they are connected by the concept of "transferability"[3]—that is, the ability of each person in a given ethclass to move to another community and take his place within the same segment of the population marked off by ethnic group and social class. This ability and the person's explicit or implicit understanding of the situation creates within him, we suggest, a mental image of a series of subcommunities much like his own existing in various communities over the land. The sum of these subcommunities interlaced by the various national institutions and organizations which are characteristic of that particular ethnic group and social class constitute the subsociety. Since substantial endogamy is one of the crucial features of the subsociety, the acid test of this formulation is in the kind of considerations which figure in the minds of parents in evaluating a prospective suitor for their daughter's hand. An upper-middle-class white Protestant family is likely not to be greatly concerned with what city Sally's new boy friend comes from. It is immaterial whether he is from Cleveland, Omaha, or San Francisco. What *is* important is whether he is white (virtually taken for granted), whether he is Protestant, and whether his father is a business or professional man.

Furthermore, within a given city or metropolitan district, a specific community need not necessarily monopolize and be restricted to one particular area. As Etzioni has suggested, "A group can maintain its cultural and social integration and identity, without having an ecological basis."[4] The telephone and the automobile have made selective socializing possible without spatial monopolization. Today, neighbors frequently do not belong to the same cliques or even the same network of cliques. While we shall find

[3] For discussions of transferability in prestige status from one community to another see Kurt B. Mayer, *Class and Society, cit. supra*, p. 54, and Milton M. Gordon, *Social Class in American Sociology, cit. supra*, p. 203.

[4] Amitai Etzioni, "The Ghetto—A Re-Evaluation," *Social Forces*, Vol. 37, No. 3 (March 1959), p. 258 (italicized in original).

concentrations of particular ethnic groups and social classes, together with their institutions, in special localities to a degree considerably greater than chance,[5] it is important to realize that modern communication techniques make complete spatial pre-emption unnecessary in the preservation of the unseen social boundaries which separate ethnic groups and classes. The subcommunity, then, is not necessarily a place on the map of the city (though in some instances it may be so). It is rather a social construct in the minds of the city's residents. But it is no less real for that.

NEGROES

The separation of America's 20 million Negroes (approximately 11 per cent of the total American population)[6] from the white population in the United States in meaningful primary group contacts and the existence of a separate Negro social world with its own institutions and associations has been attested to in such community studies and over-all surveys as those of Myrdal (a massive compilation based on many separate studies),[7] Drake and Cayton,[8] Frazier,[9] Davis and the Gardners,[10] Dollard,[11] Davie,[12] C. John-

[5] For residential concentration see, for instance, Otis Dudley Duncan and Beverly Duncan, "Residential Distribution and Occupational Stratification," *American Journal of Sociology*, Vol. 60, No. 5 (March 1955), pp. 493-503, and Otis Dudley Duncan and Stanley Lieberson, "Ethnic Segregation and Assimilation," *American Journal of Sociology*, Vol. 64, No. 4 (January 1959), pp. 364-74.

[6] Bogue, op. cit., pp. 121-5.

[7] Gunnar Myrdal, with the assistance of Richard Sterner and Arnold Rose, *An American Dilemma*, New York, Harper and Brothers, 1944.

[8] St. Clair Drake and Horace R. Cayton, *Black Metropolis*, New York, Harcourt Brace, 1945.

[9] E. Franklin Frazier, *The Negro in the United States*, New York, The Macmillan Co., 1949; and *Black Bourgeoisie*, Glencoe, Ill.; Free Press, 1957.

[10] Allison Davis, Burleigh B. Gardner, and Mary R. Gardner, *Deep South*, Chicago, University of Chicago Press, 1941.

son,[13] and R. Johnson.[14] Served by Negro weekly, semi-weekly, or daily newspapers, the leading ones like the *Pittsburgh Courier*, the Chicago *Defender*, the Baltimore *Afro-American*, and the Norfolk *Journal and Guide* having a national or regional distribution, and by Negro magazines such as *Ebony* (sometimes referred to as the Negro *Life*), *Our World*, *Jet*, *Hue*, and *Tan*, this ethnic society resounds with news of "the race" and its doings, frivolous and otherwise, and its progress against the discrimination which emanates from the "other world" which is controlled and populated by whites.

In the South this segregation is stipulated by "Jim Crow" laws, whose legality, until 1954, was unthreatened, and by customs and folkways resting on a base of racial hostility and antipathy on the part of the great majority of white people toward Negroes. Since the early 1950's, court decisions, mass demonstrations, and the impact of the federal government through the operation of military installations, civil rights laws, and executive decisions have begun to have some effect on the enforced separation in secondary group areas of contact: formal attendance at school, riding in public conveyances, using public facilities, etc. There is no evidence, however, that the existence of separate white and Negro social worlds of primary group contacts and communal associations and institutions has been affected in any significant way by these developments.

In the North, the line that divides Negroes from whites has no legal sanction, and in areas of secondary contact varies widely from

---

[11] John Dollard, *Caste and Class in a Southern Town*, New York, Harper and Brothers, 1937.

[12] Maurice R. Davie, *Negroes in American Society*, New York, McGraw-Hill Publishing Co., 1949.

[13] Charles S. Johnson, *Patterns of Negro Segregation*, New York, Harper and Brothers, 1943.

[14] Robert Johnson, "Negro Reactions to Minority Group Status," in Milton L. Barron (ed.), *American Minorities*, New York, Alfred A. Knopf, 1957, pp. 192-212.

city to city and even within a given community. Fair employment practices laws have begun to lift the "job ceiling," and Negroes in the large cities are extending the boundaries of their traditionally segregated housing areas and occasionally setting up new pockets of settlement, although few have been able to buy homes in the upper-middle-class sections of suburbs. Public facilities, with the occasional exception of bathing beaches, are generally open to Negroes. But, again, in the private worlds of intimate social contact, non-vocational organizational life, and meaningful institutional activity, Negroes and whites generally remain apart. Even in the smaller communities, if there is any significant number of Negro residents, a Negro communal life takes shape. Robert Johnson, in his report of a study of Negro life in a middle-sized upstate New York city declares that "The 'Negro community' is an isolated one. . . . Questionnaire evidence shows not only that contacts with whites are quite limited in quantity and in depth, but also that Negroes viewed many issues more as part of a psychological community of 1200 members than as part of a Hometown community of 60,000."[15] For instance, such statements or phrases by Negro respondents as "It's all over town," "the prettiest girl in town," or "the meanest man in town," had reference not to the entire city but to the Negro community. And, Johnson adds significantly, "The term 'we' usually turned out, under probe, to refer to Hometown Negroes or to Negroes throughout the country, rather than to Hometown in general."[16]

One of the most telling indexes of communal separation is the rate of intermarriage. Marriage between Negroes and whites is still legally prohibited in 22 states of the union, most of them in the South and the West.[17] These laws will probably eventually be de-

---

[15] Robert Johnson, op. cit., p. 199.
[16] Ibid.
[17] Jack Greenberg, *Race Relations and American Law*, New York, Columbia University Press, 1959, pp. 344, 397-8.

clared unconstitutional. However, even where there is no legal ban
on such unions, their rate, at present, is very small. While no over-
all national rates are available, such studies of Negro-white marriages as have been made in particular communities where their
legality is unquestioned indicate that their rates vary from none to,
at the most, three or four out of every hundred marriages involving
Negroes.[18] The percentage of whites involved in such marriages
becomes, of course, insignificant.

The internal differentiation of the Negro group into social classes
has been described in community studies such as those of Drake
and Cayton in Chicago,[19] Davis and the Gardners,[20] Dollard,[21]
and Powdermaker[22] in small communities in the South, and in
over-all surveys by Myrdal,[23] Frazier,[24] and Davie.[25] As in the white
society, class boundaries are not hard and precise, the various classes
"shade into" one another, and substantial mobility takes place
from one class to another as the socio-economic condition and occupational and educational attainment of the individual or family
shift in the fluid dynamics of American social life. Nevertheless,

[18] Ruby Jo Reeves Kennedy, "Single or Triple Melting-Pot? Intermarriage
Trends in New Haven, 1870-1940," op. cit., p. 331, ft. 2; August B. Hollingshead, "Cultural Factors in the Selection of Marriage Mates," American Sociological Review, Vol. 15, No. 5 (October 1950), p. 621; Milton Barron, People
Who Intermarry, Syracuse, N.Y.; Syracuse University Press, 1946; Gunnar Myrdal, op. cit., pp. 606 and 1360-61; Maurice Davie, Negroes in American Society, p. 410; Louis Wirth and Herbert Goldhamer, "The Hybrid and the Problem of Miscegenation," in Otto Klineberg (ed.), Characteristics of the American
Negro, New York, Harper and Brothers, 1944, pp. 276-81; Gerhard Lenski,
The Religious Factor, New York, Doubleday, 1961, p. 36.
[19] Drake and Cayton, op. cit., pp. 495-715.
[20] Davis, Gardner, and Gardner, op. cit., pp. 208-51.
[21] Dollard, op. cit., passim.
[22] Hortense Powdermaker, After Freedom, New York, Viking Press, 1939,
passim.
[23] Myrdal, op. cit., pp. 689-705.
[24] Frazier, The Negro in the United States, pp. 273-305; Black Bourgeoisie,
passim.
[25] Davie, Negroes in American Society, pp. 415-33.

the broad outlines of the Negro class system are unmistakable. The following brief account leans heavily on the studies mentioned above.

Even before the abolition of slavery, internal differentiation along socio-economic lines had begun to take place among Negroes. The free Negroes of both the North and the South, many of them mulattoes, constituted a group apart and were themselves internally differentiated according to occupation and property ownership. Within the slave group distinctions were recognized which set off from each other the privileged house servants (many of whom could claim partial white ancestry and who were able to observe and imitate the "refined" cultural behavior of their white masters), the skilled artisans, and the lowly field hands. During the years following the Emancipation, the great masses of Negroes were unskilled farm hands, and above this group such criteria as free ancestry, lighter skin color, property ownership, descent from the partially acculturated house servants, and occupational considerations, all constituted the basis for status claims and social separation. Particularly in the larger southern or border cities such as Charleston, New Orleans, Washington, and Atlanta, where a more elaborate stratification system was developed, upper-class Negro society was a "blue-vein" society—that is, it was made up of mulattoes and was highly color-conscious.[26] Occupationally, however, prior to World War I, from the point of view of the white social world, the Negro community contained little differentiation on which to base social divisions. Tailors, barbers, waiters, and undertakers mingled with a few physicians, teachers, and business men in the Negro upper class of the day.

Large-scale Negro migration from the rural South to the cities of both the North and South which began during World War I in response to the need for additional unskilled labor in the fac-

[26] By "color" is meant here not only skin color itself, but the whole complex of Caucasian facial features and hair form.

tories and processing plants of the nation created a sizable Negro proletariat which could serve as a base for increasing numbers of Negro professionals such as doctors, lawyers, teachers, ministers, and social workers, and for Negro "service" businesses such as undertaking, cosmetics, insurance, banking, and small proprietary establishments. The Negro business class, however, has never been large. The practical necessities and ideological currents of the World War II period and its aftermath, together with the increasing political participation of the northern Negro, produced further gains for Negroes in semi-skilled factory jobs, skilled trades, lower white collar work, sales work, and the professions. The result of these twentieth century trends has been to proceed some distance toward "normalizing" the Negro class structure—that is, to differentiate the group occupationally to a much wider degree than had previously been the case, and to strengthen the power of education and occupation as criteria of social class position and increasingly diminish the role of skin color and considerations of descent. An additional occupation group in the Negro community, because of job discrimination probably proportionately larger than in the white community, consists of the "shadies," those who operate, at various levels of the enterprise, the "numbers," bootlegging, and other illegal or questionable businesses. The result of all these developments is the Negro class system as it exists today. All levels of it, of course, are not found in the smaller communities. The following description is applicable to a large northern metropolis.

The Negro upper class is a relatively small group composed primarily of families whose male heads are engaged in some professional occupation such as medicine, dentistry, law, teaching, social work, publishing, and government service, but also includes successful Negro business men, writers, entertainers of national renown, and, with varying degrees of access to the social life of the rest, the top level of the "shadies." Not infrequently the wives work, also in professional pursuits. This is not a leisure class, nor with some exceptions a wealthy class, and, obviously in occupational type (and also, as we shall see, in life style) it is very similar to the upper-middle class of the white social world.

If they have a church affiliation, members of this class tend to belong to Episcopal, Congregational, and Presbyterian congregations which, situated in totally or predominantly Negro neighborhoods, are likely to be totally or predominantly Negro in membership. Services are conducted with the traditional decorum associated with churches of these denominations. The Negro minister in charge will be college and seminary trained. The social life of this class is centered around alumni groups of Negro college fraternities and sororities (the young and even middle-aged members of this class are by now mostly college trained) and an elaborate system of men's clubs, women's clubs, and, in some cases, couples' clubs, together with informal social cliques, all of which tend to be confined in membership to members of their own class. Many of the members of this class are "race men"—that is, they are active as members and leaders in Negro advancement organizations such as the National Association for the Advancement of Colored People and the National Urban League, and, as in white society, social events such as large dances frequently become the occasion for fund-raising drives for these organizations or others of a "protest" or charitable nature serving the Negro community. In recent years, with increasing prosperity, the social events of this class, according to one observer, have become increasingly elaborate,[27] and in the larger cities the Negro upper class, in parallel fashion to the white upper class, have instituted their own Debutante Balls, such as the Philadelphia "Pink Cotillion," in which the daughters of the socially prominent and ambitious are formally "presented" to Negro society.

The dominant emphasis in the Negro middle class is "respectable" public behavior, stable family life, and planning for the fu-

[27] Frazier, *Black Bourgeoisie*, pp. 195-212.

ture, either of oneself or one's children. Occupationally, it includes a wide range of ways of making a living; there are lower white collar workers, proprietors of small business establishments, skilled and semi-skilled workers, policemen, firemen, watchmen, Pullman porters, and other occupational types. Church-goers among this group are likely to belong to all-Negro Baptist and Methodist churches which frequently are large and may contain lower class members as well. (In such a case, the pastor has a difficult time adjusting the type of service to the conflicting cultural demands of both groups.) The associational life of this class is highly elaborated, and social clubs and fraternal lodges which parallel the fraternal orders of the white lower middle class abound. Some "shadies" hover on the edges of this social world. The middle class is larger than the upper class, and it is safe to assume that it is growing in relative size. However, it is still considerably smaller than the large Negro mass at the bottom of the Negro social structure which still makes up the bulk of the Negro population.

The world of the northern and metropolitan Negro lower class reflects its southern rural background. Its speech is the dialect of the lower class rural South, though its present residence is the northern urban slum. Its family and sexual patterns reflect a way of life in which the male adult frequently wanders in search of work and in which the female domestic is the surer breadwinner. Desertion, divorce, common-law marriage, illegitimacy, and violent domestic strife are routine, and the woman tends to be the dominant and stable element in the family unit. Since she is out of the house a good deal of the time earning the family income, children are frequently unsupervised and delinquency rates are high. The men, when they have work, are employed in various semi-skilled or unskilled manual labor jobs or as porters and janitors. For some, particularly the women, religion serves as an emotional outlet and an anchor of respectability. If they do not belong to one of the Baptist or Methodist churches, they support the numerous small storefront churches of the Holiness or Spiritualist variety, where the theology is Fundamentalist and the preacher, who is likely to have little education himself, knows how to whip up the congregation by means of a rambling disquisition into a "shoutin" mood—a frenzied exhibition which may include vigorous random movements as well as loud and semi-coherent expression of religious fervor. Membership in formal organizations other than the church and, lately, the union, is not characteristic of this class. It should be mentioned that there is a more stable element in this class which is trying to "live decent" or "get ahead" in spite of the handicaps of the physical and social environment. Finally, at the other end of the scale are the lower class "shadies"—the prostitutes, pimps, dope addicts, and criminals whose propinquity must be tolerated in the crowded, powerless world of the racial slum, regardless of how their behavior may be evaluated by the bulk of its beleaguered residents.

It would be too much to claim that the substantial separation of the classes within the Negro group in primary relationships and associational life has been demonstrated in rigorous quantitative fashion by the studies and surveys to which we have had reference. However, with due allowance for the imprecise nature of class boundaries in American life and some overlapping as the result, particularly, of the activities of socially mobile individuals, it may be said that the cumulative testimony of these surveys and fields reports points unmistakably to the existence of such substantial separation from each other of the intimate communal life of the classes we have described.

In evaluating the extent of the acculturation process, it will be recalled that we are using the subculture of the "core society"— middle-class white Protestants—as the touchstone. Subcultural behavior may be examined, we suggest, on three levels: extrinsic traits, or external behavior; intrinsic traits based on value systems related to inner psychological attitudes; and the nature of institutional life within the subsociety. We do not claim that the acculturation process has proceeded so far that all differences in values and norms between the middle classes, for instance, of all minority ethnic groups and the white Protestant middle class have disappeared. For one thing, the psychological and sociological experiences of belonging to a minority group must inevitably affect one's way of looking at the world, even apart from the effect of the specific content of the minority group's cultural heritage. Thus we would expect Negroes and Jews to have more liberal attitudes on civil rights issues involving ethnic segregation than Protestants, regardless of class level. Lenski, in a recent study, has demonstrated, on the basis of research on a representative sample of the population of Detroit, that there are statistically significant differences in attitudes (that is, in percentages of the given group who favor or do not favor a certain course of action) toward a complex of economic, political, familial, and educational issues related to "the Protestant Ethic" and economic advancement under capitalism among white Protestants, white Catholics, Jews, and Negro Protestants.[28] Many of these differences remain when class is "controlled" —that is, when comparisons are made among the four ethnic groups on the same class level. Davis and Havighurst, in an earlier study carried out in Chicago, comparing child-rearing practices among four groups: middle-class whites, middle-class Negroes, lower-class whites, and lower-class Negroes, found that while all differences between Negroes and whites did not disappear when class was controlled, nevertheless, that "there are considerable social class differences in child-rearing practices, and these differences are greater than the differences between Negros and whites of the same social class."[29] They go on to add that "the striking thing about this study is that

[28] Gerhard Lenski, *The Religious Factor*, New York, Doubleday, 1961.
[29] Allison Davis and Robert J. Havighurst, "Social Class and Color Differences in Child-Rearing," *American Sociological Review*, Vol. 11, No. 6 (December 1946), p. 707.

Negro and white middle-class families are so much alike, and that white and Negro lower-class families are so much alike."[30]

On the basis of the accumulated evidence, including the descriptions of institutional life in the community studies cited above, we would conclude that the subculture of the Negro upper class has many similarities, particularly in values relating to external behavior and to institutional life, to that of the white Protestant upper-middle class. The subculture of the Negro middle class appears similar in many ways to that of the white Protestant lower-middle class. Some differences in degree in particular value-areas still exist between Negroes and other groups, even at the middle-class level. The subculture of the Negro lower class testifies eloquently to the power of prejudice and discrimination to retard the acculturation process both in external behavior and internal values.

JEWS

While the United States Bureau of the Census, as a result of considerations concerning the "separation of church and state" principles, does not ordinarily ask for information on religious preference or affiliation in its surveys, in 1957 it experimented with such a question in a sample survey of the American population 14 years of age and over. In answer to the question "What is your religion?", 96 per cent of the respondents reported some religion—that is, that they were either Baptist, Lutheran, Roman Catholic, Jewish, or something else; only 3 per cent stated that they had no religion; and 1 per cent made no report.[31] On the other hand, total church membership, as reported by all of the churches and synagogues combined in the late 1950's was only about 63 per cent of

[30] Ibid., p. 708.
[31] Current Population Reports: Population Characteristics, Series P-20, No. 79 (February 2, 1958), p. 1.

the total American population.[32] This substantial difference between what might be called "church identification" and actual
church membership points up the tendency which has been commented on by Herberg[33] and, more recently, by Lenski,[34] for white
Americans to think of themselves as being part of a religious community which places them sociologically in American society, regardless of whether or not they are formally affiliated with a church
or synagogue or frequent attenders at its services.

When we speak of the Jews in the United States, then, we do
not confine ourselves to those who are affiliated with a synagogue
or temple, perhaps 50 to 60 per cent of the total number,[35] but we
refer to all those who consider themselves members of the Jewish
religio-ethnic group and are so regarded by the rest of the American
people. On this basis, the Jewish population of the United States
numbers between 5½ to 6 million, representing a little over 3 per
cent of the total population.[36]

---

[32] *Yearbook of American Churches for 1961*, published by the National Council of Churches of Christ in the United States of America, pp. 250-51. Most
Protestant bodies do not include children under 13 years of age in their totals.
However, their inclusion would not materially lessen the large gap between
"identification" and membership.

[33] Herberg, op. cit.

[34] Lenski, op. cit., particularly pp. 17-74. Lenski makes a distinction between
"associational involvement" (by which he means frequent attendance at the
church itself) and "communal involvement," which is defined in terms of the
degree of confinement to friendship and familial relationships with persons of
one's own "socio-religious group." It needs to be pointed out, of course, that
there are numerous associations or organizations within the religious subcommunity which are not affiliated with the church, and which play an important
part in the structure and life of the subcommunity.

As noted above, Lenski includes a fourth group in his analysis: Negro Protestants.

[35] Arthur Hertzberg in the *American Jewish Year Book* (1958), p. 115, estimates 60 per cent affiliation in 1956-7. A poll of all religious groups carried out
by *The Catholic Digest* in the early 1950's gave a figure of 50 per cent for Jewish membership. Cited in Herberg, op. cit., p. 210.

[36] This estimate is derived by combining data from the Bureau of the Census

Jewish Americans are a highly urbanized group, almost 9 out of every 10 residing in urban areas with a population of 250,000 or over. While Jews (and Jewish communal life) may be found in cities of varying size in all regions of the country, almost 70 per cent live in one or the other of the northeastern states, and 40 per cent of all American Jews live in the metropolitan New York area.[37] The vast majority of Jews in the country are by now native-born Americans (estimates run from 75 to 80 per cent[38]). The period of heavy Jewish immigration came to a close in the early 1920's, and neither the refugee migration of the 1930's nor the post-World War II migration of displaced persons added significantly in numbers to the steadily diminishing size of the foreign-born category.

Jewish communal life in the various cities and, increasingly, the suburbs of the nation is marked by the presence of numerous and flourishing organizations. Many of these organizations have differing ideologies or goals and so compete with one another for membership, funds, and time. In the realm of religion itself, there are congregations of the Orthodox, Conservative, and Reform varieties, named in order of their degree of adherence to the traditional rituals and practices. Contemporary American synagogues and temples (particularly those of the Conservative and Reform persuasions), like their Christian counterparts, offer a wide variety of age-graded activities in addition to worship services; afternoon Hebrew schools, Sunday schools, young people's groups, Temple Brotherhoods and Sisterhoods all offer opportunities for Jewish education and Jewish "activities." Jewish Community Centers, sometimes connected with a synagogue, more often not, together

---

report on its sample survey of Americans 14 years of age and over, cit. supra, the Yearbook of American Churches for 1961, cit. supra, and the American Jewish Year Book (1961).

[37] American Jewish Year Book (1959), Philadelphia, Jewish Publication Society of America, 1959, pp. 7, 8.

[38] American Jewish Year Book (1958), p. 14. These estimates are based on several community studies.

with Jewish "Y"s (Young Men's and Young Women's Hebrew Associations) offer programs of education and recreation with Jewish cultural content for children, youth, and adults. Active Zionists may choose between joining a chapter of the Zionist Organization of America or the Religious Zionists of America, or still others, while Jewish women are invited to join Hadassah, the Women's Zionist Organization of America, or Mizrachi. Anti-Zionists, on the other hand, can join the American Council for Judaism, a small but active group. In the larger cities, where there are hospitals under sectarian auspices, women's auxiliaries of the local Jewish hospital help to raise funds for its operation or plan the décor of the new nursing home. Jewish "defense" organizations, like the American Jewish Committee, the American Jewish Congress, and the Anti-Defamation League of the B'nai B'rith, wage never-ending educational and legal campaigns against prejudice and discrimination—not only that which is directed against Jews, but discrimination that is directed against other minorities as well. In the colleges and universities Jewish fraternities and sororities encourage socializing and dating within the Jewish group, and chapters of Hillel, sponsored by the B'nai B'rith, provide cultural and religious programs and social activities for those Jewish students who choose to participate. In many of the larger cities a weekly Anglo-Jewish newspaper (a Jewish newspaper printed in English) publishes news that is of national and local interest to the members of the Jewish community. (These may range from a syndicated article on anti-Semitism in the Soviet Union to an announcement of the program for the next meeting of the local Hadassah chapter.) Only a handful of the various voluntary Jewish organizations have so far been mentioned. It is clear, then, that American Jewish communal life is not monolithic and no one group or federation of groups can speak for all Jews in America. Perhaps the nearest thing to an overarching institution in Jewish life in America is its philanthropy—a well-organized system of fund-raising and allocations for Jewish welfare activities in this country and abroad—particularly in Israel.[39]

Some Jews, of course, participate in organizations which are community-wide and nonsectarian. Just how many do so it is difficult to say since the data are few and fragmentary. In Elmira, New York, Dean reported that "slightly over half" of the Jews belonged to "mixed organizations."[40] In "Riverton," a Middle Atlantic city of 130,000, Sklare and Vosk found that 14 per cent of the parents in their sample belonged to organizations with "predominantly Gentile memberships," whereas 27 per cent of the teen-age children did so.[41] Apparently a much larger percentage, perhaps as high as 57 per cent of the parents belonged to organizations containing *some* Gentile members.[42] In Washington, D.C., one study found that approximately 51 per cent of all Jewish women in the entire metropolitan area and 61 per cent of the men belonged to at least one nonsectarian organization and that 21 per cent of the women were affiliated with two or more such organizations.[43] Kramer and Leventman, in their study of two generations of Jews in "North City" in the American Midwest, discovered that 31 per cent of the sample of second-generation males belonged to "non-Jewish or mixed" organizations, and that only a slightly larger proportion, 37 per cent, of the third-generation sample held membership in such organizations.[44] Dean reported that in Elmira Jewish men were twice as likely to belong to nonsectarian groups as Jewish women.[45]

[39] See Herberg, op. cit., pp. 212, 213.
[40] John P. Dean, "Patterns of Socialization and Association Between Jews and Non-Jews," *Jewish Social Studies*, Vol. 17, No. 3 (July 1955), p. 252.
[41] Marshall Sklare and Marc Vosk, *The Riverton Study*, The American Jewish Committee, 1957, p. 38.
[42] Ibid. Neither this figure nor the complete table are given in the published report. The figure has been arrived at by calculations based on data which appear in the report.
[43] Stanley K. Bigman, *The Jewish Population of Greater Washington in 1956*, Washington, Jewish Community Council of Greater Washington, 1957, p. 72.
[44] Judith R. Kramer and Seymour Leventman, *Children of the Gilded Ghetto*, New Haven and London, Yale University Press, 1961, pp. 181-2.
[45] Dean, op. cit., p. 252.

A. Gordon, in his study of Jews in "suburbia," declared that Jewish women in these areas often participated and assumed leadership roles in the League of Women Voters, Community Funds, and the Red Cross, as well as in fund-raising drives for the various societies concerned with disabling illness, such as blindness, cerebral palsy, nephritis, and cancer.[46] One of the difficult points to evaluate in data of this type, in attempting to estimate the amount of interethnic contact, is whether or not chapter and area groups, and working parties of the nonsectarian national organizations are likely to be made up of persons of the same ethnic background. We also know next to nothing about the relative amount of time, effort, and emotional involvement devoted to the nonsectarian as distinguished from the ethnic organization.

A further point that needs to be made is that, while the vast majority of Jews in the United States probably belong to at least one Jewish organization (in Elmira, 90 per cent did so;[47] in "Riverton", 82 per cent[48]) and many belong to more than one (in Elmira, 25 per cent of the Jewish residents belonged to four or more Jewish organizations),[49] there are some Jews who belong to none. Many of these are doubtless Jews in the intellectual and artistic professions, who probably have a lower degree of participation in Jewish communal life than any other occupational category. More will be said about this group later in the chapter. On the whole, however, little is known from a research standpoint about those Jews who take no part in Jewish organizational life.

Organizational participation *may* involve, or lead to, primary relationships. Participation in social cliques and close friendships, however, constitute primary group activities in unqualified form. Most studies show a strong tendency for Jewish primary relation-

[46] Albert I. Gordon, *Jews in Suburbia*, Boston, Beacon Press, 1959, p. 211.
[47] Dean, op. cit., p. 252.
[48] Sklare and Vosk, op. cit., p. 8.
[49] Dean, loc. cit.

ships to be confined, ethnically, to other Jews, although the pattern is by no means absolute. Lenski, in his Detroit study, found 77 per cent of his Jewish sample reporting that "all" or "nearly all" of their close friends were Jewish.[50] In "Riverton," Sklare and Vosk discovered that among the Jewish adults 32 per cent had "close friends" who were Gentile, while, for the sample of teen-agers, 38 per cent did so. Significantly, when asked to recall their friends at the age of eight or nine, the teen-agers reported a much more frequent pattern of association with Gentiles.[51] It would thus appear that, at least in some types of communities, close association of Jews with Gentiles occurs frequently in childhood but declines with increasing age, the issue becoming decisive when dating and marriage choices enter the picture.

Kramer and Leventman claim to find differences in friendship patterns with Gentiles associated with generation. Whereas only 18 per cent of the second-generation Jewish males in "North City" report some Gentile friendships, 70 per cent of the third-generation male sample did so. It is worth noting, however, that even in this third-generation group, when the question was phrased in terms of "four closest friends," 80 per cent included only Jews in this intimate circle.[52] Furthermore, the third-generation sample in this study appears to include Jewish intellectuals in such professions as university teaching and scientific research; these individuals may already, in any realistic sociological sense, be a part of the intellectual subsociety rather than the Jewish subcommunity of the local city.[53]

Dean, in the Elmira study, found the following interesting distinction in patterns of Jewish-Gentile association. About three-

[50] Lenski, op. cit., pp. 33-4.
[51] Sklare and Vosk, op. cit., pp. 38-9.
[52] Kramer and Leventman, op. cit., pp. 175-6.
[53] See my review of *Children of the Gilded Ghetto* in *American Sociological Review*, Vol. 27, No. 4 (August 1962), pp. 563-4.

quarters of his Jewish respondents reported some socializing with
their "closest Gentile contact." However, this socializing rarely
occurred in a clique situation, "fewer than 10 per cent" reporting
participation in a mixed social clique.[54] In other words, in this
middle-sized community, the typical Jewish-Gentile friendship appeared to exist as an isolated phenomenon outside the context of
the more significant group experience of social cliquing. Gans, in
his study of Jewish communal life in the Chicago suburb of Park
Forest, discovered that 66 per cent of his sample declared that they
"see regularly socially" "only" or "mainly" other Jews.[55] He described, also, the "garden-type" suburban pattern wherein Jewish
women in the daytime participated in the social life of their particular neighborhood with other women, regardless of ethnicity,
but "in the evening and weekend social relationships of couples . . . the Jewish husband and wife turned primarily to other
Jews."[56] And A. Gordon, in his study of "Jews in suburbia" confirmed this pattern, quoting a suburban Jewish woman on the
subject of Jewish-Gentile relationships as follows:

Our husbands do business with them [Christians]. We see them in
the town's shopping area. It's always a very pleasant, "Hello, how are
you?" kind of superficial conversation. We may even meet at a meeting
some afternoon or even perhaps at a PTA school affair, but it is sel-
dom more than that. It is a kind of "9 to 5" arrangement. The
ghetto gates, real or imagined, close at 5:00 p.m. "Five o'clock
shadow" sets in at sundown. Jews and Christians do not meet socially
even in suburbia. If we do, you bet that it is to help promote some
cause or organization where they think we Jews may be helpful. But
after five o'clock there is no social contact, no parties, no home visits,
no golf clubs—no nothing!

[54] Dean, op. cit., pp. 252-4.
[55] Herbert J. Gans, "The Origin and Growth of a Jewish Community in the
Suburbs: A Study of the Jews of Park Forest," in Marshall Sklare (ed.), *The
Jews: Social Patterns of an American Group*, Glencoe, Ill., Free Press, 1958, p.
227.
[56] Ibid., p. 226.

"This is not," declares Gordon, "an isolated opinion expressed by an unhappy and unaccepted Jewish person. On the contrary, it is the most representative comment made by Jews and is generally confirmed by Jews in suburban communities all through America."[57]

One of the functions of ethnic communality and the maintenance of primary relationships exclusively or predominantly within the ethnic group is to ensure ethnic endogamy—that is, marriage within the group. All available data suggest that the Jewish group has been remarkably successful in the attainment of this goal, although the rate of out-marriage may be increasing slowly. The rate of Jewish-Christian marriage in the United States has been low at least since the late nineteenth century, when the large-scale immigration of Jews from Eastern Europe began. In New Haven, Ruby Jo Reeves Kennedy found that the rate of Jewish in-marriage (that is, marriage with other Jews) was 98.82 per cent in 1900, while in 1950 it was still 96.10 per cent, hardly a large decline in half a century.[58] A study of the New Orleans Jewish community in 1953 revealed that 7 per cent of its married members had non-Jewish spouses.[59] That this figure appears to be representative of the na-

[57] Albert I. Gordon, op. cit., p. 170.
[58] Ruby Jo Reeves Kennedy, "Single or Triple Melting Pot? Intermarriage in New Haven, 1870-1950," op. cit., p. 57. In 1948, according to a study by Hollingshead, the Jewish in-marriage rate in New Haven was 97.1 per cent (August B. Hollingshead, "Cultural Factors in the Selection of Marriage Mates," American Sociological Review, Vol. 15, No. 5 (October 1950), p. 622).
[59] Benjamin B. Goldman and Alvin Chenkin, The Jewish Population of New Orleans: 1953, Council of Jewish Federation and Welfare Funds, 1954, cited in Ben B. Seligman, with the assistance of Aaron Antonovsky, "Some Aspects of Jewish Demography," in Marshall Sklare (ed.), The Jews: Social Patterns of an American Group, op. cit., p. 63. The study of the Greater Washington Jewish population, cited earlier, found a rate for mixed conjugal families of 11.3 per cent (Stanley K. Bigman, The Jewish Population of Greater Washington in 1956, p. 124). However, this rate is not likely to be representative because of the unusually large proportion of intellectuals and professionals among the Jewish population of Greater Washington.

tion as a whole is attested to by the Bureau of the Census "religious" survey of a national sample of the American population in 1957, cited earlier, which found that of existing marriages in which one spouse was Jewish, 7.2 per cent of the husbands or wives were either Protestant or Catholic.[60] Of course, this figure represents "current mixed families," or "remaining mixed marriages" rather than the percentage of actual Jewish-Christian marriages ever contracted. If one or the other partner in a marriage converted to the other's religion, that marriage would no longer count as mixed in this form of tabulation.[61] Therefore, the actual rate of Jewish-Christian intermarriage is larger than this figure by an unknown degree.

In discussing the class system within the Jewish group—or, to put the matter conversely, the relationship of the Jewish group to the American class system—we are aided by considerable statistical data on the position or distribution of the Jews, economically, occupationally, and educationally, but handicapped by the paucity of studies which deal with the communal and cultural life of the various strata of the Jewish population. There is one perceptive study of an Eastern metropolitan Jewish upper class—that of Philadelphia —carried out by E. Digby Baltzell as part of a larger study of the Philadelphia upper class.[62] And the Kramer and Leventman study of "North City" divides the second generation sample into an upper status group, corresponding to the upper-middle and lower-upper segments of the general community, and a lower status group, which would be about lower-middle and middle-class in American society as a whole.[63] Also, there are, by now, a number of

[60] Bureau of the Census, *Current Population Reports: Population Characteristics*, Series P-20, No. 79, Table 6, p. 8.
[61] The figures for New Orleans and Washington, cited above, are similarly based on mixed families. The New Haven figures represent actual intermarriages contracted in the particular year.
[62] E. Digby Baltzell, *Philadelphia Gentlemen*, Glencoe, Ill., Free Press, 1958.
[63] Kramer and Leventman, op. cit.

additional studies of Jewish communities in various medium-sized cities or suburbs, but these have little focus on class differences, doubtless, in part, because of the high concentration of Jews in these communities in the middle class, thus narrowing the gap of class disparity. However, enough is known about the class structure of the Jewish community for the following remarks to be made. These remarks need to be prefaced by the presentation of a brief historical perspective.[64]

Although the ensuing comments constitute an oversimplification, basically there have been three waves of Jewish immigration to the United States, prior to the "modern" period which we shall date from the nineteen-thirties. The first, during colonial times, consisted of, first, Sephardim (that is, Jews of Spanish and Portuguese origin) who came directly from the Netherlands, England, or the European colonies of Central and South America, and, later in the period, Askenazim (that is, Jews of German origin), who arrived from Central Europe. This was numerically a very small migration (there were probably no more than 2500 Jews in the United States in 1790). Although the two groups mixed, they were culturally dominated by the Sephardim, who had undergone more acculturation to the Western World and the forces of the Enlightenment. These colonial Jews were largely a middle-class group of merchants, and the more wealthy and influential of them were apparently accepted into the communal life of the Gentile upper class of the day. Considerable intermarriage appears to have taken place, which led eventually to the absorption of the intermarried Jew, or at least his descendants, into the Gentile subsociety.

The second wave of Jewish immigration occurred in the middle

[64] For historical materials I have drawn particularly on the following sources: Nathan Glazer, "Social Characteristics of American Jews, 1654-1954," in *American Jewish Year Book* (1955), and *American Judaism*, Chicago, University of Chicago Press, 1957; Oscar Handlin, *Adventure in Freedom*, New York, McGraw-Hill Publishing Co., 1954; and E. Digby Baltzell, *Philadelphia Gentlemen*, op. cit., pp. 273-91.

portion of the nineteenth century and consisted, for the most part, of Jews from the various German states. Many of these immigrants arrived relatively impoverished and began their life in the United States as peddlers, fanning out to the communities of the hinterland, the Midwest, the West, and the South to sell their wares. Eventually, the peddler settled down and became a storekeeper and, in some cases, the proprietor of what became the large department store in the large city. Thus the German Jews prospered, and in the late 1840's and 1850's their ranks were swelled by German Jewish professionals and intellectuals who, along with the more numerous non-Jewish Germans, were fleeing a political climate inhospitable to democracy. The German Jews of this mid-nineteenth-century period who came to this country had had greater exposure to the freedoms and doctrines of the Enlightenment, which began to spread throughout Europe after the French Revolution, than their fellow Ashkenazim who resided in the territories of Poland and Russia to the East. These German Jews brought with them Reform Judaism, which represented a drastic refashioning of the doctrines and ritual of traditional Judaism in line with Western values. The most prosperous of the German Jews in the larger cities eventually, in the latter part of the nineteenth century, became a Jewish upper class, resting on a solid middle-class base.

Shortly before the third wave of Jewish migrants came to American shores, the Jews of the United States numbered at most a few hundred thousand. But beginning in the 1870's and swelling to substantial proportions in the 1880's and 1890's, the tide of Eastern European Jewry, fleeing persecution and economic dislocation in the lands of the Czars and hard times in the empire of the Hapsburgs, came to America seeking refuge and a new life. Before this tide was cut off, temporarily by World War I and eventually by the quota laws of the 1920's, probably two and one third million Jews from Eastern Europe had taken up residence in the United States. Some of these left their ports of debarkation and went to the smaller cities and towns as their German predecessors had done.

The vast majority, however, because of their poverty and the availability of jobs, stayed in the larger Eastern cities—particularly New York, Boston, and Philadelphia—and most of these became a part of the urban working class in the garment factories and other light industries of the time.

Although the German-Jewish community took on social work and "Americanizing" functions in relation to the hordes of Jews from Eastern Europe from the very beginning, the social chasm between the two groups, based on both cultural and class factors, persisted for some years. In the end it was to be overcome as the more recent immigrants, and particularly their children, rose in the economic and social scale during the twentieth century and were acculturated and socialized into American patterns of behavior.

The rise in socio-economic status of the Eastern European Jews and their descendants is, in fact, the greatest collective Horatio Alger story in American immigration history. By the 1940's Jews in the United States (by now, of course, overwhelmingly of Eastern European origin) had an occupational distribution which showed striking similarities to that of the high-status Protestant denominations. In a national sample studied in 1945-6 by the American Institute of Public Opinion, 36 per cent of the Jews were in "Business and Professional" occupations, as compared with 32 per cent of the Episcopalians, 33 per cent of the Congregationalists, and 31 per cent of the Presbyterians. By contrast, 14 per cent of the Catholics and 13 per cent of the Lutherans fell into this category.[65] In Lenski's Detroit sample of 1957, with the use of a two-factor (occupational status and income) scale, 43 per cent of the Jews were placed in the upper-middle-class bracket in comparison with 19 per cent of "white Protestants," and 12 per cent of "white Catholics."[66] Numerous surveys of Jews in medium-sized communities show them to

[65] Reported in Liston Pope, "Religion and the Class Structure," *The Annals of the American Academy of Political and Social Science*, Vol. 256, March 1948, p. 87.
[66] Lenski, op. cit., p. 73.

be bunched overwhelmingly in middle-class occupations, especially
as managers and proprietors in retail and wholesale trade and man-
ufacturing, and increasingly in the professions.[67]

The reasons for this phenomenal rise in occupational status are
complex, but in essence they pertain to the cultural history of the
Jews before they came to America.[68] The traditional stress and high
evaluation placed upon Talmudic learning was easily transferred
under new conditions to a desire for secular education, if not for the
parent generation, at least for the children. The restrictions of Jewish occupational choice in medieval and post-medieval Europe had
placed them in the traditional role of traders, self-employed artisans, and scholars. Thus the Jews arrived in America with the
middle-class values of thrift, sobriety, ambition, desire for education, ability to postpone immediate gratifications for the sake of
long-range goals, and aversion to violence already internalized.
These qualities meshed very well with the demands of an expanding American economy in which the need for farmers and manual
laborers was constantly contracting. Even though large numbers of
Jewish industrial workers in the large cities remained in this status,
their children were encouraged to get an education and thus rose
in the occupational hierarchy. Even the Jewish industrial workers
themselves did not display the cultural values usually associated
with a proletariat. As Glazer points out, it was not dangerous to
walk through the New York slums at night when they were in-
habited by Jews. In contrast to the usual pattern, Jewish workers
belonged to voluntary organizations in greater frequency than did
Jewish white-collar workers. A study carried out in New York City
in 1945 revealed that low-income Jews wrote letters to their con-

[67] For pertinent summaries of data from these studies, see Nathan Glazer, "So-
cial Characteristics of American Jews, 1654-1954," op. cit., pp. 25-30; see also,
Alvin Chenkin, "Jewish Population in the United States, 1957," in *American
Jewish Year Book* (1958), pp. 12-13.
[68] I draw here upon the perceptive discussion by Nathan Glazer in "Social
Characteristics of American Jews, 1654-1954," op. cit., pp. 29-33.

gressmen more frequently than did high-income Protestants and Catholics.[69] Other data could be cited to support the point,[70] but enough has been said to illustrate the thesis that the Jews arrived in America with middle-class values already internalized, even though most of them had to begin at the bottom of the socio-economic ladder. It is these cultural values which account for the rapid rise of the Jewish group in occupational status and economic affluence.

Currently, then, the social class picture among American Jews may be described as follows: In the small or medium-sized cities, most Jews are either upper-middle or white-collar lower-middle class, although there will be a small group of blue-collar workers— skilled, semi-skilled, and unskilled. (In Canton, Ohio, in 1955, the blue-collar workers constituted about 11 per cent of the Jewish population; in Des Moines, Iowa, in 1956, they formed about 7 per cent.[71]) In the large cities and metropolitan areas, a full distribution of classes from upper to lower, or working-class, will be found, and the working class will form a numerically more significant portion of the total. Perhaps as much as one-third of New York's gainfully employed Jews were still engaged in some form of manual work around 1950,[72] and two separate studies in Detroit in the 1950's, one as late as 1958, placed a little over a quarter of Detroit's Jews in blue-collar jobs.[73]

Through Baltzell's study of the Philadelphia upper class we are able to see the Jewish enclave of this class as it appeared in 1940.[74] Institutionally, it is separated from the larger Gentile group of comparable affluence and lineage. It is largely of German extraction, al-

---

[69] These studies are cited in Glazer, "Social Characteristics of American Jews, 1654-1954," op. cit., pp. 32-33.
[70] Ibid.
[71] Chenkin, op. cit., pp. 12-13.
[72] Glazer, "Social Characteristics of American Jews, 1654-1954," op. cit., p. 26.
[73] David Goldberg and Harry Sharp, "Some Characteristics of Detroit Area Jewish and Non-Jewish Adults," in Marshall Sklare (ed.), The Jews: Social Patterns of an American Group, op. cit., p. 112; Lenski, op. cit., p. 73.
[74] Baltzell, op. cit., pp. 273-91.

though by this time some Jews of Eastern European background had achieved sufficient wealth or prominence to join its ranks. Membership is held in three synagogues (or "temples," to use the preferred Reform term), one of them Sephardic Orthodox, the other two Reform. Residentially, this class is concentrated in two areas: the Old York Road section of the northern suburb of Elkins Park and the Rittenhouse Square area of fashionable apartment houses near the center of the city. Social life revolves around three organizations: the Philmont Country Club, located along Old York Road, the older Mercantile Club with family participation, and the newer Locust Club, a downtown club of Jewish businessmen which parallels Philadelphia's fashionable downtown clubs for male Gentiles.[75] No data are given on social cliquing. By the early 1960's, at the time of this writing, it is virtually certain that many more Jews of Eastern European origin have become participating members of the Philadelphia Jewish upper class, although empirical data are lacking.

A study of social clubs in the Jewish community of Atlanta, Georgia, made in 1948, also revealed internal class separation, although some overlapping in institutional affiliation was also indicated.[76] The "S" club had the highest status and its members were predominantly of German and Central European origin; however, as in the case of the Philadelphia Jewish upper class, wealthy or culturally comparable Jews of Eastern European descent had begun to be admitted to this upper-class organization. Over three-quarters of its members belonged to the Reform Temple and about half of the spouses of its male members belonged to the high-status Na-

[75] Baltzell reported that the original founders of the Locust Club had hoped to include Gentiles and the club did have a few Gentile members for a time. Gentile membership in 1940 appeared to be nominal, and the club was known in Philadelphia as "the Jewish Union League," op. cit., pp. 289-90.
[76] Solomon Sutker, "The Role of Social Clubs in the Atlanta Jewish Community," in Marshall Sklare (ed.), *The Jews: Social Patterns of an American Group*, pp. 262-70.

tional Council of Jewish Women. Gans, in his study of the suburb of Park Forest, reports that social cliquing had divided the Jewish community into four groups: upper-middle-class business and professional men, upper-middle-class professionals engaged in academic and research functions, a "suburban middle-middle-class" section (the largest), and those in lower-middle-class white-collar occupations.[77] A. Gordon also writes of class differences and divisions among Jews in suburbia. "The mass-produced suburbs built since 1946 consist in the main of lower-middle-class families," he observes. "In the older suburbs of New England and the Midwest, an admixture of both upper- and lower-middle-class Jewish families may be found. In Westchester County and several of the old well-established suburban areas of Long Island, Jewish lower-upper families reside in great numbers."[78]

In the Kramer and Leventman study of "North City," the well-to-do Jewish self-made businessmen and independent professionals who make up the upper-status "clubniks" live in fashionable and expensive neighborhoods, belong to the all-Jewish Pinecrest Country Club, affiliate with the Reform Temple, and reveal greater receptivity to Gentile values and social contacts than do the low-status "lodgniks," whose occupational, organizational, residential, and social patterns reflect both their lower position in the American class structure and their greater adherence to traditional Jewish subcultural values. It is worth noting that the upper-status group in this good-sized city in the late 1950's is overwhelmingly of Eastern European origin. The effective separation of the upper-status group from the lower-status group, though both are Jewish, is attested to in the distinctive ecological and institutional patterns, and this separation extends to the realm of informal social relationships. "Friendship circles of the clubniks and the lodgniks," report the

[77] Gans, "The Origin and Growth of a Jewish Community in the Suburbs: A Study of the Jews of Park Forest," pp. 233-4.
[78] Albert I. Gordon, op. cit., p. 14. See also pp. 15, 80-81, 203-4.

authors, "reflect their respective social positions in the Jewish community. A scrutiny of the characteristics of their Jewish social circles confirms the fact that our sample groups (and their friends) do, in fact, represent distinct social strata. The respondents' friends live in the same neighborhoods, belong to the same organizations, have much the same incomes, and are in similar occupations."[79]

While the data cited above are highly informative, we are, regrettably, unable to draw upon any full-scale study of class divisions among Jews in a large metropolitan area which deals systematically and comparatively with the full range of classes, their degree of separate communality, their cultural differences, and their possibly differential relationships with Gentiles.

With regard to the acculturation process, it is clear to any close observer of the American scene that in extrinsic culture traits, native-born Jews at various class levels are very similar to native-born non-Jews of the same social class. In dress, appearance, manner, and speech pattern, the Jewish graduate of an Ivy-League college, for instance, appears virtually indistinguishable from his Gentile counterpart. In the world of the lower-middle class, minor differences in speech patterns stemming from the intonations and inflections of Yiddish can still be detected between the Jews and the white Protestant Anglo-Saxon core group, but even these minor differences are likely to disappear in another generation. Furthermore, a few Yiddish intonations and inflections have, themselves, become a part of American popular culture, as witness the recent general popularity of Jewish comedians and humorists who make conscious use of them. Within a very few years, as the foreign-born Jewish population becomes increasingly attenuated by age, and the next generation of American Jews at whatever class level become the native-born children of native-born parents, it seems reasonable to predict that all or nearly all differences in extrinsic culture traits between Jews and non-Jews will disappear. This prognosis could be

[79] Kramer and Leventman, op. cit., pp. 104-5.

wrong if there were large-scale immigration to the United States of Jews from other countries, but this eventuality is unlikely.[80]

In the realm of intrinsic traits, or psychological attitudes and value systems, some differences in degree in some values, as previously noted, have been demonstrated between American Jews and Gentiles. Jews, for instance, are more likely to vote Democratic than white Protestants and, to a smaller degree, than white Catholics, even with class level controlled, and they are somewhat more favorable toward welfare state ideals, on the average, than Gentiles of the same class level.[81] Also, a number of studies have demonstrated that the fertility patterns of Jewish families differ in degree from those of other ethnic groups. Over the past few decades, the birth rate of Jewish women has been about 81 per cent of the total Protestant rate (including all races) and about 73 per cent of the Catholic rate.[82] Jewish wives are more favorable to the use of contraceptives for planning and spacing births than those of any other large religious classification, and Jewish families practice contraception and practice it successfully more than the other groups.[83] How-

[80] It excepts, too, the small enclaves of Hasidic Jews (The Hasidim are a mystically oriented sect stemming from eighteenth century Eastern Orthodoxy) who have come to America in recent years as a part of the post-World War II refugee influx and have settled in cohesive clusters in and around a few large cities, particularly New York. They attempt to preserve for themselves and their children (and any converts) their traditional way of life taken directly from the "shtetl," or small town, so closely identified with Eastern European Jewry. It will be interesting to see how much success they have over time. For a valuable study of this group, see Solomon Poll, The Hasidic Community of Williamsburg, New York, Free Press of Glencoe, 1962.

[81] Lenski, op. cit., pp. 125, 137; Berelson, Lazarsfeld, and McPhee, Voting, op. cit., pp. 62, 71; Laurence H. Fuchs, The Political Behavior of American Jews, Glencoe, Ill., Free Press, 1956, passim.

[82] Erich Rosenthal, "Jewish Fertility in the United States," American Jewish Year Book, 1961, p. 9.

[83] Ronald Freedman, Pascal K. Whelpton, and Arthur A. Campbell, Family Planning, Sterility, and Population Growth, New York, McGraw-Hill Publishing Co., 1959, pp. 103-15, 155-61; Charles F. Westoff, Robert G. Potter, Jr., Philip C. Sagi, and Elliot G. Mishler, Family Growth in Metropolitan America,

ever, two other sets of data bring this portrayal of differences into better perspective. When the completed fertility of a national sample of Jewish women is compared with that of Presbyterian women, it turns out to be practically identical (in fact, one percentage point higher).[84] Furthermore, when Jewish couples in a national sample were matched with groups of Protestant and Catholic couples in occupation of husband, education of wife, income of husband, duration of marriage, metropolitan character of present residence, and farm background, the differences in fertility patterns between the Jews and the Protestants were virtually eliminated, although the differences between Catholics and non-Catholics remained.[85] In other words, Jewish values on fertility which at first appeared to differ in degree from those of other Americans, turned out to be a function of urbanization and socio-economic position, and thus are seen to be the same as those of Protestants with the same socio-economic distribution and degree of urban residence.

In the area of value conflict, as distinguished from value differences, Jewish divergences from the core society are most salient in the interpretation of church-state relationships, particularly the issue of Christmas observances in the public schools. There are remnants of controversy involving some elements in Orthodox Jewry over laws requiring humane slaughter for animals, although these show signs of resolution as techniques of humane slaughter have recently been devised which appear to satisfy the requirements of both humane considerations and ultra-orthodox interpretations

Princeton, N.J., Princeton University Press, 1961, pp. 92-102; Rosenthal, "Jewish Fertility in the United States," pp. 23-5.
[84] Ibid., p. 10. The data are derived from a survey carried out by the United States Bureau of the Census in 1957.
[85] Ronald Freedman, Pascal K. Whelpton, and John W. Smit, "Socio-Economic Factors in Religious Differentials in Fertility," American Sociological Review, Vol. 26, No. 4 (August 1961), pp. 608-14.

of ritual criteria.[86] In any event, the proportion of American Jews which is exercised over this issue (at least, on the side of enforcing ritual requirements) is probably quite small, since evidence from several studies cited earlier indicate that observance of the traditional Jewish dietary laws, except on ceremonial occasions, is fast disappearing.[87]

It is in the institutional area of religious life that one would logically expect the greatest difference between Jews and non-Jews in America to appear. It is precisely here, however, that the attractions of American core society values and the success of the acculturation process are revealed in broadest outline. Reform Judaism, brought over and developed by German Jews in the nineteenth century, and now embracing many Jews of Eastern European descent as well, broke sharply with the rituals and beliefs of Orthodoxy and produced a pattern of religious worship not unlike that of the liberal Protestant denominations. In recent years Reform has reintroduced a few traditional elements, but the pattern of acculturation has not thereby been significantly affected. Of even greater sociological interest, since it has played such an important role among the much larger mass of Jews of Eastern descent, is the development of the Conservative branch of Judaism. Marshall Sklare, in a brilliant and persuasive study, has shown how Conservative Judaism arose in the second and third decades of the twentieth century as a response on the part of Eastern European Jews who had achieved middle-class status in America to the values and conditions of their new class and cultural situation.[88] The introduction of English into portions of the service and into the business affairs of the synagogue, the adoption of the sermon, changes in the func-

---

[86] Much of this controversy pertains to methods of handling the animals prior to slaughter—a matter apparently not actually covered by Talmudic law. See *Jewish Newsletter*, Vol. XVII, No. 7 (April 3, 1961).

[87] Sklare and Vosk, op. cit., pp. 11-12; Gans, op. cit., pp. 222-3; Albert I. Gordon, op. cit., pp. 129, 130-32; Kramer and Leventman, op. cit., pp. 77 and 81.

[88] Marshall Sklare, *Conservative Judaism*, Glencoe, Ill., Free Press, 1955.

tion of the rabbi, the abolition of the segregation of the sexes in
worship, the emphasis on "decorum," the institutional development of the "multi-functional" synagogue with its age- and sex-
graded recreational and educational program—all these changes
represented substantial breaks with Orthodoxy which, while they
did not go as far as the Reform movement, constituted clearly
recognizable adaptations to the standards of the American middle
class. In fact, the trend among native-born Jews in middle-class and
suburban areas away from Orthodox cultural patterns (and one
must remember that in Orthodox Judaism religion and culture are
hardly distinguishable) accompanied, simultaneously, by a strong
desire for the preservation of ethnic identity as Jews, has led to the
development of what Herbert Gans, in a perceptive discussion, has
called "symbolic Judaism." By this he means a kind of minimal
adherence to specifically Jewish cultural values or patterns, in which
emphasis is placed on a selection of nostalgic items of "Yiddish"
background (for instance, Yiddish culinary delicacies or Yiddish
phrases), the possession in the home of tangible objects denoting
Jewishness (for example, books, records, or pictures with Jewish
themes), a concern with "Jewish" problems, and a selection of
festive religious traditions which help socialize the children into an
awareness of and affection for their Jewish identity.[89]

All of this is a far cry from the Orthodoxy of the Eastern European "shtetl," or even from the life of immigrant Jews in America
in their "area of first settlement." The acculturation process, thus,
has drastically modified American Jewish life in the direction of
adaptation to American middle-class values, while it has not by any
means "dissolved" the group in a structural sense. Communal life
and ethnic self-identification flourish within the borders of a group
defined as one of the "three major faiths" of America, while at the

[89] Herbert J. Gans, "American Jewry: Present and Future," Commentary, Vol.
21, No. 5 (May 1956), pp. 422-30; and "The Future of American Jewry,"
Commentary, Vol. 21, No. 6 (June 1956), pp. 555-63.

same time its members and, to a considerable degree, its institutions become increasingly indistinguishable, culturally, from the personnel and institutions of the American core society.

CATHOLICS

In 1790, when the first official census of the American people was taken, it is estimated that there were about 35,000 Catholics in the land,[90] less than 1 per cent of the total population of approximately four million. By the middle of the twentieth century, about one out of every four Americans considered himself or herself to be an adherent of the Roman Catholic faith,[91] and this church was the largest single denomination in the United States, although its membership was still considerably exceeded nationally by all Protestants combined.[92]

Regionally, the Roman Catholic population is heavily concentrated in the northeastern states, making up about 45 per cent of the population of this area and giving this group a plurality when considered in relation to either white Protestants or all Protestants

[90] Gerald Shaughnessy, S.M., Has the Immigrant Kept the Faith?, New York, 1925, p. 52, cited in John Tracy Ellis, American Catholicism, Chicago, University of Chicago Press, 1956, p. 42.
[91] Bureau of the Census, Current Population Reports: Population Characteristics, Series P-20, No. 79, op. cit. In this sample survey of the American population 14 years of age and over, carried out in 1957, 25.7 per cent reported that they were Roman Catholics. (Table 3, p. 7)
[92] Official Roman Catholic membership for 1959, as reported in Benson Y. Landis (ed.), Yearbook of American Churches, 1961, National Council of the Churches of Christ in the U.S.A., was 40,871,302. Total Protestant membership was given as 62,543,502. Moreover, since the Roman Catholic total includes all baptized persons, whereas many Protestant denominations exclude children under 13 in their membership total, the Protestant superiority in numbers is greater than the preceding figures would indicate. See Landis, op. cit., pp. 250-52.

combined. In the North Central states and in the West, its representation is roughly identical to its percentage of the total population, whereas in the South it makes up slightly less than 12 per cent of the total. Catholics are also highly urbanized, and it is worthy of note that in urbanized areas of 250,000 or more, the representation of Catholics and white Protestants is nearly identical, the respective percentages being 37.8 and 38.4.[93] In other words, in many of the metropolitan centers of the Northeast, and, to a lesser degree, the North Central and West, Catholics are no longer, in any significant numerical sense, a minority group.

It would be a mistake, however, to conceive of the membership of the Catholic Church in the United States, either historically or currently, as a monolithic ethnic group. From the very beginning of American settlement, adherents of the Roman Catholic faith who arrived on these shores represented many different countries, cultures, and tongues.[94] At the time of the Revolution, there were already Catholics of English, Irish, and German origin in the middle colonies of the eastern seaboard, and small settlements under French Catholic influence in the western hinterland. The acquisition of the Louisiana Purchase shortly after the turn of the century added Catholics of Spanish background to the array of nationalities, as well as additional members of the faith whose ancestral language was French. Moreover, converts among the American Indians had already been made by mission priests reflecting, particularly, these last two nationality backgrounds. Thus, even before the

[93] Bureau of the Census, *Current Population Reports: Population Characteristics*, Series P-20, No. 79, op. cit., Tables 2 and 3, pp. 6-7.
[94] In this section I have relied, particularly, on the following sources: Ellis, op. cit., *passim*; John L. Thomas, S.J., "Nationalities and American Catholicism," in Louis J. Putz, C.S.C. (ed.), *The Catholic Church, U.S.A.*, Chicago, Fides Publishers Association, 1956, pp. 155-76; Fergus MacDonald, C.P., "The Development of Parishes in the United States," in C. J. Nuesse and Thomas J. Harte, C.Ss.R. (eds.), *The Sociology of the Parish*, Milwaukee, Bruce Publishing Co., 1951, pp. 45-71; and Thomas J. Harte, C.Ss.R., "Racial and National Parishes in the United States," in Nuesse and Harte (eds.), op. cit., pp. 154-77.

large-scale migrations of the nineteenth century had begun, American Catholicism's multi-national background was already apparent, and Father John Carroll, of the distinguished Maryland family, who was shortly thereafter to become the first American bishop, was forced to deal, in 1787, in his capacity as superintendent of the American Catholic missions, with a dissident German congregation in Philadelphia which agitated for and obtained a German-speaking pastor.

The large-scale migration to America of the Irish and the Germans (many of whom were Catholic) in the middle portion of the nineteenth century, and the great influx of Southern and Eastern Europeans in the last quarter of the same century and the first quarter of the twentieth—Italians, Poles, Czechs, Slovaks, Croatians, Hungarians, Lithuanians, Ukranians, and other groups—provided the Church with the opportunity for its vast growth in numbers and in proportional representation in the American population which has already been alluded to. This migration, furthermore, placed upon the Roman Catholic Church the necessity for operating for many years in the American context as primarily the church of the immigrant, with his characteristic problems of cultural adjustment and low socio-economic position. These problems and opportunities were augmented by waves of migration to the United States of Catholics from the other Americas: French-Canadians from the north, Mexicans from the south, and, most recently, the Puerto Ricans. Furthermore, during the latter period, converts had begun to be made among the traditionally Protestant American Negroes.

The earlier Catholic migrants to the United States had agitated for priests of their own tongue; in effect this was a clash between the Germans and the Irish. The later Catholic arrivals to American shores wished to join neither group in corporate worship and the communal life which such worship implied. Their own churches in the homeland had, of course, been set in the framework of their own national culture and language. These newcomers, therefore, resisted inclusion in the regular Catholic "territorial parish" and clamored to have a priest and a congregation of their own language and traditions.

The Church's response to this problem was to set up the so-called "national parish," whose congregation consisted of all persons within an inclusive area who possessed the particular nationality background and whose priest sprang from the same traditions and language. This type of parish overlapped in locality the regular territorial parish. Thus an Italian, or Pole, or French-Canadian nationality parish will be located within a territorial parish, or, more probably, overlapping several regular territorial parishes. But the Italians, or Poles, or French-Canadians have the privilege of joining their national parish even though their place of residence falls within the boundaries of the territorial parish. In addition, some territorial parishes have, in fact, a distinct national flavor as a result of the ecological concentration of people of the particular nationality background. Harte, in an authoritative discussion, distinguishes among three types of parishes: 1) the territorial parish, which is the normal and most common type; 2) the juridical national parish, officially constituted along nationality background lines; and 3) the non-juridical national parish which is officially a territorial parish but is *de facto* a nationality parish. It should be pointed out that parishes dominated by the Irish and served by Irish priests have never been designated as national parishes, since the Irish were English speaking even on first arrival, and the national parishes had their *raison d'être* in language diversity. To complete the picture one must mention that there are racially segregated parishes in the South and, to a lesser extent, in the North, whose exact canonical status is obscure.[95]

The role of the "ethnic church" in maintaining the ethnic community as a cohesive social system has been well demonstrated by

[95] Harte, op. cit., *passim*.

Warner and Srole in their study of ethnic groups in Yankee City.[96] Regrettably, however, to my knowledge, we do not have demographic trend studies of the national parish as a phenomenon in American Roman Catholicism which would provide clues to its changing role and function, or studies of a particular national parish or group of such parishes through the crucial transition from the period of the dominance of the first generation to that of the native-born second and third generations as adults. Clearly, the national parish will have its greatest attraction for the immigrant himself, who has not yet mastered the English tongue, and who brings with him his internalized cultural norms from Europe. To what extent the second- and third-generation Italians, Poles, Slovaks, etc., have remained within the national parish is unknown in any strict quantitative sense, although informal observation would lead one to believe that there is a rapid falling away from the juridical national parish on the part of the American-born Catholic, particularly if he is socially mobile and moves to a higher class area of second or third settlement, who tends then to take his place in the regular territorial parish. Certainly the policy of the Church itself is not to foster nationality communalism any longer than is necessary. In the words of Father Harte: "In general, the official position of the Church on this question of membership in juridical national parishes is clearly to encourage assimilation into a larger community by lifting all barriers to affiliation with the territorial parish for those who speak English." He goes on to add: "At the same time, however, the individual's right to make his choice freely is fully guaranteed, and the right of the national or ethnic group to perpetuate its culture is likewise protected."[97]

[96] W. Lloyd Warner and Leo Srole, *The Social Systems of American Ethnic Groups*, New Haven, Yale University Press, 1945; see, particularly, Chapter 7. Their study includes the Greek Orthodox Church and the Jewish synagogue and their respective communities, as well as an Irish-dominated territorial and a French-Canadian national parish.

[97] Harte, op. cit., p. 160.

However, the long-run prognosis is for the decline, if not disappearance, of the national parish. "As for the future of national parishes in America," declares Harte, "one may safely predict that their numerical strength and importance will decline rapidly under present immigration policies."[98]

A larger question than the fate of the national parishes, however, and one not entirely coincident with it, is the fate of the separate ethnic communal subsystems which have, historically, existed as separate units of the social structure of American Catholicism. According to the "triple melting pot" theory, these various subsystems are breaking up and dissolving into the larger subsystem of American pan-Catholicism. While there is some evidence in favor of the validity of this hypothesis, the question should be approached with caution and with proper specificity.

In the first place, there is no reason to believe that the approximately 650,000 Negroes[99] who belong to the Roman Catholic Church are integrated in any meaningful social way into the white Catholic subsociety.[100] Though some Negro Catholics, particularly in northern cities, attend mass together with whites, it should be kept in mind that the worship services of the large Catholic Church, sometimes embracing thousands of parishioners, do not necessarily promote primary group relations such as inter-home visiting, social cliquing, and cooperation in small group activities. In this respect—that of effective social segregation—the great mass of white Catholic parishioners do not appear to act any differently from their Protestant and Jewish counterparts. Moreover, similar social separation in primary group relationships and communal life

98 Harte, op. cit., p. 164.
99 This figure is taken from a report released by the Commission for Catholic Missions Among the Colored People and the Indians and described in *The New York Times*, March 4, 1961.
100 Gunnar Myrdal, *An American Dilemma*, op. cit., pp. 870-71; Joseph H. Fichter, S.J., *Social Relations in the Urban Parish*, Chicago, University of Chicago Press, 1954, pp. 47-8, 117-19, 205; Harte, op. cit., pp. 172-4.

would appear to be the current lot of the three million or so[101] Catholics of Mexican and Spanish descent located primarily in the Southwest, and of the approximately 1,000,000 Puerto Ricans[102] residing principally in New York City, but also in other metropolitan centers of the Northeast and in Chicago.[103] Thus, with regard to the inclusion of racial and quasi-racial groupings, pan-Catholicism as a sociological goal has been largely unrealized.

Among the white Catholic groups of European and Canadian origin, however, the outcome has been somewhat different. Here, there is no doubt that some "melting" into a pan-Catholic society mediated into the general American scene by the Irish and their

---

[101] Estimates of the size of the Mexican and Mexican-American (including the Hispanos) population in the United States vary from 2,500,000 to 3,500,000 people. See George Eaton Simpson and J. Milton Yinger, *Racial and Cultural Minorities*, New York, Harper and Brothers, Rev. ed., 1958, p. 811; Charles F. Marden, *Minorities in American Society*, New York, American Book Co., 1952, p. 131; Edward C. McDonagh and Eugene S. Richards, *Ethnic Relations in the United States*, New York, Appleton-Century-Crofts, 1953, p. 174; John H. Burma, *Spanish Speaking Groups in the United States*, Durham, N.C., Duke University Press, 1954, p. 36.

[102] The Migration Division of the Puerto Rico Department of Labor estimated that 946,000 persons of Puerto Rican origin resided on the mainland at the end of 1960. See *The New York Times*, August 13, 1961.

[103] For information on the communal life and social separation of the Mexican-Americans, see Burma, op. cit., particularly pp. 72-99; Ruth D. Tuck, *Not with the Fist*, New York, Harcourt Brace, 1946, pp. 122-72; Glenn V. Ramsey and Beulah Hodge, "Anglo-Latin Problems as Perceived by Public Service Personnel," *Social Forces*, Vol. 37, No. 4 (May 1959), pp. 339-48; and Ozzie G. Simmons, "The Mutual Images and Expectations of Anglo-Americans and Mexican-Americans," *Daedalus, Journal of the American Academy of Arts and Sciences*, Spring, 1961, pp. 286-99.

For similar information on the Puerto Ricans, see C. Wright Mills, Clarence Senior, and Rose K. Goldsen, *The Puerto Rican Journey*, New York, Harper and Brothers, 1950; Christopher Rand, *The Puerto Ricans*, New York, Oxford University Press, 1958; Dan Wakefield, *Island in the City*, Boston, Houghton Mifflin, 1959; Oscar Handlin, *The Newcomers*, Cambridge, Harvard University Press, 1959, p. 49-117. An interesting phenomenon among the Puerto Ricans is the relatively successful inroads made by Protestant proselytizing.

descendants has taken place. The only question is, How much?
Even more specifically, How much and with what generations? In
the absence of research focused precisely on these questions we can
give only tentative answers. However, in a preliminary way, the picture may be painted with broad strokes.

The groups made up of the immigrants themselves, the first generation, did not melt but maintained their own respective communal subsystems and, as we have seen, held out for priests of their
own nationality background and language. The Roman Catholic
Church throughout a goodly portion of the nineteenth century was,
in effect, an Irish-American church within which were clusters of
German and French parishes. Geographic separation helped to
minimize conflict among church members at the parish level although it did not eliminate it in the struggle for power and representation at the level of the hierarchy. The arrival of the Southern
and Eastern European immigrants in the last two decades of the
nineteenth century and the first twenty-five years of the twentieth
century produced additional large ethnic islands of Italians, Poles,
Slovaks, etc., but the maturation of the acculturated native-born
descendants of the Irish and the German Catholics and their geographic and social mobility began to lessen the "social distance"
between these two groups. The problem of *choosing* types of structural and cultural behavior related to the assimilation process did
not develop for those of Southern and Eastern European stock until the native-born second generation had become adolescents and
young adults—roughly, not until the 1920's and 1930's. The problems attendant upon such choice have been described in varying
contexts for the Italian second generation in studies by Child,[104]
Whyte,[105] and Gans.[106]

[104] Irvin L. Child, *Italian or American? The Second Generation in Conflict*,
New Haven; Yale University Press, 1943.
[105] William Foote Whyte, *Street Corner Society, The Social Structure of an
Italian Slum*, Chicago, University of Chicago Press, 1943. See also his "A Slum

Child, whose primary focus is psychological, poses the problem for the second-generation Italian-American as that of which group to affiliate with and which set of cultural norms to follow, the Italian or the American. He distinguishes three psychological reaction-types: the "rebel," or movement in the direction of the American system; the "in-group," in which the tendency is to adhere to the Italian group and its values; and the "apathetic," which involves a retirement from the conflict and a minimizing of the fact and significance of nationality grouping. Curiously, Child does not appear to envisage the possible creation of a subsociety in which the second-generation Italians themselves, as later adults, might man the leadership and organizational posts and thus form an intermediate group between the dwindling first-generation group and the core society; nor does he take into consideration the role of pan-Catholicism. In a sociological sense, then, the study, valuable as it may be on the psychological level, does not shed much light on the questions we are interested in.

Whyte's classic study of second-generation Italian street corner gangs in an urban slum in the late 1930's is only incidentally concerned with assimilation and acculturation phenomena, but some light is thrown on these issues by his data and observations. Two "natural" groups of single, native-born males of Italian descent in their twenties are studied in detail: the Nortons, a group of lower-class boys, and the Italian Community Club, which has some overlap with the Nortons in membership but is made up primarily of Italian-American young men from the same area who have obtained a college education and are socially mobile. It is clear that in their cliquing, dating, and organizational activities, the Nortons confine their contacts almost entirely to second-generation Italian-

Sex Code," *American Journal of Sociology,*" Vol. 49, No. 1 (July 1943), pp. 24-31.
[106] Herbert J. Gans, *The Urban Villagers, Group and Class in the Life of Italian-Americans,* New York, The Free Press of Glencoe, 1962.

Americans, and even the college group appears to be only slightly less confined. There is no melting pot bubbling away here. Two qualifications must be made, however. First, Whyte's study is known to have been made in the most concentrated Italian section of "Eastern City"; thus, ecological factors alone would dictate ethnic closure in peer groups. There are other sections of the city where Italians live in close proximity to the Irish, and here the outcome in socializing might well be different.[107] Second, we do not know the outcome in structural affiliation for these young adult men subsequent to their marriage and absorption into the married adult community. Particularly if they moved out of the neighborhood, significant social contacts across nationality background lines might well have been formed.

The latest research report on Americans of Italian descent and the one most clearly focused on the sociological problems of interest to us is Gans's participant-observer study of the life of a second-generation working-class group of Italian descent living in the West End of Boston in the late 1950's.[108] While, in accordance with the aims and methods of the study, the results, for the most part, are not presented quantitatively, the following picture clearly emerges. These second-generation working-class Italian-Americans, now old enough to have families of their own, confine their meaningful social and institutional participation to other working-class Italian-Americans, largely of the same generation and the same neighborhood. Indeed, the description and discussion of the "peer group sociability" carried on in frequent informal evening home gatherings of collateral relatives of similar age and generational position together with a few close friends, constitutes one of the principal emphases of Gans's report. Culturally, Gans finds only a

[107] I am indebted to exploratory studies on the Italians in "Eastern City" carried out by Barbara Josephs, Nina Nathanson, and Collette Ramsey, in a Sociology Seminar at Wellesley College, 1959-60, for insights into the situation of the Italian-Americans in this community.
[108] Herbert J. Gans, *The Urban Villagers*, op. cit.

few traces of the immigrant Italian way of life left in these American-born semi-skilled and unskilled workers. They still prefer "Italian cooking" in their dietary habits and they retain a speaking knowledge of their particular Italian dialect as a second language, although their own children, the third generation, are not being taught the ancestral language and will grow up knowing only English. While the structural pattern of the "peer group society" is in many ways compatible with their ancestral Italian social patterns, this emphasis on peer group sociability, as Gans demonstrates, is a general working-class cultural pattern and not peculiarly Italian. In short, this second-generation working-class Italian-American group is ethnically (and class) enclosed, structurally, but overwhelmingly acculturated to an American working-class way of life. This study, of course, cannot tell us with assurance what will happen to the third generation, nor does it deal with the adjustments made by second-generation Italian-Americans who have been socially mobile into the middle class.

Probably the most pertinent available data on the extent of the trend toward pan-Catholicism within the white group pertain to intermarriage. Kennedy's study of intermarriage rates between various national origins and religious groups in New Haven from 1870 to 1950, already referred to, is the most thorough and allows for longitudinal analysis. Her basic finding, we recall, was the increasing trend toward the breaking down of national origins barriers in marriage, but the maintenance of religious lines—the "triple melting pot" effect in which interethnic marriages tended to take place within the three major religious "pools": Protestant, Catholic, and Jewish. But this important finding as to trend must be placed alongside the also important fact that the rate of in-marriage for certain national origins groups, while declining, was still high at the concluding point of her study. The in-marriage rate for Italians, a large ethnic group in New Haven, had fallen substantially from a high point in 1900 of 97.71 per cent, but in 1950 it was still as high as 76.70 per cent. In other words, as late as 1950, three-fourths of all persons of Italian descent in New Haven selected mates who were also of Italian descent. The 1950 in-marriage rate for persons of Irish descent was 50 per cent, and for Poles 40.74 per cent.[109] Hollingshead's study of intermarriage between various social categories in the same city in 1948, including data on the marriage choices of the respondents' parents, bears out Kennedy's findings in both instances. On the basis of his results, Hollingshead declared that "the Catholics are becoming a mixture of Irish, Polish, and Italian as a result of intermarriage between these groups, but there is still a large block of unmixed Italian stock in New Haven and smaller blocks of Irish and Polish."[110]

Fichter's studies of various aspects of Catholic life in parishes in a large southern city and what appears to be a medium-sized midwestern city include data on national origins intermixture; these data indicate that the process of ethnic merger within the boundaries of the Church has proceeded more rapidly outside the areas of heavy Catholic settlement in the Northeast and the large metropolitan areas of the Midwest. In the southern parish, only 42 per cent of his households contained spouses of the same nationality background,[111] and in his midwestern city parish, as few as 28 per cent of his sample of families were ethnically unmixed.[112] These studies, of course, do not tell us what is happening in this regard in such large midwestern cities as Chicago or Detroit.

It is clear from the data reviewed above that the process of creating a white all-Catholic subsociety out of the descendants of the

[109] Kennedy, "Single or Triple Melting-Pot? Intermarriage in New Haven, 1879-1950," p. 56.
[110] August B. Hollingshead, "Cultural Factors in the Selection of Marriage Mates," *American Sociological Review*, Vol. 15, No. 5 (October 1950), p. 624.
[111] Joseph H. Fichter, S.J., *Southern Parish: Vol. I, Dynamics of a City Church*, Chicago, University of Chicago Press, 1951, p. 27.
[112] Joseph H. Fichter, S.J., *Parochial School: A Sociological Study*, Notre Dame, Ind., University of Notre Dame Press, 1958, p. 438.

various immigrant nationalities has begun, and in some types of communities has made considerable headway. But it is perhaps too early to read the "nationalities" out of the picture entirely. The structures of these ethnic subsocieties—that is, their organizations, institutions, newspapers, formal and informal gathering places, and informal network of social cliques, still remain, even if in attenuated form.[113] What we do not know in significant quantitative form, and need clearly focused research to find out, is to what degree the members of the second and third generations participate in the social structure of the national origins subsociety and come to man its command posts as the old immigrant generation dies out. Warner and his associates, on the basis of their studies in several small communities, have advanced the proposition that the pull of the American class system tends to loosen the ties of the ethnic person to his ethnic collectivity, so that as he rises in class status—particularly as he reaches the upper-middle class—he is drawn into association with the general American community of similar class background.[114] However, this hypothesis fails to emphasize two important points: 1) city size and its consequence, the size of the ethnic community itself, which, in some cases, is large enough to develop an upper-middle or even upper class within itself that is made up of others of the same ethnic background, and 2) the rise of the religious subsociety (e.g., white pan-Catholic), as a solvent rather than the "Old American" subsociety. It is certain that in most large urban concentrations, the Catholic population as a whole is large enough and sufficiently diverse occupation-

[113] I am indebted to students in my Sociology Seminar at Wellesley College, 1959-60, for valuable exploratory studies into these "nationality" subsocieties (Catholic, Protestant, and Orthodox) in "Eastern City." Besides the three students mentioned in footnote 107, the following contributed papers: Lucy Davis, Linda Fleger, Tamsen Knowlton, Anne Moffat, Nancy Norris, Margaret Rives, and Cynthia Simon.

[114] Warner and Srole, op. cit.; W. Lloyd Warner, *American Life*, Chicago: University of Chicago Press, 1953, p. 170-71, and Warner and Associates, *Democracy in Jonesville*, New York: Harper, 1949, Chapter 11.

ally to be able theoretically to develop Catholic-confined institutions at all class levels. In view of the trends adduced above, it would seem that the development of a white Catholic subsociety in which national origins will become of increasingly minor importance is likely to be the dominant outcome, although the completion of this developmental stage is still some distance away.

The above considerations pose pertinent questions relating to the socio-economic position of Catholics in American society, and the development of class differentiation and parallel, class-confined institutions within the Catholic group. Historically, after an initial brief period when the small number of Catholics in Federal America were led and signified by well-established English families in Maryland and other Middle Atlantic states, and by English and French priests, Roman Catholicism in the United States has been predominantly the religious institution of the impoverished immigrant manual laborer, especially the Irish, and later the Italians and Slavs. Gradually, the descendants of these immigrants, very much in the order of their ancestral arrival, began to work their way up the American ladder of social opportunity. By the end of the first third of the twentieth century, a few had made substantial fortunes which allowed them to aspire to an upper-class way of life, a larger but still small number had become upper-middle-class professionals and business men, and entrance into the lower-middle class of white collar and highly skilled manual workers had been accomplished on a scale of some magnitude.[115] The business boom which accompanied World War II and continued into the post-war period saw Catholics share significantly in the socio-economic gains made by most segments of the American population during this recent era. At the present time, then, while American Catholics as a whole are still concentrated in the lower part of the class structure, particularly the upper-lower and lower-middle sectors, to a greater extent than Jews or all white Protestants com-

[115] See Warner and Srole, op. cit., pp. 1-102.

bined (although their class distribution appears to be remarkably similar to that of the Baptists, except for a rural-urban difference), there are now large numbers of Catholic college graduates engaged in business and professional careers and living a general upper-middle-class style of life, as well as an increasing number who have the wealth and social ambition to project definitely upper-class life styles.[116] The result has been the development of Catholic institutions, organizations, and primary group life appropriate to, and in a *de facto* way, confined to, the upper levels of the class structure and paralleling the social structure at these class levels already developed among Protestants and Jews, respectively.

It is regrettable that there are as yet no substantial and clearly focused sociological studies of the development of Catholic upper-class institutions in America. Those few studies of "typical" Catholic parishes which have appeared,[117] though they include discussions of the role of social class, are precluded from study of the upper reaches of the Catholic social structure by the very nature of their population selection. The following brief glimpse, then, into this sector of Catholic life is based on several interviews which I carried out with key Catholic individuals in the Boston area, on an exploratory study of upper-class institutions in Boston executed by one of my students,[118] perusal of the "society" pages of The

[116] For confirmation of the points made in this paragraph, see, in addition to Warner and Srole, op. cit., John J. Kane, "The Social Structure of American Catholics," *The American Catholic Sociological Review*, Vol. 16, No. 1 (March 1955), pp. 23-30; Liston Pope, "Religion and the Class Structure," *Annals of the American Academy of Political and Social Science*, Vol. 256, March 1948, pp. 84-91; Will Herberg, *Protestant—Catholic—Jew*, op. cit., Chapter 9, pp. 227-46; David Goldberg and Harry Sharp, "Some Characteristics of Detroit Area Jewish and Non-Jewish Adults," op. cit.
[117] In addition to the studies of Joseph H. Fichter, S.J., already mentioned, there is Joseph B. Schuyler, S.J., *Northern Parish*, Chicago, Loyola University Press, 1960.
[118] Nancy Norris, "A Description of Assimilation into Boston Society," Term Paper, Sociology Seminar, Wellesley College, 1959-60.

New York Times and the *Boston Herald* for an extended period, scanning of *The Pilot,* the weekly official newspaper of the Archdiocese of Boston, for over a year, and on referral to such published materials as may be relevant, particularly Baltzell's study of the upper class of Philadelphia.

Of primary importance is the fact that Catholics have begun to develop a network of private academies, both day and boarding, and fashionable colleges, which enroll the children of Catholic families who have attained upper-middle-class status or higher. These private schools, it must be emphasized, exist in clear distinction from the parochial schools; the latter are official units of the parish and the diocese, and serve as mass educational institutions for Catholic children of lower and middle socio-economic position; the former are usually created and staffed by various Religious Orders of the Church, particularly, in the case of the girls' schools, Orders of French derivation, and are usually small and aristocratically oriented. Thus, in the Boston area, fashionable or socially mobile Catholic girls, if they do not go to secular or Protestant institutions, may be sent to the Academy of the Sacred Heart in Newton, and then on to the College of the Sacred Heart in the same suburban area. In the New York City environs, they can choose between Marymount College or Manhattanville College of the Sacred Heart, among others, and in Washington, they will probably be sent to Trinity College, one of the most aristocratic and nationally oriented of them all. Upper-class Catholic boys may prep at two fashionable New England boarding schools, Portsmouth Priory and Canterbury, which parallel Groton and St. Paul's, and then, if they eschew Harvard, Princeton, or Yale, are likely to be found at Notre Dame University, where they can date Catholic girls of comparable status at nearby St. Mary's College, or at Georgetown University, which is conveniently located in the same community as Trinity. It is clear, then, that one of the latent functions of this upper-class Catholic educational system is to separate, at a crucial time in the socialization and dating processes, upper-class Catholic adolescents from, on the one hand, lower- and lower-middle-class Catholics, and on the other hand, Protestants and Jews of a class background comparable to their own.

Even more recent than the development of the fashionable private school and college is the rise of the Catholic debutante ball. It would appear that a few Catholic families, mostly of English and French descent, have participated in the "general" American upper class from the very beginning. This participation varied from city to city, being particularly strong in Baltimore and New Orleans, and perhaps particularly weak in the old established aristocracies of Boston and Philadelphia which traditionally have been almost exclusively Protestant. However, the rise in social and economic position of families of Irish, and most recently, Italian descent, created a whole new set of conditions—conditions which the established institutions of the Protestant upper class were either unwilling or unable to meet. Consequently, in parallel fashion to the "general" upper-class debut ball, there has developed the Catholic upper-class debut ball. Thus, in New York, at the annual Gotham Ball, Catholic debutantes are formally presented to Cardinal Spellman, and the financial proceeds of the ball are donated to a worthy Catholic charity. In Boston, the St. Nicholas Cotillion, with Cardinal Cushing officiating, performs the same function. In addition, in Boston, the Colony Ball, privately sponsored, is principally for Catholic debutantes, although a few Protestant girls may also be invited.

In Boston, fashionable Catholic women, primarily of Irish, but also of Italian and other national origins, are likely to belong to the Ace of Clubs, which parallels the "proper Bostonian" Chilton Club in the general upper-class institutional system. Upper-class and upper-middle-class women are likely to work for the Church through the League of Catholic Women; upper-class Irish Catholic men may affiliate with the Clover Club; and upper- and upper-middle-class Catholic men of whatever national origins may well be found in the Serra Club, an international Catholic club which parallels Rotary.

The development of Catholic private academies, fashionable colleges, debutante balls, and relatively exclusive men's and women's clubs does not necessarily signify, of course, that all upper-class and upper-middle-class Catholics make use of these institutions, nor that some interreligious contact does not take place at the primary group level among the upper classes. For one thing, many Catholics from the upper part of the class structure send their children to nonsectarian or Protestant oriented fashionable schools and colleges where they are bound to fraternize to some degree with non-Catholics. Nevertheless, the development of a vigorous institutional life at the upper-class levels of American Catholicism clearly indicates that there will be increasing opportunity for those economically and socially favored Catholics who wish to do so to confine primary group contacts and sources of cultural influence, for themselves and for their children, to those individuals and institutions which share *both* their religious affiliation and their socio-economic position.

The general question of the degree of Catholic "separatism" from Protestants and Jews in primary group relationships is one not easily answered by existing research. Again, as in the case of upper-class Catholic institutions, one can easily discover that the institutional world of Catholic communal life is extensive, bustling, and growing in scope. As Will Herberg has forcefully described the situation:

The Catholic Church in America operates a vast network of institutions of almost every type and variety. The social and recreational activities in the Catholic parish—from baseball teams to sewing circles, from bowling leagues to religious study groups—are only a beginning. Every interest, activity, and function of the Catholic faithful is provided with some Catholic institution and furnished with Catholic direction. There are Catholic hospitals, homes, and orphanages; Catholic schools and colleges; Catholic charities and welfare agencies; Catholic Boy Scouts and War Veterans; Catholic associations of doctors, lawyers, teachers, students, and philosophers; Catholic leagues of policemen, firemen, and sanitary workers; Catholic luncheon clubs and recreation fellowships; there is the Catholic Youth Organization, with some six million members; there is even a Catholic Audio-Visual Educators Association. This immense system constitutes at one and the same time a self-contained Catholic world with its own complex interior economy and American Catholicism's resources of participation in the larger American community.[119]

The existence of this vast network of communal institutions is indisputable. What is more difficult to determine is what percentage of American Catholics make use of it and to what degree, whether exclusively, predominantly, equally with other institutional systems, minimally, or not at all. We know from the researches of Fichter that the formal parochial societies engage the active participation of only a small percentage of parishioners. But Fichter also testifies to the growing importance of the supraparochial and even supradiocesan Catholic societies based on common interests and common vocation,[120] and his research on the parochial school system demonstrates the substantial effect which the financing and directing of extracurricular activities such as sports and other recreation, not to speak of the Parent-Teachers' Association or the Catholic-equivalent Home and School Association, have in bringing Catholic parents of parochial school children into communal association.[121]

[119] Herberg, op. cit., pp. 168-9.
[120] Fichter, *Social Relations in the Urban Parish*, Chapter 11, pp. 138-53.
[121] Fichter argues that many of these activities also bring Catholic parents into contact with members of other faiths in city-wide and regional meetings of the various organizations. It would appear, however, that most of these latter contacts are of a frequency and type which make them secondary rather than primary relationships. See Fichter, *Parochial School: A Sociological Study*, Chapter 17, pp. 427-53.

Precise quantitative data on the extent of primary group relationships between Catholics and non-Catholics in cliques and other
close friendship relationships are exceedingly scarce. In Lenski's
sample of white Catholics in Detroit, 44 per cent reported that all
or nearly all of their close friends were Catholic.[122] On the basis of
this figure, Lenski classifies the "communal bond" among white
Catholics as "medium" in strength, comparing the figure with the
comparable percentage for Jews of 77 per cent, and for white
Protestants of 38 per cent. Fichter, on the basis of his study of
three southern white parishes, reports "close, cordial, and multiple"
social relations of Catholics with non-Catholics of their own social
class level, but presents no exact figures.[123] The same investigator,
however, in his study of a midwestern parochial school, provides
data on the friendship patterns of Catholic school children which
are highly suggestive. All pupils from the parochial elementary
school are compared with Catholic pupils attending the same
grades in a nearby public school on the question of the religion of
their three best friends. Approximately 50 per cent of the parochial
school children have only Catholics as their three best friends. This
compares with a figure of 2 per cent having all Catholic "best
friends" for the Catholic pupils in the public school. Of the parochial school children, 31 per cent named two Catholics in their
group of three best friends, in comparison with 11 per cent of the
public school Catholic children who fall into this category. Cumu-
latively, these figures show that over 80 per cent of the parochial
school children had either all Catholics, or two Catholics out of
three, as their three best friends, while the comparable figure for
Catholic children in the public schools was approximately 13 per
cent.[124]

[122] Lenski, op. cit., pp. 35-6. This sample of self-identified Catholics undoubtedly
includes many whom Fichter would call "marginal" and "dormant" Catholics.
[123] Fichter, *Social Relations in the Urban Parish*, p. 49.
[124] Fichter, *Parochial School: A Sociological Study*, p. 222. The investigator
goes on to make the following significant observation: "The [parochial school]

One of the ultimately decisive criteria of communality is the intermarriage rate. Hollingshead found a rate of Catholic intermarriage with other faiths (in New Haven in 1948) as low as 6.2 per cent,[125] while Kennedy's study reported a religious intermarriage rate of 27.4 per cent for Catholics of Italian, Irish, and Polish extraction in the same community in 1950.[126] Thomas, on the basis of diocesan records cumulated for the nation, found that Catholic marriages to non-Catholics which were sanctioned by Catholic nuptials in the decade 1940 to 1950 approached 30 per cent of all Catholic marriages.[127] This figure does not, of course, include Catholic mixed marriages not sanctioned by the Church. Thomas also reports that the Catholic intermarriage rate fluctuates widely from community to community, varying inversely with the percentage of Catholics in the total population and the presence of cohesive national origins groups, and positively with the socioeconomic status of the Catholic population in the area.[128] The sample survey of the American population made by the Bureau of the Census in 1957 found a rate of *existing* Catholic mixed marriages of 22 per cent.[129] The difference between Thomas's figure of 30 per cent and the latter figure might well indicate the approximate magnitude of the rate of conversion of one of the spouses to the faith of the other. In fact, some data of Lenski's for Detroit white Protestants and white Catholics combined indicate how

children who have non-Catholic playmates are mainly those in the lower grades of St. Luke's school, but there are also a few in the upper grades, mainly pupils who have transferred from a public school."
[125] Hollingshead, "Cultural Factors in the Selection of Marriage Mates," p. 622.
[126] Kennedy, "Single or Triple Melting-Pot? Intermarriage in New Haven, 1870-1950," p. 57.
[127] John L. Thomas, "The Factor of Religion in the Selection of Marriage Mates," *American Sociological Review*, Vol. 16, No. 4 (August 1951), p. 488.
[128] Ibid., pp. 489-91.
[129] United States Department of Commerce, Bureau of the Census, *Current Population Reports: Population Characteristics*, Series P-20, No. 79, February 2, 1958, p. 2, and Table 6, p. 8.

frequent the conversion process may be and how it may be trending. Of this combined sample, 85 per cent reported that they and their spouses were of the same major faith, but only 68 per cent, it was discovered, had been reared in the same religion. Furthermore, among the members of the third generation, born in the North, who had contracted marriages of mixed faith there appeared to be a greater tendency toward conversion of one spouse to the faith of the other than among the comparable first and second-generation members of the sample. Not only is conversion of spouses in mixed marriages quite extensive, then, but, as Lenski notes, it increases with increasing Americanization.[130] These last points should alert the observer to pose the question of whether interfaith marriage in American society today serves as an effective bridge between the major religious groups or simply as a preliminary step to the entrance of the intermarried couple into the sub-society of one or the other of the faiths of the spouses. Current research on intermarriage in the United States tells us little or nothing about the answer to this query.

Our final point concerns the acculturation of white Catholics in America. With regard to extrinsic culture traits, it is a matter of commonplace observation that the descendants of the Irish and other Northern European Catholic immigrants of the nineteenth century are indistinguishable in appearance and manner from core group members of the same class, and the descendants of the later arrivals from Southern and Eastern Europe are rapidly approaching this acculturation stage. In this process, attributable in essence to the overwhelming attraction of American core culture for the native-born generation of whatever ethnic background, the history of the Roman Catholic Church and America and the modifications which it, itself, has undergone in the light of American conditions, have played an important role.[131] The dominant

---

[130] Lenski, op. cit., pp. 49-50.
[131] I draw here upon the persuasive discussion of these modifications by Herberg, op. cit., Chapter 7, pp. 150-85.

national origins group in the Church from the middle of the nineteenth century to the present time has been the Irish, an English-speaking people who were able to play a mediating role between the later-arriving foreign-language groups, on the one hand, and American society and culture, on the other. Efforts to fragment the Church in America along diocesan lines on a national origins basis ("Cahenslyism"—so called for the German promoter of the scheme), which would have effectively retarded the development of an English-language pan-Catholicism, were decisively defeated in the late nineteenth century by firm ecclesiastical action. (From this point of view, ecclesiastical sanction of the "national parish," a more modest step, turns out in retrospect to have been an inspired "middle ground" position which met the needs of the immigrants themselves without compromising the future needs of their descendants.) The development of the American Church along activist lines corresponding to the American ethos, its fusion with American nationalism in the minds of its adherents, the modification of its traditional and formal position on the desirability of state "establishment" of Catholicism under American conditions, the *de facto* acceptance of, and empirical comfortableness with, the pluralistic nature of American religious life with its "three great religions of Democracy"—all of these developments, as Herberg has noted, represent modifications in traditional Catholic orientations which reflect the nature of the pervasive social forces emanating from American life and conditions, and constitute a measure of the substantial degree of acculturation which the institutionalized Catholic Church has undergone in America.

The foregoing does not deny or attempt to minimize in any way the significant value conflicts in the area of civic life which exist today between faithful Catholics and most other Americans. These conflicts center, for the most part, around the crucial issues of birth control, divorce, and public support for private schools. There are signs, however, that even in these areas the pull of non-Catholic American values is strong and, particularly on the divorce and birth control issues, may account in part for the rather substantial defection or "leakage" from the ranks of active Catholic parishioners.[132] With regard to the general question of intrinsic culture traits, both the evidence and the interpretations vary as to the extent and significance of differences between Catholics and non-Catholics, and the degree of success of the Catholic subsociety in fostering specific Catholic values. One strategy for studying this question has been to compare Catholics who have had parochial school training with Catholics who have been educated in the public schools, as well as with Protestants and other Americans; this strategy rests on the assumption that the attitudes and behavior of parochial school Catholics are more likely to constitute a measure of the success of the Catholic effort to inculcate Catholic values in members of the faith. The Rossis, after surveying several studies of this nature carried out on adults, mostly in New England, conclude that:

We have been unable to find strong evidence that parochial-school Catholics are very different from other Catholics. The influence of the school is shown most dramatically in areas where the Church has traditionally taken a strong stand, for example, on support for religious education, or on the performance of ritual duties. In other areas of life the parochial-school Catholic is only marginally differentiated from other Catholics."[133]

Fishman, after an analysis of many studies of various types on Catholic school children, comes to an even more negative conclusion on the effect of Catholic schooling in developing distinctive values among its representatives: "Thus it seems," he declares, "that the child arrives at the Catholic parochial school with already established attitudes and needs in relation to his total American environment, and that the school itself is not strong enough to

[132] See Fichter, *Social Relations in the Urban Parish*, Chapters 5 and 6, pp. 56-79.
[133] Peter H. and Alice S. Rossi, "Some Effects of Parochial School Education in America," *Daedalus, Journal of the American Academy of Arts and Sciences*, Spring, 1961, p. 324.

change these attitudes, even when it regards change as desirable." And he adds: "The tireless efforts of Catholic leaders to employ parochial education to transmit the deep philosophical and religious differences which separate Catholicism from American Protestantism and from secularism have been most consistently embarrassed by the strivings of Catholic parents, young people, and children."[134]

Fichter, too, in his study of a midwestern parish, found few differences between Catholic parochial elementary school children in the upper grades and comparable public school children of all faiths. On the California Test of Personality, which includes such subsections as "social standards," "freedom from anti-social tendencies," and "family relations," there were virtually no differences between the two sets of children. On other tests dealing with current social issues, he found the parochial school children scoring in the more liberal (as conventionally defined) and humanitarian direction in attitudes on such subjects as "refugees," "foreign aid," and "labor unions." (The differences were small, averaging about four percentage points.) When asked to choose their favorite movie and TV stars, the parochial school choices were, in order, Tab Hunter, John Wayne, and Debbie Reynolds, while the public school children chose Tab Hunter, John Wayne, and Rock Hudson, the latter a group of choices which, while monotonously male, hardly seem distinguishable in any other way from the parochial school favorites. Both sets of students also selected as the greatest persons in history, in the same order, George Washington, Abraham Lincoln, and Christopher Columbus. However, when asked to name the "greatest men living today," the parochial students chose Pope Pius XII, President Eisenhower, and Cardinal Mindzenty, while the public school group selected, in addition to President

134 Joshua A. Fishman, "Childhood Indoctrination for Minority-Group Membership," *Daedalus, Journal of the American Academy of Arts and Sciences,* Spring, 1961, p. 337.

Eisenhower, Vice President Nixon and Elvis Presley! On the whole, the picture presented is one of rather substantial similarity in values and tastes on the part of the two groups of children in the face of the general stimuli emanating from American popular culture.[135]

On the other hand, Lenski, in his Detroit study, found significant differences between white Catholics and white Protestants (even with social class controlled) in attitudes toward a complex of economic, political, familial, and educational issues related to economic and social mobility, authority and freedom, and civil rights and liberties. What is more, he found that some of these differences were accentuated by a Catholic parochial school education, and were greater in the middle class, the third generation, and urban groups, representing future trends among the American population, than in other social categories.[136] It is difficult to say in the absence of additional strategic comparative research, whether the difference in results and conclusions in the studies and interpretations reviewed briefly above are due to differences in the time or place of their undertaking, differences in methodology, or to other variables. To this observer, however, it would appear that although value conflict and variation in statistically significant degree on selected value-issues unquestionably exist between Catholics and non-Catholics in the United States, the degree of similarity in values, as a reflection of the similar response to the common stimuli of American mass culture, constitutes at least an equally significant phenomenon.

A NOTE ON WHITE PROTESTANTS

If Negroes, Puerto Ricans, Mexican-Americans, Jews, and white Catholics are, in varying but significant degree, involved in the

[135] Fichter, *Parochial School: A Sociological Study*, pp. 109-31, 442-6, and 452-3.
[136] Lenski, op. cit., *passim*, and p. 291.

communal institutions and cliques of their own subsocieties, it is clear that, by a process of reduction, the white Protestants must, to some extent, be doing the same. Thus, what is usually referred to as "general American society" turns out in reality, insofar as communal institutions and primary group relations are concerned, to be a white Protestant social world, colored and infused with the implicit assumptions of this particular ethnic group. To be sure, it is the largest ethnic group in the United States, and like other large ethnic groups it is divided in major fashion by social class.[137] Denominational, rural-urban (unlike Jews and white Catholics, white Protestants are significantly represented in the rural population), and regional differences also play a role in dividing the Protestant group, although this role is a distinctly minor one; furthermore, Protestant denominationalism tends to be structured along class lines[138] so that its additional divisiveness, except for isolated rural enclaves, is negligible.

Essentially, then, the important fact is that Protestants are distributed throughout the class system, and it is the intersection of Protestant ethnicity with social class that forms the boundaries of the communal system within which Protestant primary group relations tend to be confined. For example, upper-middle-class white Protestants who form the bulk of the resident commuter population in such suburban communities as Ardmore, Pennsylvania, Scarsdale, New York, Short Hills, New Jersey, or Wellesley, Massachusetts, would appear to be as closely articulated and easily recognizable a communal group as most such groups in America. In this connection two types of data may be cited. As already noted, in Lenski's Detroit study, 38 per cent of the white Protestants declared that all or nearly all of their close friends were also Protestant.[139] This is not a startlingly large figure, although it indicates

---

[137] For analyses of the "general" American class system, see the works cited in Chapter 2, ft. 16 and the discussion on pp. 40-47.
[138] Liston Pope, op. cit.
[139] Lenski, op. cit., pp. 35-6.

that nearly four out of ten white Protestants in the sample were "communally" enclosed in primary relations. We are not told how this tendency varies by class, and, of course, we do not know what the figure would be for communities where other variables obtained. To this information, moreover, should be added other data from Lenski's study. Of the white Protestant group, 76 per cent reported that all or nearly all of their close relatives were also Protestant, and 73 per cent of the group had married someone raised as a Protestant, while 86 per cent were currently married to someone of the Protestant faith.[140] In the Bureau of the Census sample survey of the entire adult American population, carried out in 1957, the Protestant rate of what may be called "current religiously homogeneous marriages" was over 91 per cent. This figure was only slightly below the Jewish rate of 93 per cent and was substantially above the comparable Roman Catholic rate of 78.5 per cent.[141] White Protestants, of course, being the largest ethnic group in America, the culturally dominant group, and the group whose historical role has the greatest degree of popularly accorded legitimation, can afford to be relaxed about their own communalism, indeed, as seems frequently to be the case, can even afford to be unaware of it; but to an objective observer, the difference in communalism in relation to other ethnic groups is a difference not in kind, but only in degree.

It is worth noting that Protestant communalism has probably increased over the past few decades, partly at least, as a result of the vigorous—even aggressive—growth in the institutional life of the other religious denominations. In this connection, it is instructive to consider that many national organizations, presumably of a community-wide nature and originally instituted within such a framework, have become religiously (not to mention racially) frag-

[140] Lenski, op. cit., p. 35.
[141] United States Department of Commerce, Bureau of the Census, op. cit., Table 6, p. 8.

mented at the local level in recent years. Two salient examples are the Boy Scouts of America and the Girl Scouts of the United States of America.[142] A generation or so ago, boys and girls who joined these organizations in their local communities were likely to find themselves participating in troops organized on an all-community basis (even when, in some cases, under Protestant church auspices) and thus to be thrown together with young people of faiths other than their own. In the mid 1930's, Catholic officials and the Catholic Youth Organization accepted Scouting as a part of the Church's program for its young people on the basis of arrangements under which sponsorship of local troops would be undertaken by Catholic institutions and such troops would be considered as reserved primarily for Catholic boys and girls. The Scouting organizations, anxious to spread the principles of their respective movements, have (separately and in varying ways) acceded to arrangements of this type. There are now many Scouting groups sponsored by Protestant and Catholic Churches and Jewish synagogues, as well as by YMCA's, YMHA's, parochial schools, Jewish community centers, and other sectarian groups. The percentage of religious sponsorship in Scouting has steadily risen; well over 50 per cent of all Boy Scout troops are now under some form of sectarian sponsorship and about a quarter of all Girl Scout troops are so organized.[143] It is true that some religiously sponsored troops con-

[142] I draw here upon two exploratory research projects carried out by my students in a Wellesley College Sociology Seminar in 1959-60 (one on the Boy Scouts by Jean LeMatty, the other on the Girl Scouts by Florence Craig), and also on research reports based on interviews with Scouting officials carried out by Martha M. Gordon during 1959. Other members of the Sociology Seminar who contributed useful reports on the relationship of ethnicity to organizational life were Abby Alt, Linda Fleger, Susann Hayes, Joan Kaplan, Collette Ramsey, and Susan Ruppert.

[143] For Boy Scouts (1959) see official table, Classification of Scout Units by Chartered Institutions, provided by Boy Scouts headquarters and inserted in paper by Jean LeMatty cited above. For Girl Scouts, see "Girl Scouting and Religious Groups" (pamphlet), Girl Scouts of the U.S.A.

tain members of more than one faith and that all-community and regional activities bring some Scouts together from different troops (although most of the latter type of activity would seem to be of a secondary rather than a primary group nature). However, the basic trend in Scouting would appear to be *de facto* religious separation at the local level, a phenomenon which both derives from and reinforces religious communalism at the adult level.

THE INTELLECTUALS

It is my hypothesis that intellectuals in the United States interact in such patterned ways as to form at least the elementary structure of a subsociety of their own, and that this subsociety is the only one in American life in which people of different ethnic backgrounds interact in primary group relations with considerable frequency and with relative comfort and ease. Research which would definitively prove or disprove this hypothesis does not exist. The intellectuals have discussed themselves and their role with abiding passion,[144] but empirical studies of intellectuals which would be related to the verification of our thesis are few and far between. Those that have been found will be mentioned briefly below. But first some remarks on a definition of the term "intellectuals" are in order.

Intellectuals are "people for whom ideas, concepts, literature, music, painting, the dance have intrinsic meaning—are a part of the social-psychological atmosphere which one breathes."[145] Occupationally, they are characteristically found in the professions, particularly college teaching, research, and the upper reaches of journalism (to a lesser degree, law and medicine), and in the arts,

---

[144] See George B. de Huszar (ed.), *The Intellectuals: A Controversial Portrait*, Glencoe, Ill., The Free Press, 1960.
[145] Milton M. Gordon, "Social Class and American Intellectuals," *American Association of University Professors Bulletin*, Vol. 40, No. 4 (Winter, 1954-55), pp. 518-19.

either as creators or performers. If they are engaged in business, they are likely to be in communications or publishing. Not all persons in each of these occupational categories are intellectuals, and intellectuals will at times be found in other occupations. The academic world of teaching and research, supplemented now by the world of the Foundation, which either carries out or commissions research, is the most salient concentration point of the intellectual life, and this becomes increasingly so as writers, artists, and musicians begin to take on the role of faculty members and "artists-in-residence," alongside professors of the humanities and the natural and social sciences.

As Lipset has noted, the number of intellectuals in the United States is now so great and this number is so dispersed over the vast geographical area of the country, that it is impossible for the American intellectual, in contrast to his counterpart in some European countries, to know personally more than a tiny fraction of his peers.[146] There are about 9000 college and university teachers in the Boston area alone, 14,000 or so in northern California centered on the San Francisco area, over 20,000 in and around New York City.[147] By the same token, however, this abundance of academics should make it apparent that the numbers which make an enclosed communal social life possible are unmistakably present. The intellectual world, furthermore, because of its wide array of different occupational specializations, is more like a loose network of subgroups with varying degrees of articulated social relations between them than a tightly integrated enclave. People in the theater, for instance—playrights, directors, and actors—form a closely knit group, as do those in the dance, in the visual arts, and so on. Even college professors (though this varies considerably with the per-

---

[146] Seymour Martin Lipset, "American Intellectuals: Their Politics and Status," *Daedalus, Journal of the American Academy of Arts and Sciences,* Summer, 1959, pp. 470-72.
[147] Lipset, op. cit., p. 470.

sonality of the individual) in the larger universities are likely to form a large part of their friendships along departmental or divisional lines.

As we pointed out earlier, any subsociety is likely to be composed of numerous subcommunities, each geographically located in a particular area, whose personnel are interchangeable. Therefore, the geographical dispersion of intellectuals by no means argues against the existence of an intellectual community. Furthermore, the abundant reading which intellectuals engage in, either as a part of their occupational role or their avocational interests, tends to create a common framework of leadership, reference groups, and conventions of discourse. For instance, most intellectuals read what is, in effect, the national newspaper of the intellectuals—*The New York Times*; they read it selectively but they read it either daily or Sunday, and they have some idea from the Book Review of what books are being written, from the drama section of what plays are being produced, from the music section of what orchestras, conductors, artists, and ensembles are appearing in New York, and from the news section, of what the current serious national and international events and controversies may be. The magazines on their coffee tables, apart from the professional journals they read, are likely to be selected, according to taste and interest, from *Harper's, The Atlantic Monthly, The New Yorker, The Reporter, Commentary, The Saturday Review, Daedalus, Consumer Reports,* the literary quarterlies, and a few others. If they have a television set ("for the children") they turn it on, themselves, only rarely to watch Leonard Bernstein, the Play of the Week, or the contemporary equivalent of Omnibus. If they are musically inclined, they will turn on their Hi-Fi sets to listen to solid classical music, either in orchestral or chamber music form, or to good jazz, or to both, but to nothing in between. They buy and read, if somewhat harriedly, books, not only in their professional fields, but also of a general nature such as biography, history, and analyses of current events. In other words, they bypass to a very large degree the popular culture which makes up the mass communications stimuli received with bemused attention, although somewhat selectively according to social class, by the rest of American society. I have argued elsewhere that, from the point of view of status position and the ordinary amenities of life style, the intellectuals fall within the ranks of the upper-middle class.[148] Even so, their basic frame of reference, outside these ordinary amenities, is likely to be not the frame of reference of the other members of the upper-middle class, but that which is peculiar to them as intellectuals. Thus, when intellectuals meet, they recognize each other and can communicate easily with one another, just as a lower-middle-class white Protestant non-intellectual, to take just one of a number of possible examples, recognizes and speaks with confidence and an awareness of common assumptions to another person who shares both his ethnic and his class background.

Intellectuals, of course, like other individuals have ethnic backgrounds and some of them do not venture beyond the ethnic fold. The man of ideas and the arts is a Negro, a Jew, an Irish or Italian Catholic, or something else.[149] As the culturally assimilating forces of the American social class system exert pressures which bring him into contact with persons of different ethnic but the same social class position, the containing walls of ethnic communality are threatened—but not necessarily broken. The intellectual, because his interests are sharper and rarer, simply faces this conflict in a more acute form than do others. On the basis of his resolution of the conflict and the personality style which significantly influences it, we may distinguish three "ideal types" of response to the dual pressures of ethnicity and intellectualism. The representatives of

[148] Gordon, "Social Class and American Intellectuals," op. cit.
[149] The discussion and typology contained in the following few paragraphs is taken, mostly verbatim, from my article, "Social Class and American Intellectuals," op. cit. (by permission).

these three types may be called "the actively ethnic intellectual," "the passively ethnic intellectual," and "the marginally ethnic intellectual."

The "actively ethnic intellectual" remains within his ethnic group and focuses his intellectual interests precisely on his ethnicity. He is the cultural historian of the group, the theologian, the communal leader, the apologist, the scholar of its art, its music, and its literature. While he maintains a respectable acquaintanceship with the broader ideological currents and events around him, his primary interests and passions are reserved for the racial, religious, or nationality background ethos in which he considers his roots to be firmly placed. His is a confident approach, and he appears to be spared many of the problems of marginality. He may be a white Protestant as well as a member of a minority, since white Protestants are simply the largest American ethnic group.

The "passively ethnic intellectual" is the second distinguishable type. Finding it easier, safer, or more in line with his personality style, this individual remains predominantly within the subsocietal boundaries of his ethnic group and social class. If he is a Negro, most of his friends may be intellectuals but they will also be Negroes. If he is a Jew, he confines his friendships primarily to other Jewish intellectuals. While his interests are mostly of the broader, nonethnic variety, he gratifies them within the borders of ethnic communality. Occasionally, he looks wistfully beyond the ethnic boundaries at other intellectuals but he is not moved, or not able, to cross these boundaries in any substantial sense.

The "marginally ethnic intellectual" is, from our point of view, the most interesting and the most significant type. It is he who enters and makes up the intellectual subsociety. As the appellation indicates, he wears his ethnicity lightly, if not in his own eyes at least in the eyes of the world. Whatever his social psychology, he finds ethnic communality unsatisfactory and takes his friends, and probably even his spouse, where he finds them, so long as they share his fascination with Kafka and his passion for Heinrich Schuetz. To other, more conventional ethnics he is very occasionally a traitor, sometimes a snob, not infrequently, in Lewin's term, a "leader from the periphery." Mostly they let him alone; if he is successful, they will claim him—and he will be pleased by their claim.

In the absence of relevant research, it is impossible at this time to specify the relative numerical strength of these three types of intellectuals either as a whole or in relationship to particular ethnic groups. We would hypothesize that Type 1 is numerically small but relatively stable in proportion to the size of the ethnic group; that Type 2 is larger in numbers but tends to be unstable in size and composition as the resources of the ethnic community are increasingly perceived by the intellectually inclined ethnic group member as inadequate for his needs. According to this hypothesis, then, Type 3, the "marginally ethnic intellectual," is the numerically largest category and the one which constantly expands in size, forging along with its numerical increase, the structure of the intellectual subsociety.

Empirical data which would either verify or disprove our hypothesis concerning the existence of an intellectual subsociety are scarce. Seeman, in a largely qualitative study of forty assistant professors in a midwestern university, found that his respondents, in discussing themselves and their role as intellectuals, used the language and mechanisms which frequently characterize the responses of ethnic minority groups in self-discussion. While the language and mechanisms alluded to were negatively oriented toward the image of intellectuals, and while overt acceptance of intellectual status was rare, it is possible to infer from the protocol materials presented a covert awareness of both intellectual group identity and a subjective feeling of alienation from the broader society.[150]

Survey data from a study by Hajda of over 2000 native-born

150 Melvin Seeman, "The Intellectual and the Language of Minorities," *American Journal of Sociology*, Vol. 64, No. 1 (July 1958), pp. 25-35.

graduate students in twenty-five American universities bear somewhat more directly on our hypothesis.[151] Of the sample, 47 per cent
defined themselves as intellectuals—that is, answered in the affirma-
tive to the question: "Do you think of yourself as an 'intellectual' "?
This proportion rose to 53 per cent of the students in the humanities and 51 per cent of those in the social sciences. About two-
thirds of the entire student group felt alienated from the larger
society (alienation being measured by an index based on responses
to a series of questions dealing with how the students felt in the
presence of non-academic people). Thus, while Hajda's data do
not suggest that all graduate students are either self-defined intellectuals or feel estranged from the larger society (or that alienation
is ever complete), the percentages in each category are noticeably
large. Moreover, another of Hajda's findings, namely that "alienation, coupled with intellectual orientation, is generally characteristic of those who expect to stay in the academic world after gradua-
tion,"[152] bears even more suggestively on the validity of our hypothesis of the existence of an intellectual subsociety. Furthermore,
this investigator's description of the sociological profile of the
alienated intellectual indicates the minimization of structural affiliation with the institutions and organizations of the larger society
which is characteristic of this group: "The alienated intellectuals
among graduate students are persons committed more or less exclusively to the academic community. They are most prone to
regard the larger society as anti-intellectual; to have no religious
affiliation, or merely formal church membership; to have less intense attachment to their parental families than other students; to
have few if any friends from high school days. Their personal career
is marked by dissent from religious traditions in which they were
reared and by a history of conflict with parental authority. The only

[151] Jan Hajda, "Alienation and Integration of Student Intellectuals," *American
Sociological Review*, Vol. 26, No. 5 (October 1961), pp. 758-77.
[152] Ibid., p. 772.

THE SUBSOCIETY AND THE SUBCULTURE IN AMERICA

non-academic organization that sometimes commands their loyalty is a liberal political movement."[153] In this last connection, a finding of Lazarsfeld and Thielens in their study of the reactions of a national cross-section of nearly 2500 college teachers in the social sciences to the pressures for ideological conformity in the decade following World War II deserves mention. In answer to the question, "Are the people you see the most of socially mainly from your department, from the faculty generally, or from the community?" 62 per cent reported that their main social contacts were confined to the university faculty. This figure rises to above 70 per cent for faculty members in the more distinguished and prestigeful colleges and universities.[154]

A final piece of evidence—of a highly qualitative nature, to be sure—may be cited from the pages of *Commentary*, the monthly magazine of high intellectual distinction published by the American Jewish Committee. In the spring of 1961, the editors of this periodical published a symposium on the theme of "Jewishness and the Younger Intellectuals." The symposium consisted of the replies of thirty-one American intellectuals of Jewish birth, none of them over the age of forty and most of them under thirty-five, to a series of questions dealing with their attitudes toward a series of issues relating to Jewish culture and the Jewish community in America.[155] Their replies, while highly varied and complex, as might be expected from a group of this nature, revealed an overwhelming estrangment from the ideologies, issues, and concerns of Jewish communal life in America. The anguished and angry "letters to the editor" received from a number of Jewish communal representatives and published in subsequent issues of the maga-

[153] Ibid., p. 775.
[154] Paul F. Lazarsfeld and Wagner Thielens, Jr., *The Academic Mind*, Glencoe, Ill., The Free Press, 1958, pp. 31-2.
[155] "A Symposium: Jewishness and the Younger Intellectuals," *Commentary*, April 1961, pp. 306-59.

zine[156] testified to their perception of this estrangement and their
negative evaluation of it.

In short, empirical evidence of the existence of an intellectual
subsociety in America is in short supply, indicating the need for
research focused directly on the hypothesis. However, much of that
evidence which does exist suggests that the outlines of such a subsociety have begun to take shape in the United States. The implications of this development for intergroup relations will be discussed in the concluding chapter.

[156] See the "Letters From Readers" column in the June and July 1961 issues of
Commentary.

This is not to say that the symposium contributors disclaimed having been
influenced by Jewish culture. But their interpretation of Jewish culture tended
to be in the direction of emphasizing the universalistic prophetic tradition of
social justice rather than those elements of the cultural heritage which foster
specific ethnic concerns.

8

Assessment and Implications
for Intergroup Relations

We are now ready to assess the meaning of the foregoing analysis for the field of intergroup relations. As noted on the opening page of this volume, we are concerned ultimately with problems of prejudice and discrimination; however, our study has focused directly not on individual psychological states and activities related to ethnically prejudiced behavior, but rather on the nature and structure of group life itself in the United States. We have pursued this line of analysis not out of a conviction that individual psychological states are unimportant in explaining the phenomena under consideration but rather because of a firm belief that group life and social structure constitute the matrix in which cumulative psychological states are embedded, that the latter cannot be thoroughly understood without reference to the former, and that social structure and group life have been relatively neglected as dynamic factors in etiological analysis of racial and cultural prejudice.

To put the matter in another way, one may consider racial and cultural prejudice in America in two different contexts. One is to think of 190 million American individuals, some of whom happen to be white Protestant, some white Catholic, some Jewish, some

Negro, etc. We then ask why some of these individuals are ethnically prejudiced and others not, or only partly so, and then concentrate on studying the personality syndromes (and their etiological roots) of the various types along the prejudice continuum. Much valuable research has been carried out along these lines. Our inquiry has been substantially different, although the two approaches can be considered complementary rather than competing or mutually exclusive. We have chosen to focus on the nature of group life itself in the United States as constituting the social setting in which relationships among persons of differing race, religion, and national origin take place. For these 190 million Americans are not just individuals with psychological characteristics. They belong to groups: primary groups and secondary groups, family groups, social cliques, associations or formal organizations, networks of associations, racial, religious, and national origins groups, and social classes. And the nature of these groups and their interrelationships has a profound impact upon the way in which people of different ethnic backgrounds regard and relate to one another.

In particular, we have called attention to the nature of the ethnic group itself as a large subsociety, criss-crossed by social class, and containing its own primary groups of families, cliques, and associations—its own network of organizations and institutions—in other words, as a highly structured community within the boundaries of which an individual may, if he wishes, carry out most of his more meaningful life activities from the cradle to the grave. We have pointed to the considerable body of evidence which suggests that the various ethnic varieties of Americans, excepting the intellectuals, tend to remain within their own ethnic group and social class for most of their intimate, primary group relationships, interacting with other ethnic and class varieties of Americans largely in impersonal secondary group relationships. The United States, we have argued, is a multiple melting pot in which acculturation for all groups beyond the first generation of immigrants, without eliminating all value conflict, has been massive and decisive, but in which structural separation on the basis of race and religion—structural pluralism, as we have called it—emerges as the dominant sociological condition. The implications of this analytical description of American group life for intergroup relations will now occupy our attention. The following remarks will vary considerably in the generality of their theme and the specificity of their conclusions and recommendations. Furthermore, they will, from time to time, call into play certain ideological premises which will at such times be carefully identified. With these considerations in mind we are ready to proceed to a discussion of the implications of our analysis seriatim.

Structural Separation, Functional Consequences, and Prejudice: Recent studies have pointed to the role of intimate equal-status contact between members of majority and minority groups in reducing prejudice.[1] Structural separation, by definition, denotes a situation in which primary group contacts between members of various ethnic groups are held to a minimum, even though secondary contacts on the job, on the civic scene, and in other areas of impersonal contact may abound. In view of the tendency of human beings to categorize in their psychic perceptions and reactions and to form in-groups and, frequently, out-groups on the basis of fa-

[1] Samuel A. Stouffer, Edward A. Suchman, Leland C. DeVinney, Shirley A. Star, and Robin M. Williams, Jr., *The American Soldier: Adjustment During Army Life*, Princeton, N.J., Princeton University Press, 1949, pp. 586-95; Morton Deutsch and Mary Evans Collins, *Interracial Housing*, Minneapolis, Minn., University of Minnesota Press, 1951; John Harding (ed.), "Intergroup Contact and Racial Attitudes," *Journal of Social Issues*, Vol. VIII, No. 1, 1952; Gordon W. Allport, *The Nature of Prejudice*, Cambridge, Mass., Addison-Wesley Publishing Co., 1954, pp. 261-82; Daniel M. Wilner, Rosabelle Price Walkley, and Stuart W. Cook, *Human Relations in Interracial Housing: A Study of the Contact Hypothesis*, Minneapolis, Minn., University of Minnesota Press, 1955; George E. Simpson and J. Milton Yinger, *Racial and Cultural Minorities*, New York, Harper and Brothers, Rev. Ed., 1958, pp. 751-7.

miliar experiences and contacts,[2] it may be plausibly argued that just as intimate primary group relations tend to reduce prejudice, a lack of such contacts tends to promote ethnically hostile attitudes. It should be carefully noted that we are not thereby concluding that prejudice and discrimination cannot be reduced under conditions of structural pluralism; nor, indeed, that structural pluralism is necessarily undesirable from a philosophical point of view. Obviously, even from a sociological viewpoint, the matter is one of degree and should be discussed in that context.

On the one hand, structural separation of ethnic groups, brought about in part by the prejudices of the majority and in part by the desire of most such groups to maintain their own communal identity and subculture, can proceed to a point which is dysfunctional both for the creation of desirable attitudes and relations between the groups and for the workable operation of the society itself. The operation of modern urbanized industrial society is predicated upon the assurance of the easy interchangeability and mobility of individuals according to occupational specialization and needs. The fulfillment of occupational roles, the assignment of living space, the selection of political leaders, and the effective functioning of the educational process, among others, demand that universalistic criteria of competence and training, rather than considerations based on racial, religious, or nationality background, be utilized. The subversion of this principle by ethnic considerations would appear bound to produce, in the long run, confusion, conflict, and mediocrity. American society has not moved as far in this direction of "compartmentalization" or "columnization" as have certain other countries such as Holland and Lebanon,[3] but a trend toward this

[2] Gordon W. Allport, op. cit., pp. 17-67.

[3] Gerhard Lenski, *The Religious Factor*, op. cit., pp. 326-30; and David O. Moberg, "Social Differentiation in the Netherlands," *Social Forces*, Vol. 39, No. 4 (May 1961), pp. 333-7. On the question of dysfunctional consequences of excessive pluralism in the Netherlands, see Moberg, pp. 334-7. The following quotation is instructive: "Community solidarity and efficiency [in the Nether-

type of structural organization in America may well be in the making. As Lenski has cautioned, after surveying the data from his study of socio-religious groups in Detroit:

Currently we seem merely to be drifting into a type of social arrangement which Americans of all faiths might well reject if they became fully aware of all it entails.

This problem should be of special concern to religious leaders. Our current drift toward a "compartmentalized society" could easily produce a situation where individuals developed a heightened sense of religious group loyalty combined with a minimal sense of responsibility for those outside their own group. In a more compartmentalized society there is good reason to fear a weakening of the ethical and spiritual elements in religion and a heightening of the ever dangerous political elements. Such a development would be a serious departure from the basic ideals of all of the major faiths in America, sharing as they do in the Biblical tradition. Hence, on both religious and political grounds, Americans might do well to study more critically than they yet have the arguments advanced by advocates of pluralistic society.[4]

With regard to prejudice itself, it would seem reasonable to conclude that excessive compartmentalization or structural separation, since it prevents the formation of those bonds of intimacy and friendship which bind human beings together in the most meaningful moments of life and serve as a guard-wall against the formation of disruptive stereotypes, sets up the conditions under which ethnic prejudice will grow and flourish. It is possible that even a

---

lands] are diminished. Not only is group set against group in political affairs, but even when there are community-wide activities with cooperative planning there must nearly always be representation from all major confessional groupings of the community. As a result, incompetence is often evident; considerations of religious politics are placed above competence in the appointment or selection of personnel for community organizations and committees. Even when federated activity cuts across the religious columns, actual association of persons with different religious views takes place only among the small proportion of the population which holds positions of leadership. 'Water-tight' partitions separate the rank-and-file members." (Moberg, op. cit., p. 336).

[4] Lenski, op. cit., pp. 329-30.

modest degree of structural separation will tend always to have as a sociological concomitant a low, endemic degree of prejudice among the various ethnic groups (varying considerably, of course, for individuals). This is by no means a counsel of despair and is in no way meant to discourage the attempts to combat prejudice and discrimination by those standard means currently being used by various agencies, private and public. At the very least, however, it suggests that one may not be able to eat *all* of one's cake and have it too, and it puts high on the agenda the carrying out of research focused on the causal relationship between degrees and types of structural separation and the holding of ethnically prejudiced attitudes. It makes mandatory, too, careful consideration by those ethnic agencies, institutions, and officials (of whatever religion, race, or nationality) of the desirability of program and policy measures calculated to produce a heightening of the level of structural separation now existing among the various ethnic groups in America. Furthermore it raises questions about the ultimate desirability of the acquiescence by manifestly community-wide civic agencies and programs (of which the Boy Scouts and Girl Scouts are salient examples) in organizational segregation at the local level according to religion, as a result of the stipulations of religious communal leaders and officials.

The characteristic disclaimer by denominational communal leaders that "We want out people to participate actively in *both* denominational organizations and activities *and* community-wide organizations and affairs" must be measured against the simple reality that people's time and energy are not infinite in extent and, in fact, are bounded by substantial limitations. If the ordinary citizen is continually exhorted by his ethnic leaders to participate unreservedly in the ever-expanding array of ethnic-enclosed communal institutions springing up at all age levels, he will, in fact, have little or no resources of time and energy left to participate in those agencies and activities of the broader community that through their broader perspective and membership bind the religious, racial, and nationality groups of America into a viable nation—a nation that for reasons of both sociological health and traditional political ideals must strive to be substantially more than an instrumental federation of mutually suspicious ethnic groups.

Structural and Cultural Pluralism: Legitimation and Relationship to Democratic Values: Although we have just finished warning of the dangers of an excessive degree of structural pluralism, our second point calls attention to the overwhelming reality of this form of social organization in America, to the extreme unlikelihood that its essential outlines will be changed in the foreseeable future, and to the need for demonstrating to the public consciousness that structural and cultural pluralism in moderate degree are not incompatible with American democratic ideals. The evidence we have examined indicates that, apart from the subsociety of the intellectuals, intimate primary group relations between members of different racial and religious groups in the United States remain at a minimal level. This structural separation provides for the preservation of the communal nature of the ethnic group, and, in the case of the major religious denominations, makes for the retention of a core of differentiated religious beliefs, values, and historical symbols important to the loyal members of the faith. To this extent, one is entitled to say that structural pluralism in America is accompanied by a moderate degree of cultural pluralism as well. There is certainly nothing in the democratic value-complex shared by most Americans and anchored in the country's historical traditions which dictates that these differentiated historico-religious values and their cultural concomitants should perforce be merged into one over-all religious system, or that Catholics and Jews should abandon their religion and convert to Protestantism. Nor does the American democratic value-creed imply that the citizens of this land do not have the right to choose their intimate friends and

their organizational affiliations on the basis of whatever criteria of
likeness and congeniality they find it convenient and desirable to
utilize. To put it another way, subsocietal affiliation and participation in America, so far as the state is concerned, are voluntary matters (notwithstanding the fact that informal social pressures ascribe
such affiliation on the basis of birth—that is, on the basis of the
parents' affiliation), and the voluntary selection of structural and
subsocietal affiliations, within functional limits, is well within the
area of personal choice provided for by democratic values.

This position, of course, in no way justifies the use of racial or
religious criteria in employment, housing, education, access to
public facilities, or any other area in which functional benefits
crucial to the fulfillment of human personality and the general
welfare are concerned. In other words, it does not justify *discrimination*. But it does reserve the matter of choice in intimate primary group relationships for personal decision on whatever grounds
the individual may elect to use. By the same token, it enjoins the
state or any private citizen or group of citizens from interfering
with those individuals who wish to form primary group relationships *across* racial or religious lines. There is no justification, for
instance, in the value system of either political democracy or the
Hebraic-Christian religious tradition for state or municipal laws
forbidding social relationships between whites and Negroes (or
other racial groups) up to and including the marriage relationship.

Finally, then, if a moderate degree of structural and cultural
pluralism are legitimated by the American Creed, legitimation
should be made salient in the public consciousness. For to legitimate and explain the system as it actually operates is to justify it
and help to draw away the animus that many Americans have
toward minority groups which, in their minds, do not "assimilate"
or "melt"—in other words, do not merge into the white Protestant
population, give up their communal identity, and relinquish their
cultural differences in crucial areas of belief and practice. As we

have indicated, for those who do not wish to "merge" to this extent, ample justification in the American value system exists. The legitimation of pluralism and the projection into the public consciousness of its justification and its reality on the American scene would also help to dispel the erroneous conclusion that it is only this group or that group that desires to maintain communal separation. In this respect, the Jews have frequently been singled out as a "separatist" minority; "clannish" is the adjective often applied. As our study has shown, although they do not succeed with the intellectuals, all of the major religious faiths—Jews, Catholics, and Protestants—operate functionally so as to perpetuate ethnic communality in the general population. The Protestants are least aware of the process since their majority status and historical precedence in America tend to make them unaware of the Protestant assumptions and criteria operative in many of the institutions which are labeled as "American" and "community-wide." Being the majority group, numerically, also tends to lessen objectively the possibility of the erosion of Protestant ethnic communality and cultural values through the process of intermarriage and other types of interethnic primary relationships. Thus Protestants have less to lose in encouraging ethnic mixture.

Our point, in sum, is not that interethnic primary group contacts are undesirable. Quite the contrary. It is rather that since many, perhaps most, members of the major faiths (and, among racial groups, notably the American Indians) basically desire some form of ethnic communality and subcultural preservation, both the reality of the system and its justification in the American value creed should be clearly brought home to the American population as a whole.

Pluralism and Assimilation: Guidelines for Agencies Concerned with Orienting the Immigrant to American Life: The analysis which we have made of the assimilation process, the factoring out

of the various subtypes of assimilation, and the discussion of the
interaction of these subtypes, theoretically and empirically on the
American scene, suggest a number of guidelines for those agencies
and institutions concerned with the adjustment of immigrants and
their descendants to American life and culture. These may be
listed as follows:

1) Structural assimilation of immigrants to the United States
(that is, the first generation arriving as adults), who enter the
country in numbers substantial enough to make feasible a communal life of their own, is both impossible of attainment in most
cases and undesirable as a goal toward which pressure on the immigrant might conceivably be exercised. While exceptional individuals will occasionally assimilate structurally into a native American
subsociety—in many cases, the community of intellectuals—the
great majority of newcomers to the country will need and prefer
the security of a communal life made up of their fellow-immigrants
from the homeland. This generalization is particularly applicable
to immigrants of peasant, working-class, and lower-middle-class
backgrounds, whose perspectives and orientations, on a statistical
basis, will be inevitably narrow; however, it encompasses the great
majority of immigrants of higher class origins, as well, who, in any
case, are less likely to arrive in large numbers. Thus, efforts, however well-intentioned, to force structural assimilation on the immigrant are likely to be both futile and tension-producing. The
newcomer needs the comfortable sociological and psychological
milieu which the communality of his own group provides. Even
those individuals who eventually will make major structural contact with native subsocieties can profitably use the communal base
of their own group to make their initial adjustment and to fall
back upon if their tentative interethnic primary group contacts
prove unsatisfactory. Immigrant-adjustment agencies, then, should
not waste their time and energy in attempting to promote structural assimilation on a massive scale but should accept the func-

tional desirability of immigrant communal life with good grace. In this area, they might well limit their efforts to making significant opportunities for primary group contacts with native Americans available as alternatives on a thoroughly voluntary basis for that relatively small minority of immigrants who wish to and can meaningfully make use of such opportunities for broadening their communal life.

2) The major efforts of immigrant-adjustment agencies, then, should be directed toward acculturation, or cultural assimilation, and even here in modest degree and in selected areas. The basic goal should be the adjustment of the immigrant to American culture and institutions in those areas of secondary group and institutional contact which permit him to obtain and keep a job commensurate with his potential and training, to receive appropriate retraining and education where necessary, to perform adequately his role as a potential future citizen of both the nation and the local community, and to raise his children in ways which will neither do emotional violence to the traditions of the homeland nor subvert the family socialization process congenial to child-rearing in a basically middle-class American culture. This places the emphasis on the provision of instrumental skills: adequate use of the English language not at the expense of (nor denigration of) but in addition to the native tongue, occupational training, orientation to standard technological devices, knowledge of how to make use of the vast array of American educational opportunities, sophistication in citizenship adjustment, voting behavior, and participation in the political process generally. The functional goal would be the successful relationship of the immigrant, both culturally and structurally, to the secondary groups and instrumental institutional areas of American life. Changing the direction or nature of his intimate, primary group communal life would be excluded as a feasible or desirable product of directed effort.

3) The institutional and subcultural life of the immigrant com-

munity should be regarded not only as a necessary concession to the sociological and psychological health of the new American but as providing a positive and effective means of enabling such a degree of acculturation as is posited as desirable and feasible in the paragraph above. The forms and devices of the immigrant community face two ways. On the one hand, providing the indispensable comfortable milieu, they continue the newcomer's orientation to the culture of the old country and the old locality, to its familiar ways of doing things, to its current history and its current gossip. On the other hand, they gradually incorporate elements of the American culture, interpret that culture to the newcomer in ways which he can understand, and sift its elements and bring them to his attention in a degree and at a pace which muffles and makes bearable the shock of cultural collision. The immigrant's burial and insurance societies, his indigenous church, his "foreign language" press, his favorite cafés and coffee houses, his old-style theatrical entertainments, his network of social cliques and "nationality" organizations, his ceremonies and folk dances, are never created or recreated simply as replicas of old country elements; they always progressively reflect the influence of American conditions and American events, serving as a sturdy bridge between the old and the new. In a word, the immigrant subsociety mediates between the native culture of the immigrant and the American culture. The recognition of this fact is the indispensable prerequisite for effective use of the communication channels and influence networks of the immigrant's communal life to aid and encourage the achievement of worth-while acculturation goals.

4) The American-born children of immigrants, the second generation, with exceptions based on the existence of a few rigidly enclosed enclaves, should be realistically viewed as a generation irreversibly on its way to virtually complete acculturation (although not necessarily structural assimilation) to native American cultural values at selected class levels. Exposed to the overwhelming accul-

turative powers of the public school and the mass communications media, the immigrants' children will proffer their unhesitating allegiance to those aspects of the American cultural system which are visible to them in their particular portion of the socio-economic structure. The feasible and necessary task of the immigrant-adjustment agencies, in this area, is to aid in making this acculturative transition as smooth as possible, in view of the many potential difficulties, for both the children and their parents.

The tendency will be for native-born children to become alienated from their immigrant parents and the culture they represent, as they respond affirmatively to the higher status American cultural values. The challenge for social welfare agencies and institutions in the immigration field is, without mounting a doomed effort to stem the inevitable tide of American acculturation, to aid the second-generation child to gain a realistic degree of positive regard for the cultural values of his ethnic background, which will hardly retard the acculturation process, but which will give the child a healthier psychological base for his confrontation with American culture and for his sense of identification with and response to his parents. Such an effort should not preclude, of course, the encouragement of the development of effective English language skills, since this development is indispensable to adequate adjustment to American life. Nor do these counsels obviate the need to deal with the interconnected problems that the second-generation child traditionally faces as a member of a minority group, subject to some degree of prejudice and discrimination, and as a person being socialized in the lower and underprivileged sector of the socioeconomic environment.

Desegregation, Integration, and the Role of Government: Our sociological focus on the phenomenon of ethnic communality in the United States suggests certain important implications for the current controversies surrounding the attempts to eliminate racial

discrimination by law—a series of events launched into full motion
by the Supreme Court school desegregation decision of 1954.

The basic theoretical distinction which it is necessary to make in
the types of processes involved in these turbulent happenings has
been well delineated by Kenneth Clark, who points to the differences between *desegregation* and *integration*.[5] Desegregation refers
to the elimination of racial criteria in the operation of public or
quasi-public facilities, services, and institutions, which the individual is entitled to as a functioning citizen of the local or national
community, equal in legal status to all other citizens. It is the
achievement in full of what is usually referred to as his "civil
rights." Integration, however, embraces the idea of the removal of
prejudice as well as civic discrimination and therefore refers to
much more. In Clark's words, "Integration, as a subjective and
individual process, involves attitudinal changes and the removal
of fears, hatreds, suspicions, stereotypes, and superstitions. Integration involves problems of personal choice, personal readiness, and
personal stability. Its achievement necessarily requires a longer
period of time. It cannot come about 'overnight.' It requires education and deals poignantly with the problems of changing men's
hearts and minds."[6] To which we would add that, in social structural terms, integration presupposes the elimination of hard and
fast barriers in the primary group relations and communal life of
the various ethnic groups of the nation. It involves easy and fluid
mixture of people of diverse racial, religious, and nationality backgrounds in social cliques, families (i.e., intermarriage), private organizations, and intimate friendships. From this basic distinction
between desegregation and integration, and the relation of this
distinction to both sociological realities and the American democratic value system, a number of conclusions follow:

1) Desegregation—the process of eliminating racial discrimina-

[5] Kenneth B. Clark, "Desegregation: The Role of the Social Sciences," *Teachers College Record*, Vol. 62, No. 1 (October 1960), pp. 16-17.
[6] Ibid., p. 16.

tion in the operation of public and quasi-public institutional facilities—will not lead *immediately* or, in the intermediate future, *necessarily* to integration in the sense of the dissolution of ethnic communality and the formation of large-scale primary group relationships across racial and religious lines. The tendency toward ethnic communality, as we have demonstrated, is a powerful force in American life and is supported, once the ethnic subsociety is formed, by the principles of psychological inertia, comfortable social immersion, and vested interests. Even if all southern public schools and other public facilities were to be immediately desegregated, there is no reason to suppose that the Negro and the white subcommunities would merge into one another or that the traditional barriers to intimate friendships and relationships between Negroes and white would at once come tumbling down. Certainly there is no basis for the belief that Negroes and whites, respectively encapsulated in their own subcommunity and subculture, would rush to marry each other. This sociological insight, it will be noted, is offered here in a spirit of scientific neutrality and not as a conclusion which is either good or bad from the point of view of some particular value system. I have already pointed out that, on the basis of traditional American democratic values, Negroes and whites should have the right to make close friendships and to marry across racial lines at their pleasure. But sociological realities do not indicate that these phenomena would be likely to take place in significant volume in the immediate future, even if all public and institutional discrimination were to be eliminated. If die-hard segregationists who now bitterly oppose the granting of full civic equality to Negroes could be made to understand this fact, it is possible that the debate over desegregation could be carried out in a less emotional and a more rational climate of discussion and action. It is necessary to repeat that this point is not a concession to any *right* of segregationists to bar interracial primary group relationships; it is a statement of sociological probabilities which, if correctly understood, might clear the way for more rapid and effective action in such areas as public education, public transportation, public recreation, jobs, housing, and the operation of ordinary institutional facilities which belong to all Americans on an equal basis.

2) The proper role of government in racial and ethnic matters, under the American democratic system, can be defined in three steps:

a) It is the responsibility of the government to effect descgregation—that is, to eliminate racial criteria—in the operation of all of its facilities and services at all levels, national, state, and local. The American democratic value system and the specific constitutional expression of these values in the Fifth Amendment and the three Civil War Amendments to the Federal Constitution, particularly the Fourteenth, with its clause enjoining the state from depriving any person of the "equal protection of the laws," provide the legal mandate for such a ban, and the execution of this mandate demands action (some of which, it should be noted, has already been taken) in the form of legislation, court orders, or executive orders, in such areas as jobs, housing, voting, education, service in the armed forces, and access to public facilities. Since the national government, through grants, loans, and purchasing, now has a hand in so many types of activities which were once exclusively private or, if public, purely within the scope of states and municipalities, the way is opened for entirely legitimate pressure to be exerted by the national government on recalcitrant or hesitant local governments, businesses, institutions, and individuals who still want to preserve the old segregated pattern but are reluctant to dispense with federal largesse. There will inevitably be some areas of activity where the question of whether there actually is governmental participation of sufficient scope to warrant a judgment that "state action" applics will be unclear;[7] these matters can only be decided

[7] For a discussion of one interesting case where the definition of "state action" was crucial and controversial, see Milton M. Gordon, "The Girard College

by subsequent judicial decision. Nevertheless, the major goal of getting the government—the focal expression of the will and welfare of all the people of the country—out of the business of supporting racial discrimination, either directly or indirectly, remains both clear and irreproachable.

b) It is neither the responsibility nor the prerogative of the government to attempt to impose integration, as here defined—that is, to take official notice of personal attitudes and preferences (beyond the ordinary teaching process in the public schools where standard facts and interpretations underlie the curriculum), and to interfere in any way with those personal choices in primary group relationships and organizational affiliations which make either for ethnic communality or interethnic mixture, as the case may be. I except here specific incitations to violence and, of course, paramilitary operations which threaten law and order. In short, the ordinary processes of communality, whether intra-ethnic or interethnic are beyond the scope of governmental interference or concern.

c) It is neither the responsibility nor the prerogative of the government to use racial criteria positively in order to impose desegregation upon public facilities in an institutional area where such segregation is not a function of racial discrimination directly but results from discrimination operating in another institutional area, or from other causes. If institutional area A is *de facto* segregated not because of the direct use of racial criteria but because institutional area B is segregated and because there is a relationship between institutional areas A and B, then the place to fight discrimination is not A but B. The obvious case in point is the operation of the public school system. The attempt by well-meaning "race liberals" in a number of northern communities to desegregate public schools by overturning the principle of neighborhood

Case: Resolution and Social Significance," *Social Problems*, Vol. 7, No. 1 (Summer, 1959), pp. 15-27.

assignment—that is, to positively promote Negro-white intermixture by means of racial assignment across neighborhood lines—is,
in my opinion, misguided. It is misguided because it does exactly
what is in principle wrong, regardless of how laudable the goal.
It puts the government in the business of using race as a criterion
for operating one of its facilities. This is precisely what the government should not be doing, either negatively or positively. The
genius of the American political tradition, in its best sense, in relation to race is that it dictates that racial criteria are *not* legitimate
in the operation of governmental facilities and should be rigorously
eschewed. To bring racial criteria in by the front door, so to speak,
even before throwing them out the back, represents, in my opinion, no real gain for the body politic and has potentially dangerous
implications for the future. If racial criteria are legitimate criteria
for government consideration (which I firmly argue they are not),
then the way is left open for many ominous disputes as to the
merits of any particular racial clause in governmental operations.

It should be understood that I am making no specific plea here
for the particular merits of the principle of neighborhood assignment to public schools. This is a matter which the educationists
can debate among themselves. Furthermore, where inferior facilities in a school in a predominantly Negro area exist, or Negroes or
members of any ethnic group are not appointed to teaching positions on the basis of individual qualifications, then we are in the
presence of legitimate cases of racial discrimination which call for
effective remedy.[8] My basic point, however, is that if *de facto*
segregation of public schools in many northern cities exists because of segregation in housing (which, of course, it does), the
place to fight the battle of civil rights is housing, not the public

[8] Another qualification is necessary here. If school districts were gerrymandered
originally for the sake of instituting all or predominantly Negro schools, then
this initial act of discrimination should be fought and redress should be demanded.

school system, and the way to fight it is to eliminate racial criteria from the routes of access to housing space, not to inject them into the operation of the educational system.

d) It is unwise and unjustifiable for the government to create programs labeled and reserved for the benefit of any special racial group, or to set up racial quotas in any area of activity such as employment, as is currently demanded by some civil rights proponents. It is undeniable that the burden of unemployment bears most heavily at present on Negroes, as a result of the cumulation of past discriminatory events. However, there are white, Indian, and Oriental unemployed workers who need aid, also, and any government program designed to retrain or upgrade the job skills of occupationally disadvantaged Americans should include them as well. In other words, it should be set up as an all-inclusive "functional" rather than an exclusive racial program. It goes without saying that job hiring and promotion at all levels should be made on the basis of individual merit, not racial quotas, however "benignly" the latter may be motivated. Present wrongs do not solve the problems created by past injustices and only assure that the underlying social evil will further plague the future. We do not want "see-saw discrimination" in American life; we want the dismantling of the discriminatory apparatus.

In sum, the proper role of government is to deal equitably with all persons under its jurisdiction without taking into consideration their racial background for any purpose.

Desegregation, Integration, and Private Institutions: The distinction between the processes of desegregation and integration is not nearly so vital for assessing the role of private institutions and organizations in racial and ethnic matters. For one thing, in many types of private social institutions—for instance, fraternities and social clubs—desegregation automatically implies integration because of the kind of social relationship implicit in the operation of the institution. In other private institutions of larger scope, as, for instance, the private university, college, or academy, desegregation may or may not lead to integration depending upon particular factors associated with the life of the institution such as size and the presence or absence of segregated or self-segregated subgroups. Moreover, the arguments surrounding the choices of segregation, self-segregation, or desegregation are more varied, more complex, and more conflicting than in the case of government. However, several insights and guide-lines to action are suggested by the direction and scope of our previous analysis:

1) Some types of private organizations are those for whose goals and operation ethnic background is functional and centrally relevant. Quite obviously, a Methodist mission society, a Catholic sodality, a Jewish Temple sisterhood, or a club instituted to insure social welfare benefits for Polish immigrants and their descendants cannot reasonably be expected to throw open its membership to persons of other faiths or nationalities, as the case may be. Here one can confidently assert that there is no discrimination but simply a functionally relevant definition of membership.

2) Private organizations and institutions which serve a more general purpose, while they may be, under some circumstances, technically free to restrict membership on an ethnic basis, must face a series of crucial queries. Do they receive any assistance from the public treasury either in the form of grants or exemption from the payment of taxes? Can they justify an exclusionary policy on the basis of major functional relevance to the goals of the organization? Do they claim to operate under the general principles of American democracy, Hebraic-Christian brotherhood, and fair play? Do they perform a quasi-public function such as providing general education? If, in many cases, the answers to these questions should suggest the inappropriateness of an exclusionary policy, then the way is certainly left open for efforts to institute a policy which is nondiscriminatory. If such efforts by concerned members make the

segregationists in the organization unhappy, it must be pointed out that initiating change in the policy of a voluntary organization at the will of a majority of its members is a thoroughly democratic procedure. Thus the ethnic practices of private organizations can frequently be settled by the dynamics of policy-making in a democratic setting where traditional procedures are subject to current examination in a changing society.

The Built-in Tension Between the Goals of Ethnic Communality and Desegregation: Earlier in this chapter we stated that desegregation in public and quasi-public facilities was unlikely to lead to the rapid breakdown of barriers between the primary group communal life of the various ethnic groups in America, and that the fears in this area of the segregationists, however unworthy, were thus unfounded. Here we examine a point which may appear at first to repudiate the above conclusion, but which, in fact, does not, but only qualifies it.

Desegregation—or, put positively, the achievement in full of civil rights for all groups—creates situations on the job, in the neighborhood, in the school, and in the civic arena, which place persons of different ethnic background into secondary, frequently equal-status, contacts with each other. These secondary contacts will not necessarily lead to primary group relationships, such as clique friendships, common membership in small organizations, dating, and intermarriage, and in the immediate or intermediate future will probably not seriously disturb the basic outlines of ethnic communality which have been shown to exist in America. However, over a sufficiently extended period of time, these new secondary group relationships between people of diverse ethnic backgrounds will presumably lead to an increase in warm, personal friendships across ethnic lines, a broadening of cultural perspective, an appreciation of diverse values, and in some degree a rise in the rate of interethnic marriage. All of these last-named developments run counter to the sociological requirements, whether realized or admitted, of ethnic closure and ethnic communality. Here, then, is another major area of social reality where the advocates of cultural pluralism (and, by implication, structural pluralism) cannot eat their cake and have it, too. There are built-in tensions between the simultaneously desired goals of ethnic communality and full civic equality, and these tensions create for the cultural pluralists a poignant dilemma. The dilemma is particularly acute for the two large minority religious groups—the Jews and the Catholics—who do not wish to see their young people "lost" to the numerically and culturally dominant Protestant subsociety or to the community of intellectuals and yet who ardently support the fight to secure full civic equality for all persons in American society. The racial groups approach the problem somewhat differently: the Negroes, apart from the new crop of "black nationalists," have never been ideologically committed to racial communality, however much they have been forced to create it; however, those whites who desire the full complement of civil rights for all, but who are reluctant to support the idea of racial intermarriage, must wrestle with the possibility that the rate of racial intermarriage will eventually increase under conditions of full equality. The nationality groups which still hope for subcultural survival are fighting such a rear-guard and eventually futile action that the dilemma for them has less realistic overtones.

There is, I believe, no clear course of action which neatly resolves this dilemma to the complete satisfaction of all parties concerned. My point, in this section, has simply been to make the conflicting considerations apparent. It is a dilemma which is certainly close to the center of the social problems attendant upon the presence of groups of diverse cultural origins and background in a modern industrial society. I shall leave my own "solution" of it for the concluding remarks of my analysis.

The Intellectual Subsociety and Its Significance: The existence of an intellectual subsociety in America which draws upon appropriate individuals from all ethnic groups for its membership and, to some degree, allows them an institutional setting for primary group relationships, has several discernible consequences—or, to put it otherwise, serves several functions, both positive and negative.

First, it serves as an institutional safety-valve for those individuals who, because of a wide-ranging interest in ideas, the arts, and people, find ethnic communality personally uncongenial. If these individuals intermarry across ethnic lines, they find the need for the intellectual subsociety sociologically pressing, since this subsociety is the only real "neutral ground" in American life and the only communal group which looks either with favor or unconcern at interethnic marriage. (This is, of course, a matter of degree; interracial marriages, especially Negro-white, are still problematic even for the intellectual subsociety.) Even those who do not intermarry find the interethnic or nonethnic social environment with its emphasis on ideas and common interests rather than on ethnic background a comfortable and necessary one. Perhaps one should say that ethnic background is not ignored in the intellectual subsociety, as witness the great interest in this milieu in ethnic folk dancing and folk singing; it is rather that ethnicity becomes an interesting but subsidiary issue rather than one which colors and dominates the rest of life. Were such a social environment and subsociety not available, individuals of the aforementioned interests and inclinations would be rebellious and unhappy as they chafed at the restrictive bonds of ethnic communality.

Second, the intellectual subsociety with its ethnic intermixture serves the rest of the nation as a symbol of the possibility of interethnic harmony and integration at the meaningful primary group level of communal living. It is true that the process of achieving such integration is still incomplete even among intellectuals; the Negro, most notably, is still only partly and imperfectly encompassed in the communal life of the intellectual group. Nevertheless, partial as ethnic integration may be within it, the intellectual subsociety still serves as the most salient example of the possibility of a truly integrated society. As such, it provides a testing ground for the problems and processes inherent in the achievement of such a society and stands as a symbol of its potential development in larger scope.

A third functional consequence must be stated in negative terms, or perhaps it would be more accurate to say that a question must be raised the probable answer to which has negative implications. The question is this: What are the consequences for the several major ethnic subsocieties in America of the fact that many, perhaps a large majority, of the most intellectually inclined of their birthright members are siphoned off, as it were, into a subsociety of their own, retaining only a minimal concern, if any, for the communal life and issues of their parental group? Put more specifically, if intellectuals of Jewish, Catholic, and Protestant background become alienated from the subsocietal life and concerns of their respective groups, what functional consequences result for these ethnic groups and for the general quality of American life of which these groups make up the overwhelming part? Some intellectuals, to be sure, remain within their ethnic origins groups as clergymen, communal leaders, or ordinary laymen, but the general trend is as otherwise described. Does this outflow of intellectuals from the religio-ethnic groups of America, their subsequent estrangement from the life of these groups, and the resultant block in communication between the ethnic subsociety and the intellectual have dysfunctional consequences? Do the major decisions both in the society as a whole and within the ethnic subsociety come to be made with the intellectual excluded from the decision-making process? Is there a mediocrity and stereotypy in American popular culture and in the subcultural life of each major ethnic group which results from this withdrawal of the intellectuals into a social world of their own? Do the intellectuals themselves lose out in breadth and vision as a result of this estrangement? And is this estrangement or alienation inevitable—in the very nature of things, given the scope and nature of individual genetic differences—or is it subject to elimination or modification as a result of measures not yet thought of or implemented? These are questions, the answers to which, in the absence of relevant research and exploration, are not entirely clear. Nevertheless, they point to a series of problematic areas in American life resulting from the alienation of the intellectual from popular society and culture.

The Ethnic Subsociety and Its Internal Responsibilities: The ethnic subsociety can be counted on to marshall its institutional resources to carry out the fight against racial and religious discrimination and prejudice on the American scene. Various aspects of the strategy of this indispensable effort have been discussed in previous pages. We turn now to a related but ostensibly different question: What should be the attitude of the leaders and leading organizations of the ethnic subsociety toward the subsociety itself—to the constituency which it serves—with regard to its relationship to the larger community? This topic will be considered by reference to two subquestions.

The first deals with the appropriate attitude of the institutional leadership of the ethnic subsociety toward facts and occurrences which appear to reflect unfavorably on the ethnic group. While the illustrations used below deal with the Negro group, other ethnic groups, including the white Protestant majority, could well have been utilized.

Not long ago, a journal dedicated to the cause of advancing the position of the Negro within the framework of equal rights, raised the question of whether it should devote an entire issue to the topic of delinquency and crime among Negroes. There are those who will argue that the correct answer is No—that special consideration of the above-average rates of crime and delinquency among Negroes focuses undesirable attention on this phenomenon and plays into the hands of the racists who are only too quick to point with alarm and to attribute higher Negro delinquency rates to some innate racial predisposition or inferiority.

I disagree with such a strategy. In the first place, national atten-

tion has already been called to the high rates of Negro crime in the
slums of the large cities through articles in such periodicals as *Time*
and *Life*, and metropolitan newspapers raise the issue whenever
local outbreaks of Negro "muggings" and allied violence take place.
It is therefore impossible to keep the issue from public attention
even if it were considered wise to do so. More realistic and desirable
goals are 1) to make the public understand the sociological rather
than "racial" causes of the higher Negro rate—that is, to comprehend its source in racial discrimination and the substandard conditions, both physical and cultural, in which the great mass of
Negroes are forced to live as a result of discrimination and prejudice; 2) to advance research in discovering the causes of crime and
delinquency generally; 3) to research in detail the particular sociological causes for the higher Negro rate; and 4) to eliminate racial
discrimination. None of these goals is advanced by an ostrich-like
policy of avoiding recognition of the higher Negro crime and delinquency rate and by misguided restriction of informed and responsible discussion of the issue.

In the larger sense, it may be said that truth and understanding
are the necessary preludes to informed and constructive action in
the field of interethnic group relations. Donald Young stated this
principle effectively over a decade ago:

It is good technique to keep members of both races accurately informed about interracial questions. There is no better way to answer
false assertions, kill tension-breeding rumors, and build a solid foundation for democratic action. This principle is generally accepted, but it
is commonly misused because of fear that if the truth is not entirely
laudatory of the Negro it may lead to greater prejudice. Also, because
Negroes are sensitive and quick to infer insults . . . , racial liberals
are reluctant to risk giving offense. The twisting or omitting of facts,
exaggeration and plain prevarication in defensive arguments about
race and crime, industrial skill, educational and scientific achievement,
military accomplishment, literary and artistic products, etc. are commonplace. But the unvarnished truth alone contradicts racial dogma,

checks rumors, and in precluding specious rebuttal is more effective than the most kindly white lie. Unless the established facts are adhered to rigidly, and both weaknesses and strengths honestly included in interracial educational campaigns, the main results are likely to be a lack of public confidence and a weak foundation for action programs.[9]

The principle applies with equal force, of course, to Jews, Catholics, white Protestants, or any other ethnic group.

The second subquestion may be phrased as follows: Does the ethnic subsociety have any special responsibility to guide the behavior of its members with respect to avoidance of those forms of action which are patently injurious to society? Certainly if we phrase this question in terms of the attitudes of institutions in the white subsocieties toward racists, the answer appears clear enough. We expect white Protestant and Catholic churches and Jewish synagogues, for instance, to urgently preach doctrines of racial brotherhood, to support desegregation both in the church itself and in the larger society, and to actively oppose prejudice and discrimination. And we take the position that civic organizations, generally, stemming from the white subsocieties, should take a similar stand. Suppose we ask the question, however, with respect to a minority subsociety, and suppose some form of anti-social behavior may be particularly salient within its ranks as a result of the forces generated by prejudice and discrimination. Here, let us again use as an example the Negro community and the high rate of delinquency found in the Negro lower class.

Does the "Negro community" have, in fact, a special responsibility and role to play in the prevention of delinquency among Negro youth? The argument against any special responsibility, of course, runs something like this: Rates of delinquency and crime are the product of general sociological and psychological forces which are within the control and responsibility of the total com-

---

[9] Donald Young, "Techniques of Race Relations," *Proceedings of the American Philosophical Society*, Vol. 91, No. 2 (April 1947), pp. 157-8.

munity and not in any special way of the Negro community. Furthermore, wherever higher rates of Negro delinquency are present, these higher rates are the result of prejudice and discrimination shown by whites and embedded in the institutions of the total community. Therefore any attribution of special responsibility to the Negro community is both morally unjustified and logically fallacious. There is much to be said for this argument, and, in a strict theoretical sense, I would agree that the Negro community should accept no attribution of responsibility for Negro delinquency which implies either a special ethical obligation to deal with it or an acceptance of the fallacious thesis that its sources are fundamentally indigenous to Negro communal life.

However, I would not be content to rest here. I would say that while the Negro community does not bear a special *responsibility* in the matter of Negro crime, it does, in terms of the sociological realities, have a special *opportunity* in practical terms to focus, voluntarily, a portion of its resources on the problem of reducing the Negro delinquency rate. The existence of specifically Negro organizations and institutions, the sense of identification with the Negro group on the part of Negro individuals, the *de facto* restriction of social participation to the Negro community—all these components of Negro communal and subcultural existence—are sociological realities. The sociological reality of the Negro subsociety thus provides special opportunities for Negro communal leaders acting through Negro communal institutions to play a special role in the reduction of rates of anti-social behavior by Negroes.

To particularize: Negro communal leaders may 1) be in a position to provide special insights into the dynamics of social processes within the Negro lower classes and Negro lower-class family life which contribute to the excessive delinquency rate; 2) be able to do more effective ameliorative field work in standard social work processes because of the greater rapport which is likely to exist between lower-class Negroes and Negro social workers, and to supplement existing social work measures directed toward the Negro community which are currently in short supply; and 3) be in a position to devise and carry through institutional counter-measures whose particular effectiveness would derive from their source within the Negro community. To ignore these opportunities, it seems to me again, is to adopt an ostrich-like policy with regard to the multiplicity of specific variables which combine to produce the higher Negro delinquency rate, and correspondingly to make possible the multiplicity of counter-measures which offer special opportunities for action by the Negro community itself. To put it succinctly, simply because the *ultimate causes* of the higher Negro delinquency rate stem from broader social forces in the general community does not signify that *some effective counter-measures* cannot be taken at existing levels of structure and process by the Negro community itself. Thus I would argue that while the Negro community does not have, in the strict philosophical sense, a special *responsibility* to concern itself with Negro delinquency, it does have, in realistic sociological terms, a special *opportunity* to devote some attention and resources to this phenomenon. In short, my point is that the ethnic subsociety, whatever its racial, religious, or nationality background, from a sociological point of view has special opportunities to deal with particular behavior problems which may be related to its social history and current situation, and these opportunities should not be bypassed, even though the more basic roots of the problem lie in the institutions and practices of the larger society.

Nothing I have said suggests, of course, in any way that the Negro community should curtail or diminish its increasingly insistent and effective efforts (aided by many white liberals) toward achieving the broader long-range goals of eliminating prejudice and discrimination from American life. In the last analysis, the attainment of equal opportunities in education, employment, housing, and access to public facilities, and the development of mutual respect for America's varied racial, religious, and national backgrounds among all her citizens constitute the ultimate effective solution to problems of social disorganization which bear unequally on particular minority groups.

Pluralism, Democratic Values, and Long-Range Goals for America: Our final remarks deal with the implications of our analysis of ethnic communality and the assimilation process for long-range goals in American social life with regard to intergroup relations. Into this analysis we must interpolate, too, the significance of democratic values as we understand them.

The struggle to eliminate racial and religious prejudice and discrimination from American life—a struggle, the unequivocal rightness of which, sociologically and ideologically, this volume takes for granted—goes on against the underlying social reality of ethnic communality tenaciously maintaining itself in an industrial urbanized society. We have described the nature of this ethnic communality as, basically, structural pluralism accompanied by an ever-decreasing degree of cultural pluralism. The relationship of this kind of a society to the problems inherent in attempting to eliminate ethnic prejudice and discrimination have been discussed in the preceding pages. What, now, of the future? What are the viable goals for America with regard to ethnic communality, given the desire to eliminate or reduce prejudice and discrimination, the nature of sociological realities, and commitment to the American democratic value system?

The system of cultural pluralism (which ultimately depends on structural pluralism) has frequently been described as "cultural democracy," since it posits the right of ethnic groups in a democratic society to maintain their communal identity and their own subcultural values. We have already argued that since ethnic communality rests principally on personal choices in primary group relations and private organizational affiliations, it falls well within the scope of those areas of free choice guaranteed by democratic values. Reversing the coin, however, we must also point out that democratic values prescribe free choice not only for groups but also for individuals. That is, the individual, as he matures and reaches the age where rational decision is feasible, should be allowed to choose freely whether to remain within the boundaries of communality created by his birthright ethnic group, to branch out into multiple interethnic contacts, or even to change affiliation to that of another ethnic group should he wish to do so as a result of religious conversion, intermarriage, or simply private wish. If, to the contrary, the ethnic group places such heavy pressures on its birthright members to stay confined to ethnic communality that the individual who consciously wishes to "branch out" or "move away" feels intimidated or subject to major feelings of personal guilt and therefore remains ethnically enclosed, or moves but at considerable psychological cost, then we have, in effect, cultural democracy for groups but not for individuals. Realistically, it is probably impossible to have a socialization process for the child growing up in a particular ethnic group that does not involve some implicitly restrictive values; nevertheless, the magnitude and intensity of such restrictive norms must be kept within bounds if we are not to be left with a system which provides cultural democracy for groups but enforced ethnic enclosure for individuals.

Probably the vast majority of Americans, as revealed in their choices in primary group relations and organizational affiliations, desire ethnic communality, at least in essential outline. Their preferences are reinforced by the self-perpetuating pressures generated by the nature of subcommunity organizational life and by the demands and exhortations, grounded in ideological conviction, of their ethnic community leaders. As we have suggested, some individuals, as a result of their particular inclinations and perspectives, move out into an amorphously structured intellectual subcommunity which contains people of all ethnic backgrounds. All of these recurring processes are probably inevitable and basically irreversible.

Thus the prognosis for America for a long time to come is that its informal social structure will consist of a series of ethnic subcommunities criss-crossed by social class, within which primary group relationships will tend to be confined, that secondary group relationships across ethnic group lines will take place in abundance as a result of the requirements of an urbanized industrial society, and that the intellectual subsociety will grow somewhat both in numbers and in institutional articulation as a result of the constant increase in the magnitude of higher education.[10]

The major problem, then, is to keep ethnic separation in communal life from being so pronounced in itself that it threatens ethnic harmony, good group relations, and the spirit of basic good will which a democratic pluralistic society requires, and to keep it from spilling over into the civic arena of secondary relations to impinge on housing, jobs, politics, education, and other areas of functional activity where universalistic criteria of judgment and assignment are necessary and where the operation of ethnic considerations can only be disruptive and even disastrous. The attainment of this objective calls for good sense and reasonableness on the part of the average American citizen, regardless of ethnic background, and in addition to these qualities, a high degree of civic statesmanship on the part of ethnic communal leaders who will be tempted at times, out of their own convictions and enthusiasms, to emphasize ethnic exclusion and the demands in time and resources from their particular constituents which are likely to make for exclusion and separation, regardless of intent.

In sum, the basic long-range goal for Americans, with regard to ethnic communality, is fluidity and moderation within the context

[10] I do not mean to indicate that all, or even most, college graduates become "intellectuals" or interacting members of the intellectual subsociety. By no means. However, the spread of higher education opens the doors of possible entrance into the intellectual subsociety to an increasing number of those who are intellectually or temperamentally suited for it.

of equal civic rights for all, regardless of race, religion, or national background, and the option of democratic free choice for both groups and individuals. Ethnic communality will not disappear in the foreseeable future and its legitimacy and rationale should be recognized and respected. By the same token, the bonds that bind human beings together across the lines of ethnicity and the pathways on which people of diverse ethnic origin meet and mingle should be cherished and strengthened. In the last analysis, what is gravely required is a society in which one may say with equal pride and without internal disquietude at the juxtaposition: "I am a Jew, or a Catholic, or a Protestant, or a Negro, or an Indian, or an Oriental, or a Puerto Rican;" "I am an American;" and "I am a man."

Index

267

English, 92-3
Equal-status contact, 235
Essien-Udom, E. U., 15n
Ethclass, 51-4, 160
  definition of, 51
  relation to transferability, 162-3
Ethnic affiliation, 151-4
Ethnic communality, 5, 105-7, 126-7,
  154-5, 132-6, 239, 253-4, 263
  desegregation and, 247-8, 253-4
  relation to viable goals, 261-5
Ethnic group, 23-30, 34-8, 234
  area pre-emption, 132-3, 141-2,
  150-51
  definition of, 23-4
  definition of, in America, 27-8
  historical development of, 23-6
  relation to social class, 47-9
Ethnic groups
  communal life, 5, 105-7, 126-7,
  132-6, 253-4
  contributions of, 73, 76n
  during Colonial times, 86-7
Ethnic identity, 26, 76n-7n
  right of choice, 151-4
Ethnic subsociety, internal responsibilities of, 257-62
Ethnicity, 23-30
  law and, 4, 35
  politics and, 35-6
  see also Ethnic group
Etzioni, Amitai, 162n

Fairchild, Henry Pratt, 64n
Fichter, Joseph H., S.J., 6n, 65, 200n,
  206, 209n, 213, 214, 218, 219-
  20
Filler, Louis, 141n
Fishman, Joshua A., 72, 112, 218-20
Flower, Elisabeth F., 144n
Francis, E. K., 24n, 28n, 54n
Franklin, Benjamin, 89, 146
Frazier, E. Franklin, 163, 166, 169

Freedman, Ronald, 191n, 192n
Frenkel-Brunswik, Else, 7n
Frontier, relation to melting pot
  theory, 117-20
Fuchs, Laurence, 191n
Fürstenwaerther, Baron von, 94

Gans, Herbert J., 180, 189, 193n,
  194, 202-3, 204-5
Gardner, Burleigh B., 163, 166
Gardner, Mary R., 163, 166
Garis, Roy L., 89n, 93n
Gaudet, Hazel, 36n
Germans, 89, 92, 99-100, 132-3, 134,
  197
  of the Jewish faith, 184
Giddings, Franklin, 53
Girl Scouts, 223-4, 238
Glazer, Nathan, 109n, 133n, 134n,
  183n, 186-7
Goldberg, David, 187n, 209n
Goldhamer, Herbert, 166n
Goldman, Benjamin B., 181n
Goldsen, Rose K., 201n
Golovensky, David I., 56n
Gordon, Albert I., 178, 180-81, 189,
  193n
Gordon, Milton M., 40n, 41n, 47n,
  48n, 53n, 57n, 67n, 82n, 157,
  162n, 224n, 227n, 248-9n
Gouldner, Alvin W., 7n
Government
  and communal life, 249
  desegregation and, 248-51
  integration and, 249
  racial quotas, and, 251
  recommended role of, 246-51
Graham, Frank P., 144n
Grant, Madison, 97-8
Gray, Ailsa, 7n
Green, Arnold W., 56n, 66-7
Greenberg, Jack, 165n
Groupculture, 39-40

Parochial schools
  effect on primary relationships, 214
  effect on values, 218-20
Petegorsky, David W., 82n
Participational identification, 52-4
Pfeffer, Leo, 144n
Pluralism. *See* Cultural pluralism;
  Structural pluralism
Politics and ethnicity, 35-6
Poll, Solomon, 191n
Pope, Liston, 185n, 209n, 221n
Potter, Robert G., Jr., 191n
Powdermaker, Hortense, 166
Prejudice
  effects of structural separation on,
    235-9
  implications of assimilation analysis
    for, 233-65
  relation to assimilation variables,
    81-2
  relation to communal life, 3
  social science studies of, 7
Price, C. A., 68n
Primary group, definition of, 31
Primary group relationships, 54n
  see also Primary relationships
Primary relationships, 32, 34, 70, 80
  democratic values and, 240-41
  of ethnic groups in United States,
    77-8
  prejudice and, 235-6
  relation to deviance and marginal-
    ity, 54-7
  relation to ethclass, 52
  relation to integration, 246
Private organizations and desegregation, 251-3
Protestants, 89, 109-10; *see also*
  White Protestants
Public schools and racial assignment,
  249-51
Puerto Ricans, 75-7, 109, 201
  in assimilation paradigm, 76

Putz, Louis J., C.S.C., 196n

Race, definition of, 27
Racial quotas and government, 251
Racism, 97-8, 102-4, 136, 259
  relation to Anglo-conformity, 102-4
Ramsey, Glen V., 201n
Rand, Christopher, 201n
Rea, Samuel, 101
Redfield, Robert, 23, 61
Redlich, Frederick C., 49n, 72n
Regional residence, relation to sub-
  society, 47-8, 50-51
Reissman, Leonard, 40n
Religion
  conversion in mixed marriage, 215-
    16
  demographic data on, 173-4
  institutional changes of, among
    Catholics, 217
  institutional changes of, among
    Jews, 193-4
  role of, in Scouting, 223-4
Reuter, Edward Byron, 64n
Richards, Eugene S., 201n
Riesman, David, 23, 56n
Robbins, Richard, 88n
Roberts, Bertram H., 49n
Roche, John P., 82n
Roosevelt, Theodore, 121-2
Rose, Arnold, 66, 82n
Rosenthal, Erich, 191n, 192n
Rossi, Alice S., 218-19
Rossi, Peter H., 218-19
Ruesch, Jurgen, 72n
Rümelin, Carl, 135n
Rural-urban residence, relation to sub-
  society, 47-8, 50-51

Sagi, Philip C., 191n
Sanford, R. N., 7n
Saveth, Edward N., 117n, 120n,
  121n, 122

"Triple melting pot," 122-4, 200
Tuck, Ruth D., 201n
Turner, Frederick Jackson, 50, 117-20
Tylor, E. B., 32

Value conflict, 18, 159
  of Catholics, 77n, 217
  of Jews, 192-3
  see also Assimilation, civic
Value differences
  of Catholics, 218-20
  of Jews, 191-2
  of Negroes, 170-73
Vickery, William E., 79n, 81n, 85n,
  157
Vosk, Marc, 177, 178, 193n
Voting and ethnicity, 36

Wakefield, Dan, 201n
Walkley, Rosabelle Price, 235n
Warner, W. Lloyd, 42, 44-5, 199n,
  207n, 208n, 209n
Washington, George, 89-90, 128, 219
Watson, Goodwin, 144n
Weber, Max, 69

Wendell, Barrett, 143n
Westoff, Charles F., 191n
Whelpton, Pascal K., 191n, 192n
White Protestants, 111, 113, 126,
  221-4
  class differentiation among, 221; see
    also Social class
  communal life of, 221-4
  communality and, 241
  intermarriage of, 222
  primary relationships of, 214, 221-2
  upper-middle-class, 221
  see also Protestants
Whitman, Walt, 156
Whyte, William Foote, 202, 203-4
Williams, Robin, 50, 235n
Wilner, Daniel M., 235n
Wilson, Woodrow, 101, 121-2
Wirth, Louis, 166n

Young, Donald, 258-9
Yinger, J. Milton, 201n, 235n

Zangwill, Israel, 120-21
Zubrzycki, J., 68n